THE REAL DEAL
MAGAZINE

THE CLOSING

INTERVIEWS WITH
NEW YORK CITY'S
TITANS OF
REAL ESTATE

Books by *The Real Deal* may be purchased. For information, please email info@TheRealDeal.com or write to: Book Sales Department, *The Real Deal,* 158 West 29th Street, 4th floor, New York, NY 10001

Printed in the United States of America
Book design by Juan Zielaskowski and Kéziah Makoundou
The Real Deal is a registered trademark of Korangy Publishing Inc.
The selections in this book first appeared in issues of *The Real Deal.*
ISBN-13: 978-0-9907287-0-2

For more about our publications and events, email info@TheRealDeal.com,
visit www.TheRealDeal.com or call 212-260-1332.

Other publications from Korangy Publishing:

_____

In print:
The Real Deal
Luxury Listings NYC
The South Florida Market Report
The Data Book

_____

Online:
TheRealDeal.com
TheRealDeal.com/Miami
LuxuryListingsNYC.com
TheRealDeal.com/Research

_____

Film/TV:
"Building Stories: New York Through the Eyes of an Architect" (produced for PBS)

> "I'm a deal junkie. It's not just about the money. It keeps me young."

JEFF WINICK
CEO & Founder, **Winick Realty Group**

TABLE OF CONTENTS

> "Very early, I realized real estate in New York is like the celebrity in L.A. We are consumed by it."

OFER YARDENI
Co-chairman & CEO, **Stonehenge Partners**

> "Architects are much more interesting than movie stars and what we do is much more enduring."
>
> ROBERT A.M. STERN
> Founder, **Robert A.M. Stern Architects**

TABLE OF CONTENTS

> "This job is kind of like when you were a kid and you played a game of Monopoly that lasted for days."
>
> BOB KNAKAL
> Chairman, **Massey Knakal Realty Services**

"I liked the idea that you could create
your own destiny in real estate."

PAMELA LIEBMAN
President, **The Corcoran Group**

TABLE OF CONTENTS

"It's easy, if you work like a dog."

HOWARD LORBER
President & CEO, **Vector Group**

"Character is destiny."
—Heraclitus

●●●●●

Larry Silverstein grew up on the top floor of a seven-story walk-up. Charles Kushner spent his time in prison mentoring younger inmates. Faith Hope Consolo never took any of her husbands' last names so she could keep the same monogram on her luggage. Bob Knakal could have been a professional baseball player. David Walentas wishes he could tell his younger self what he now tells his son, Jed.

Since I started *The Real Deal* in 2003, we've covered the New York City real estate market's booms and busts, the companies that have dominated the industry and those who have fallen hard after billion-dollar losses. We've written about record-breaking deals that have helped shape the skyline and the bitter lawsuits that inevitably spring up when deals sour.

But at its heart, real estate is an industry full of characters. From the beginning, we've tried to reveal the personalities behind the deals, with all their passions and quirks. Nowhere does that shine through more than in The Closing interview, which appears on the back page of *The Real Deal* magazine each month.

Starting with Howard Lorber, chairman of Douglas Elliman, the city's largest real estate brokerage, more than 100 real estate icons — developers, agents, architects, lawyers and politicians who have shaped the face of the city — have been profiled in The Closing interviews that touch on both the personal and the professional, accompanied by portraits from award-winning photographers Hugh Hartshorne, Ben Baker and Marc Scrivo.

Just as we planned for the magazine to be a chronicle of the industry, "The Closing: Interviews with New York City's Titans of Real Estate," our first book based on these featured interviews, relays how these tenacious individuals became the best in their field, and as significantly, held onto their perches. As we all know, this is a city where every square foot is battled over, so that's no easy feat.

Never wanting to do puff pieces on the industry's elite, we have always asked the tough questions about deals gone bad, career setbacks and heartbreaks that inevitably occur in even the most charmed lives. Our subjects have experienced detours or outright failures, only to rise again stronger. Some have overcome the loss of loved ones or dealt with bankruptcy, failed partnerships or jail time.

Along with making for a fascinating read, this book confirms that our time on earth is entirely our own, and with a combination of luck and a lot of hard work, no obstacle is too large to cage human ambition, even when it come to the toughest real estate market in the world.

●●●●●

●●●●●

We debated what to call this book: A primer. A snapshot. A how-to. Maybe it is all of these things, hopefully it is more. It is for sure required reading for the real estate-obsessed, which let's face it, is nearly everyone here in New York City and many gawking from outside.

Each month our readers skip ahead to the magazine's back page, where they find an interview with an elite individual driving the real estate industry. It's been one of our most popular fixtures at *The Real Deal* since this feature launched in 2006 and it is called, fittingly, The Closing.

These 100 dialogues, following the model of the Proust Questionnaire made famous by French writer Marcel Proust, have been culled from more than a decade's worth of issues. (Readers can note the interview date in the bottom right corner of each page; the answers have been edited and condensed for clarity.) I want to thank all *The Real Deal* reporters who have been responsible for collecting these interviews over the years.

From the beginning, it was clear the people we interviewed had achieved success, but more importantly, attained wisdom and experience. (Yes, that includes Donald Trump.) They range in age from former city agency head Seth Pinsky, born in 1971, to brokerage founder Julian Studley, born in 1927.

Those we spoke to had to piece together for themselves what worked and what didn't in order to succeed in the blood sport that is New York real estate. Like any good business book, here you will find clues about what it takes to make it to the top. Think of it partly as a "How to Win Friends and Influence People" for real estate.

The interviews also offer a glimpse at how these 1 percenters spend their time and money when they are not in the boardroom or glued to their phone, from their favorite restaurants to where they have their vacation homes. There are the lunches at the Four Seasons, the power breakfasts at the Loews Regency Hotel and the summerhouses in the Hamptons. Wealth allows for rarefied hobbies, so some pursuits are further afield: private equity investor Richard Mack likes to off-piste in Chamonix with his kids. (We had to look up where that is and what it was — it's basically skiing in France.) Chris Schlank of Savanna is really into Gyrotonics. (We looked that one up too.)

So is it possible from all these conversations to glean some common characteristics of those who've achieved great success? Yes — and perhaps unsurprisingly, some traits are positive and others are less so.

Many of the deal-making stories we offer here hinge on character. Whether our subjects identify it or not, many choices they make highlight the subject of integrity. The small-time mom-and-pop operator who doesn't honor a handshake agreement — there are plenty of these working in New York City real estate — will only make it so far, and their kind are (mostly) not to be found in this book.

Character is a theme that financier John Pierpont Morgan stressed when he said, "The first thing is character before money or anything else. Money cannot buy it. A man I do not trust could not get money from me on all the bonds in Christendom. I think that is the fundamental basis of business."

Of course, many of those who are the most successful in real estate are those who aren't afraid to take "no" for an answer either. On cold-calling as a young buck early in his career, retail broker Robert Futterman said he would always shoot as high as possible and see what happened. "I'd ask for Harry Helmsley, I'd ask for Trump. If they directed me somewhere else, then so be it." Residential broker Michele Kleier got her first big celebrity deal by sending around a handwritten note to each hotel in the city that Warren Beatty might be staying at after she heard he was looking for a place.

That kind of hustle is what helps shape our skyline, deal-by-deal, block-by-block, and has been integral to the birth of the modern-day American city. It's part of our history. In "Babbitt," the 1922 novel by author and Nobel Prize-winner Sinclair Lewis about a real estate broker (and about American hucksterism in general), we get a chronicle of property speculation and big city deal making. If "Babbitt" is a literary depiction of people hustling to make a buck in real estate, we'd argue these interview subjects are modern day, real-life equivalents.

Putting up big buildings typically requires tremendous confidence, too — otherwise known as ego. Castles, churches, grand arches and spires have all served throughout the ages as testaments to a human desire to flaunt wealth and power while reaching toward the heavens. Skyscrapers are their modern-day successors, and continue to rise even higher and higher in the city each year. Perhaps fittingly, there is

●●●●●

no shortage of unbridled ego to be found in the pages of this book.

Resilience is a quality that seems to go hand-in-hand with ego. And those responsible for the Ground Zero rebuilding and the city's new tallest tower, One World Trade Center, have shown that resilience in abundance. We sat down with developer Larry Silverstein, construction honcho Dan Tishman, architect David Childs and others who picked up the pieces — and helped lift back up the city — following Sept. 11.

But there can be a dark side to ego, too, and this book raises the question, "Does it pay to be a jerk?" Tough taskmasters accomplish great things but they sometimes are not well-liked. Every mini-mogul and tycoon must grapple with the balance between their hard-charging drive and living in a world with other people. "For the most part, people who have worked for me tell me they didn't like me much, but they learned a lot," said investor Jeff Greene. "I'm very proud of that. It would be worse if they said, 'Boy, he was a sweet guy, but I learned nothing.'" Developer Miki Naftali struck a softer note. "Some people might say that I'm, maybe, too aggressive. I hope that people see me as fair."

Not everyone who has made it to the top comes on so strong. To me one of the great things the interviews in this book show is that there is no one path to success, save for smarts. For example, making it in real estate in New York is not necessarily all about glad-handing and looking the part. Developer Ian Schrager said he is comfortable in business meetings, but holds his wife's hand at cocktail parties and is happy staying on the sidelines. Steiner Studios' Doug Steiner's casual attire often gets him mistaken for a bike messenger when he goes to business meetings in Midtown, which he doesn't mind. And commercial real estate superbroker Darcy Stacom said she learned early on that wearing a business suit or playing golf wouldn't get her anywhere.

Of course, it all boils down to money. Money is the real language of real estate, not square feet or number of stories. Money is often a measure of how far people have traveled from their past.

And it's also what people argue about the most. This book shows you the myriad ways people can screw one another — and it's almost always about money. The pros here tell you how to prevent it. "In business, anything you decide to do should be put in writing. Even with friends," said Dottie Herman, CEO of brokerage Douglas Elliman.

These conversations also show how, as F. Scott Fitzgerald once pointed out, "the rich are not like you and me." Our conversations reveal the sometimes-outlandish private lives of the rich and successful. Surprisingly, not one but two people here — broker Daun Paris and Tishman — keep llamas. And developer Kevin Maloney has chicken coops on the terrace of his Upper West Side penthouse for the fresh eggs. We have a fair number of dog lovers too. Of course at this stratosphere, "dog lover" means something else. For example, brokerage doyenne Elizabeth Stribling used to have a dog that understood French. And celeb broker Barbara Fox's dogs are provided for in her will.

Success in real estate is a family affair for some of our interview subjects. We spoke to members of the city's real estate dynasties such as Bill Rudin, Jonathan Tisch and Douglas Durst. For Rudin, the path to the company started by his grandfather first took him briefly to an entirely different industry — in his case, film — before realizing his heart lay in the family business. Call it the return of the prodigal son.

But not everyone in real estate is born rich, not by far. There have always been opportunities in real estate for immigrants and up-and-comers. Read the rags-to-riches interviews with hotelier Sam Chang and commercial real estate broker Stephen Siegel. Chang labored as a dishwasher while Siegel got his start in a humble mailroom.

We often ask Closing subjects for the key to balancing work and family. Some, like Forest City Ratner's MaryAnne Gilmartin and Cushman & Wakefield's Bruce Mosler credit their spouses. "I think this is key to any person's success in life: To have a partner who gets it," said Mosler.

Collecting these stories over the years has been personally valuable to me. The Related Companies CEO Jeff Blau, a father of three, said he doesn't see his kids in the evening. So his prescription — to be with his children 100 percent on the weekend and not let work interfere — influenced the kind of parent I am. (I try not to sit down at the computer at least until the kids are tucked in.)

The subjects of our 100 Closings here have attained the kind of wisdom that is the prerequisite for real success in work and life. We hope you'll find their interviews as inspiring as I have.

STEPHEN ROSS

CHAIRMAN | **THE RELATED COMPANIES**

Ross is a billionaire developer, and his firm is building the Hudson Yards mega-project on Manhattan's Far West Side, the largest development in U.S. history. The $20 billion project will include 16 skyscrapers and total 17 million square feet of office, residential, retail and community space. The company has already developed over $22 billion in real estate and has a $15 billion portfolio nationwide, including 6,000 luxury rental units, 9 million square feet of commercial properties and 45,000 affordable and workforce housing units. In New York City the firm has also spearheaded massive projects like the Time Warner Center and a slew of high-end residential and mixed-use properties. Ross, who also owns the Miami Dolphins, founded Related in 1972
Interview by Katherine Clarke

"I was in trouble a lot. The principal told my parents, 'You've got to discipline him, but don't break him.'"

What's your date of birth?
May 10, 1940.

What were you like as a kid in Detroit?
I was a free spirit. I was in trouble a lot. School was kind of secondary. The principal told my parents, "He has a strong personality. You've got to discipline him, but don't break him."

What did your parents do?
My dad was an inventor. He was a hard worker, so I didn't see him much, probably about as much as my kids see me. He was very creative, but he wasn't a good businessman, and he didn't have much success economically.

What did he invent?
The coffee vending machine was probably the first big thing he invented. He had patents for it and sold them. But he went with the wrong company. By the time he found out the company wasn't successful, other companies had already caught up.

Why did you move from Detroit to Miami Beach?
We moved for my dad to manage a hotel my grandfather owned. It was hard; it was the middle of freshman year in high school, and I'd just established myself at a new school.

Did you always want to go to the University of Michigan?
My parents took me to a football game in Ann Arbor when I was about eight years old. I was so enamored. ... I started at the University of Florida, but worked hard because I knew it was my last chance. I ultimately got high enough grades to transfer.

When did you come to New York?
I came to New York after law school [at Wayne State University] to get a master's in tax law at NYU. It was really the first time I'd spent any time in New York. Being single and looking to really work hard and play hard, there was no greater city in the world.

Where do you live now?
In the Time Warner Center, which I built.

You work there, too. Are there days you feel like you never leave the building?
When the weather's bad, I've gone for two or three days without going outside. I eat at the restaurants and go to Dizzy's [the nightclub at Jazz at Lincoln Center].

Do you have other homes?
I spend weekends at our home in Palm Beach, and I have a place in Southampton.

How long have you been married?
I first got married when I was 40, and that lasted for 11 years. This time? 12 years.

You left marriage until late in life then.
I was enjoying single life, but more importantly, I was intent on establishing a career and building a company.

How did you meet your wife, Kara?
On a blind date. She was a jewelry designer and had her own company. ... Since then, she's really built a brand, and she sells in Bergdorf's and other great retailers. She has a store now on 60th Street, just off Madison.

How many kids do you have?
Four. I have two girls, and she has two. I'm way outnumbered.

How did you get your start in real estate?
I got fired from two jobs, at Bear Stearns and [investment bank] Baird all within a two-year period. You had all these young people vying for the top. Everyone thought they were the masters of the universe. At Bear Stearns, the person I was working with had an inferiority complex. He wanted me to be totally subservient and that didn't work for me. I knew I couldn't go back for another interview so I made a business plan.

What was the business plan?
I started in affordable housing so I could learn the business using my skills as a tax attorney. Meanwhile, I was selling the tax shelters that accompanied the projects to wealthy investors. The financial arm eventually became the largest supplier of debt and equity for affordable housing.

The likelihood of success without money or a family history in real estate must have seemed slim.
I look back and see where I am today and I can't believe it. I have to pinch myself. **TRD**

DONALD TRUMP

PRESIDENT | **THE TRUMP ORGANIZATION**

Trump started his career working alongside his father, real estate developer Fred C. Trump, in Brooklyn and Queens. Today, his firm, the multibillion-dollar Trump Organization, is the most recognizable real estate brand in the world, with holdings like Trump Tower on Fifth Avenue and Trump Park Avenue, as well as hotels and golf courses. Trump has authored several books, including the best seller "The Art of the Deal," and is a partner in the Miss Universe and Miss USA Pageants. In 2004, he began producing and starring in the television reality show "The Apprentice." Among his current projects is an 18-hole public golf course in the Bronx. *Interview by Candace Taylor*

"Ideally you want to watch other people and learn from their mistakes, because that's less costly."

How old are you?
63.

Where did you grow up?
Jamaica Estates, Queens. My father lived there, in the same house on Midland Parkway, up until his death.

He amassed a fortune in his lifetime — why didn't he ever move?
My father loved Queens and he loved Brooklyn, and that's where he did his business. He never came to Manhattan.

You live here in Trump Tower. What other homes do you have?
I have a home in Bedford, N.Y.; I have a home in Palm Beach, Florida. I have homes in other locations, but I generally split my time between Bedford, Palm Beach and Manhattan.

Which is your favorite?
Nothing can top, to me, Trump Tower. But Palm Beach is great. I stay at the Mar-a-Lago Club. That's where I had my wedding [to third wife Melania Knauss in 2005].

Did you always know that you wanted to go into real estate?
I learned so much from my father. He enjoyed what he did so much, it made him happy. I saw that, and it rubbed off on me.

You've taken a very different path from the other old New York real estate families, like the LeFraks.
That's true. It's a very different track than probably has ever been taken in real estate. Richard LeFrak — who's a great friend of mine — was a host recently on the Miss Universe Pageant, which I own. He was on "Celebrity Apprentice" and he did a fantastic job.

How has being a TV star changed your life?
I was well-known before "The Apprentice," but certainly I'm much better known now. It's very hard to walk outside, whereas before I was able to do that. When you have a major hit television show, it's a different level than anything else.

You have five children, including a 4-year-old son, Barron. How are you different as a parent this time around?
I think I appreciate it a little bit more. I think when you're getting older and you have a young baby, it makes you appreciate all of them more.

Your daughter [Ivanka] was recently married [to real estate scion Jared Kushner]. How do you feel about her marrying into another prominent real estate family?
I thought it was great. She married a wonderful guy and I really like the family. Charlie Kushner is a fantastic guy.

Do you and Jared have bonding activities?
We have bonded. He's very smart; he's a very good person. I'm very happy with Ivanka's choice.

Was it an issue that she converted to Judaism?
No, not for me it wasn't. That was her decision.

When you look back at your career, what would you do differently?
You have to learn from your successes and your failures. And if you don't learn from mistakes, then you're a fool. Now, ideally you want to watch other people and learn from their mistakes, because that's less costly and less traumatic. But ... I wouldn't want to do it much differently. For instance, I was told, 'Don't do "The Apprentice" because it can never succeed on television, because very few shows do succeed.' And I did it against the wishes of many people so you have to just sort of go by your wits.

Which of your decisions have gone the other way?
Many decisions don't go well because of timing. You'll buy a building, make a great deal on a building, and then the market crashes. All of a sudden your great deal isn't so good.

What lessons did you take from the recession of the early 1990s?
I think I became much more conservative. We're sitting on a lot of cash and I'm looking to buy, whereas in the early '90s I can honestly say it was the exact opposite. So I either learned something, or was luckier — maybe a combination of both.

Which parts of your holdings would you be most worried about in a down market?
Frankly, if the market went down, I'd be extremely happy because we're not sellers, we're buyers. I think the market will stay at pretty low levels and then ultimately start getting better, but it could go down further. On a selfish basis, if it did, I wouldn't be unhappy.

What is something people don't know about you?
I think my image is a lot different than the fact. The image is a tough image. I'm actually a nice person who has a lot of compassion for people. I like doing the right thing. And I happen to be a very honest guy, sometimes too honest. My honesty gets me into trouble.

Did the 'you're fired' thing give people the wrong impression?
Actually, people like me better now that they see me on television and all I do is fire people. What does that tell you about my reputation before? It couldn't have been so great. **TRD**

June 2010

Photo by Hugh Hartshorne

DARCY STACOM

VICE CHAIRMAN | **CBRE GROUP**

Stacom got her start at the commercial brokerage Cushman & Wakefield, where her late father, Matthew Stacom, was a veteran broker and was involved in developing and leasing the Sears Tower. Her late mother, Claire, became a Cushman broker after marrying her father, and her sister Tara Stacom is a top broker as well. Darcy left Cushman in 2002 for competitor CBRE, where she's vice chairman and has since brokered more than $60 billion in deals. Stacom represented the seller of the GM Building, which fetched the highest price ever paid for a single office property in the U.S. at $2.8 billion. She also set records when she represented MetLife in the $5.4 billion sale of Stuyvesant Town and Peter Cooper Village in 2006. *Interview by Candace Taylor*

"I've always been a non-conformist. I've never owned a business suit and I never will."

What's your date of birth?
November 24, 1959.

Where did you grow up?
I grew up primarily in Greenwich, Connecticut. I was born in New York and briefly lived in Ridgefield, but really pretty much Greenwich.

Where do you live now?
New York City in Midtown, in a rental building. I'm the shoemaker with no shoes.

Have you always rented?
Yes. Every time we [Stacom and husband Chris Kraus, a managing director at Jones Lang LaSalle] thought we were going to buy, for some reason we decided not to. I love the location that I'm in. We've been there for over 20 years. I was only seven blocks from my office when we started to have kids. We've had different-sized apartments in the building: We started in a one-bedroom, went to a two-bedroom, then went to a three.

Are you in a rent-stabilized apartment?
No, we're fair market. When the rent hit a certain level many moons ago, we just said, 'OK, fair market.'

Do you have any other homes?
We have a home in Connecticut that we do own.

How long have you been married?
This is a big year for our family because we have been married 25 years, we're both turning 50 and our two girls [Teal and Amber] are turning 13 and 16.

What are you doing to celebrate?
We are planning a big family vacation but are vacillating between Europe and South America.

How do you juggle a career with being a mom?
I think if I had stayed home I would have driven them crazy, so it was a good balance. You just prioritize. If you have to work from 9 p.m. to midnight to make up for the fact that you were gone from 5 p.m. to 8 p.m., you do it. I'm proud of one thing: My daughters and I get along great. I can't say I fight with my daughters.

Do you think it's been good for them to see the success you've had in your career?
Sometimes they're like, 'OK, yeah, you sold that building,' but in general I'm hoping it will have been a good, positive influence. My mom worked and that was a good, positive influence on me. My dad was a little worried I was going to be the ne'er-do-well of the family.

Why?
I was a bit of a slacker as a kid. If a class really appealed to me I did well; if a class didn't appeal to me I didn't do so well. But when I got into real estate, I loved it.

When did you start in real estate?
The first summer I worked in the Cushman & Wakefield mailroom, I was 14.

Was it difficult that there were so few women in the field when you started?
Actually, it was a very positive challenge. I've always been a non-conformist. I've never owned a business suit and I never will. It's just not me. A lot of brokers use entertaining as a means of creating new relationships and establishing new clients. I just didn't do that. I remember once being scheduled to play golf with clients and then they found out what my handicap was and they cancelled. I realized that socializing wasn't going to get me anywhere.

If you've never owned a business suit, what's your standard work outfit?
I'm just very eclectic in my dress. I'm sitting here today in a hot-pink top over a long black skirt and wedge heels and earrings that come down to my shoulders. You never know; it's whatever I feel like in the morning.

You come from a family of brokers. What was the dinner conversation like?
Growing up it was a lot of real estate a lot of the time. When dad sold the land for the Sears Tower, that took up conversation for a very long time.

What's your secret to winning a negotiation?
I only lose my temper once a deal. When I lose my temper, and I do have a temper, it is very clear that I'm adamant about what I'm speaking. There's always some point in the transaction where somebody's going to finally push the deal too far. You've got to be prepared to really take a stand and say, "Look, it's now or never."

Do you treat yourself to a big gift after closing a deal?
Usually I will pick some eclectic piece of clothing or a cool piece of costume jewelry and add to my collection. Early in our marriage my husband tried to buy me real jewelry. I said, 'Can you just get me costume stuff?'

Why do you like the costume stuff?
Because you can buy more of it. **TRD**

May 2009

DANNY MEYER

FOUNDER & CEO | **UNION SQUARE HOSPITALITY GROUP**

Meyer's company operates such hot-ticket New York City restaurants as Gramercy Tavern, Union Square Cafe, Blue Smoke, Maialino and North End Grill, as well as the Whitney Museum eatery Untitled and restaurants in the Museum of Modern Art. Union Square Hospitality also runs the rapidly expanding chain of Shake Shack burger joints, with locations in New York, Florida, Washington, D.C., Dubai, Kuwait City and elsewhere. Meyer has co-authored several books, including the business tome "Setting the Table." In January 2012, Related bought a portion of Meyer's Union Square Events, with plans to partner on future ventures at Related's Hudson Yards. *Interview by Lauren Elkies*

"I'm sometimes frustrated we haven't shared in the real estate boom that we have helped make happen."

What's your date of birth?
March 14, 1958.

Where did you grow up?
St. Louis, Missouri. I'm still a Cardinals fan.

Where do you live now?
I live in a co-op in the neighborhood where most of our restaurants are, so in Flatiron-Gramercy, in the 20s.

Why so close to your restaurants?
To stay as close to our staff members, our guests and our community as possible.

How'd you get into the restaurant business?
I wanted to be in New York. The first job I got was as a salesman selling electronic tags to stop shoplifters. I worked out of my apartment. My uncle reminded me that all he had ever heard me talk about was food and restaurants, so I started taking a restaurant management class.

How did you and your wife meet?
We met in 1984 at my first restaurant job at a [now-defunct] restaurant called Pesca on 22nd Street. I was the assistant lunch manager and Audrey was an actress waiting on tables.

Who does most of the cooking in your home?
During the weekdays, Audrey and our four kids. During the weekends, our kids and me. They are 12 through 18. Our oldest daughter just won the Iron Chef competition at Yale University as a freshman.

I hear you worked as a tour guide in Rome for a summer when you were a student at Trinity College.
My dad's company sold group tours in about eight European cities. When my sister, my brother and I each turned 20, we got to work as a tour guide in a country that my dad did business in. I picked Italy.

Do you speak fluent Italian now?
I do. And that eventually led to a restaurant, Maialino, which is really an homage to Rome. Because I was working for my dad's company during that summer, I was called Meyerino — which means "little Meyer." I consistently took my tours to a local trattoria. All I ever ate there was the roast suckling pig, so my name changed to Maialino. It means "little pig." So they were calling me Little Pig all summer.

Being a successful restaurateur is partly about real estate, of course. How do you pick your locations?
We don't ever open a restaurant unless a number of us fall in love with a location.

Does your company own any of the buildings where your restaurants are situated?
We own the space that is Gramercy Tavern.

Is that the only one?
Sadly. I'm sometimes frustrated we haven't shared in the real estate boom that some of our restaurants have helped make happen.

What are your favorite dishes at your restaurants?
The pimento cheeseburger at Untitled is the stuff of dreams. The bacon and maple croissant at North End Grill — if that were the last thing I ate before dying, I'd be pretty happy. And Nancy Olsen's chocolate bread pudding at Gramercy Tavern.

If you had to eat at Burger King, McDonald's or Wendy's, which would you choose?
I wouldn't. If someone said, 'You've got to eat your next two meals at American fast-food restaurants,' I would do one meal at Chipotle and one meal at Popeyes fried chicken.

When you opened the original Shake Shack in Madison Square Park (which pays rent to the city and the park), did you ever think it would become so popular?
I had been one of the co-founders of the Madison Square Park Conservancy. We never saw it as being anything other than an amenity for this park, to raise money and to increase the population of park users. It did both of those things, and then some. We actually opened our second Shake Shack in hopes that it would help reduce the line a little bit; if anything, each time we've opened another Shake Shack it's only increased the length of the line.

What has been your greatest setback?
Probably the biggest setback was closing [Tabla, in 2010]. Because, somehow, I had this sense that everything was forever.

Why'd you close it?
After 12 years, the restaurant was not able to fill its 283 seats on a consistent basis every lunch and every dinner. It was our biggest restaurant in terms of seats, in terms of overhead. It was also our most narrowly focused concept. It was Indian cuisine. Keeping Tabla as busy as we did for 12 years was actually a great accomplishment.

At the beginning of the year, Related purchased a portion of Union Square Events, the catering division of your company, to partner on future ventures. Why did you do that deal?
Related won the opportunity to develop the Hudson Yards. Union Square Events is overlooking the Hudson Yards, at 640 West 28th Street. We've always had an interest in that area. And what we've found to be somewhat taxing, for a company whose specialty is food service and hospitality, is the amount of time we were spending just trying to source locations for clients' events. **TRD**

May 2012

JEFF WINICK

CEO & FOUNDER | **WINICK REALTY GROUP**

Winick has personally leased more than 1 million square feet of retail space in New York as a broker and represents clients like Duane Reade, AT&T and Starbucks, as well as many major landlords. His 50-agent firm has leased more than 15 million square feet over the past 30 years, among the most of any retail firm in the city. *Interview by Katherine Clarke*

"I'm a deal junkie. It's not just about the money. It keeps me young."

What's your date of birth?
August 2, 1950.

What can you say about growing up in Queens?
My junior high school and my high school faced a cemetery. You get out of high school, you go to college and then you get buried in the cemetery. But that cemetery has been filled up for a long time, so [thankfully] I don't have to worry about going there.

What were you like as a kid?
Athletic. I played baseball, basketball and football.

Where did you go to college?
I didn't. After high school, I went straight into fashion, designing ladies accessories. My family was in the accessories and trimming business. If you bought a dress, they made the trimmings. Belts, lace and ruffles — all that stuff. I did that from 1968 until 1976. In 1973, I won a design award from the leather industry for my belts.

So how did you end up going into real estate?
Someone knocked on my door one day and wanted to buy my apartment. I told her my apartment in Manhattan was a rental, but she said it was going co-op. I started buying tenants' rights in buildings that were going co-op. I would buy the apartments or flip them to third parties. That was my beginning in real estate. At one point, I had 168 furnished apartments in New York.

But then you moved into retail.
Residential wasn't fashionable enough for me. I sold off my residential portfolio and went into retail in the '80s. I opened up a company with about 15 brokers and here we are today. My first deal was for a 2,000-square-foot store on 97th and Broadway. The tenant was probably a Subway or a Blimpie's.

Where do you live?
In a very modern apartment on 54th Street and First Avenue. That's why our office is on 42nd and Third.

Do you have any other homes?
Yes. In Southampton. I go out there on weekends in the summer. I love boating. I love the ocean and the beach.

Are you married?
I was married for a couple of years a long time ago. My ex-wife [Lizzete Winick] is a residential broker at Corcoran. My daughter, Danielle, is 20.

Are you single and looking?
Are you married? Let's go out tonight.

What would you put in your personal ad?
I pull no punches, and you better have a lot of energy to stay up with me. I love the sun and I love fast cars.

Do you have a collection of cars?
I have three cars. I love my Mercedes convertible. When I was growing up, someone pulled up next to me in a Corvette and wanted to drag race. I said, 'This is not for me.' I've been in a Mercedes ever since.

You recently lost a lot of weight.
I lost 55 pounds. I wanted to get rid of the diabetes, which I was diagnosed with 10 years ago. I'm self-cured. Three months ago, I went off all medication. I went to see some really good doctors and watched what I ate. I quit smoking, too.

What inspired the change?
Certain people come along and they change your life. Plus, my daughter kept on beating me up saying, 'Dad, I want you around for my wedding.'

Is there a special lady in your life you're talking about?
There was a lady. I'm not sure what status it's in right now. She's a photographer.

Tell me about your daughter, Danielle.
She interned at Vornado last year. She was the only intern there with a sales license. She's going to come here this summer and work for us. She's my whole life.

Did you ever want to have more kids?
I wouldn't rule out having another child. They keep you young. Maybe someday, if someone will put up with my personality.

Who are your closest industry friends?
Joe Moinian, Larry Gluck, Meyer Chetrit, Richard Wagman, Joey Jacobson and David Berley.

Are you a tough boss?
If you can survive me, you can become a very successful broker. I don't hold peoples' hands.

Do you live extravagantly?
I collect Rolexes. My favorite is the one I'm wearing, which is the cheapest one they make.

You're renowned for your wild parties at ICSC. What are they really like?
We have a pool party and a couple of tables at the club at night, that's all. It's just a bunch of people having a good time. You wrote that I fill my pool in the Hamptons up with Cristal every weekend. I'd have to be a billionaire to do that. They wouldn't have enough Cristal in the country to fill up my pool.

People say you're an aggressive deal-maker.
I don't think being a passive broker makes you successful. I'm not afraid to tell a tenant when he's wrong or a landlord when he's wrong.

Are you a workaholic?
I'm a deal junkie. It's not just about money. It keeps me young. I get a big rush from it, whether it's a $5,000 commission or a $100,000 commission. **TRD**

May 2014

THE CLOSING

KEVIN MALONEY

FOUNDER | **PROPERTY MARKETS GROUP**

Maloney's firm has built projects including Walker Tower, a condo conversion it developed with JDS Development at 212 West 18th Street. The penthouse for this project sold for more than $50 million, a record for downtown Manhattan. The two firms are also building a 1,350-foot hotel and condo at 111 West 57th Street, which is slated to be one of the tallest residential towers in the city. Among PMG's other projects, it's planning to bring a 44-story building with nearly 400 residential units to Long Island City, and has several projects in the works in Miami. *Interview by Katherine Clarke*

"We were just guys begging and borrowing to try to get deals closed."

What's your date of birth?
December 5, 1958.

What were you like as a kid growing up in upstate New York?
I was difficult. I never could follow rules. My father was [a lawyer] in the Marine Corps, so that made for a very interesting dynamic.

What kind of trouble did you get into?
I was always in trouble with the police, just bucking the system. I took the truck from the family farm when I was 14, put three or four shotguns in the back and a case of beer. I had no license or insurance, and we took it out and were shooting mailboxes. I got picked up by the state troopers, and my father had to come get me.

You were recruited by Chemical Bank out of college. How did you like the finance world?
I worked at 30 Rock, on the 60th floor, before it became famous [for NBC being there]. It was old, musty, and full of asbestos I'm sure, but it was the heart of New York City. I think they paid me $18,000 a year. I thought I was so rich.

How did you get into real estate?
In college at SUNY Buffalo, I was off-campus in student housing. I quickly figured out the rents and cost of the houses in the neighborhood. The next semester I took my state student loan and bought a house, renovated it and leased it to students. By the time I left college, I had accumulated a few properties. When I left Chemical, I ended up working for Ensign, a $2 billion federal bank, where I ran real estate.

Were your parents surprised by your success given your childhood antics?
They fully expected to come visit me in Attica or another penitentiary, but for some reason it all fell into place.

Where do you live?
My official residence is in Miami. I have a house on the beach in Golden Beach. I also have a beautiful penthouse on 84th and West End Avenue. My wife and daughter live in Miami November through May and in New York May through November. I commute back and forth every week.

What's your penthouse like?
We have a large terrace where we keep a lot of chickens. We get fresh eggs every day. We have to watch [the chickens] because the hawks have taken a couple of them.

Do you have any other homes?
We have a small ranch outside of Aspen and a flat in London. My wife, Tanya, is from London.

How did you meet your wife?
I was coming back from swimming at a community pool one morning and I saw a woman bent over a silver Porsche being frisked by two policemen. I was driving by and she looked really cute. I knew one of the cops so I stopped. He thought she was coming back from an all-night party and was drunk, but her position was that she was just a really bad driver. It turned out that she is really a bad driver.

What's Tanya like?
She's pretentious and she's British so she's got no sense of humor. She drives like an old lady. ... I intervened, and he let her go.

How many kids do you have?
I have one daughter who's 8 months old. Her name is Madeleine Rose. I also have two adopted children because I lived with a woman who had two kids. They're college-age now.

How does it feel to become a dad again at this age?
You've got to be nuts to have a kid at 54, but I'm going to get the first 12 to 14 years before she becomes a lunatic teenager. Then I'll be dead, so her mom can deal with all that stuff ... We have a nanny who lives with us and travels with us, so we get to sleep through the night, which is a big thing.

In the early days of PMG, you worked with Ziel Feldman [now of HFZ Capital] and Gary Barnett [now of Extell Development]. What was that like?
We had a little tiny office with no heat and Home Depot card tables for desks. We were just guys cobbling deals together, begging and borrowing to try to get deals closed.

People have said that you won't work with Michael Stern of JDS again. Why is that?
There's probably not a good fit for us to work together going forward. We're very different personalities. I don't know that it's productive for any developer to stand up and get too much on his soapbox, saying, 'look at all the great things I did.'

What's your bad habit?
Not returning phone calls. Everyone wants something from you, and I'd just rather not deal with it.

What are your hobbies?
I'm a pilot. I fly my plane to Florida regularly. It's a TBM, a high-speed jet turbine.

Why did you get into flying?
Because of my fear of flying. I was living with a woman at the time, and we went to Italy on vacation. I think I'd taken a Xanax, an Ambien and a few glasses of wine and I was still awake wondering what was happening with the airplane. You're not in charge, so it's very uncomfortable for me. She said, 'I think it's a control thing.' She bought me a flying lesson for my birthday that year. **TRD**

IAN SCHRAGER

CHAIRMAN & CEO | **IAN SCHRAGER COMPANY**

Schrager established his hotel and real estate development firm in 2005, and his high-profile New York projects include the 2006 redesign of the Gramercy Park Hotel as well as residential properties such as 40 Bond and the Gramercy Park Hotel's 50 Gramercy Park North condos. Schrager, who brought the urban resort to Miami with his groundbreaking Delano Hotel, is famous for pioneering the boutique hotel concept. But he is also known for more value-oriented hospitality — having launched the mid-priced Public hotel chain. Additionally, he is working with Marriott to bring his Edition hotel chain to New York's Madison Square Park Clock Tower. Prior to starting the Ian Schrager Company, Schrager was at the Morgans Hotel Group, which he co-founded in 1984 with the late Steve Rubell. Schrager is best known for the legendary nightclub Studio 54, which he created with Rubell in 1977. *Interview by Lauren Elkies*

"We lost everything. We had nothing. But we were able to come back and pick ourselves up off the floor."

What's your date of birth?
July 19, 1946.

Where did you grow up?
In East Flatbush, Brooklyn.

Do you still live in the 8,500-square-foot penthouse at 40 Bond?
Yes.

Do you have any other homes?
In Southampton.

How many kids do you have?
I have two kids from a former marriage. My wife has two kids, and we have a one-year-old baby son. His name is Louis. He's named after my father.

How'd you and your wife [of three years, Tania Wahlstedt] meet?
She used to dance with the New York City Ballet. I knew her because my first wife also danced with the ballet. For some strange reason, I have a preference for ballerinas.

What were you like as a kid?
Very active, obsessed with basketball — the way I became obsessed with business — and very competitive. I played guard. I had a bunch of scholarship offers, but my father wanted me to concentrate on my studies, so I didn't play in college.

Describe your personality back then.
I was always kinda passionate and competitive, but also very shy. And it's still the same. I can get up and talk about my work in front of a million people, no problem, but when I go to a cocktail party, I'll hold onto my wife's hand and gravitate toward the corner. Funny.

How'd you first get into the nightclub business?
I was a practicing lawyer for a couple of years. I didn't really like it. I happened to be Steve Rubell's lawyer at the time.

Is that how you two met?
Actually, we met in college [at Syracuse University].

Didn't you date a woman at the same time as him?
He was a few years older. He was dating her and then I got up to school and I started dating her while he was dating her. We weren't friends at that point. But I think it's the way that we dealt with each other through that process that made us become friends.

What was your favorite celebrity sighting at Studio 54?
[Legendary pianist] Vladimir Horowitz because he was such an unlikely person to be there. He came to watch with earplugs in.

Crate & Barrel named a sofa "Ian" in your honor and you sued them. Why?
Because they didn't even have the courtesy to ask. They kinda have this attitude that they can do whatever they want to do. They had to withdraw the name. If they would've asked I probably would've said no ... but they just went and did it and then they had the nerve to tell me that it had nothing to do with me — even though the [store merchandise] buyer said it was inspired by Ian Schrager.

What's your favorite hotel to stay in?
It's really only my hotels that I like 100 percent.

Do you think some of the W hotels in New York City are similar to yours?
No. To me, the Ws have no ethos, no originality, no vision. They're replications of what they see. It's like between Coca-Cola and Royal Crown Cola. ... My customers don't go to the W. It's not their cup of tea.

What's your biggest pet peeve with hotels today?
I think I'm kind of bored with this over-the-top design with no reason for it, no vision for it. It's not authentic.

Do you think you're compromising your hip, sleek, cool brand by partnering with the Marriott?
No, not at all. I'm a consultant to Marriott. It's my own private label.

You've moved into the value-oriented hotels sector with Public. Why?
It'll have a bigger impact on the industry than the boutiques had. ... They're value-oriented hotels with great service and style. That's the new twist. I got the idea from an Apple store. When I went in there, with the Genius Bars and the way everything is so much like a cult, where you get great service by their brand ambassadors, I came out thinking, 'Is that luxury service, or what is that? It's essential.' Everything you needed they gave you [without the] array of services nobody really cares about.

In 1979, you and Rubell pleaded guilty to income tax evasion at Studio 54 and served nearly two years in prison. What did you take away from that?
It was unreported $400,000 in gross income. I guess I must've been thinking the rules didn't apply to me. It didn't take away my enthusiasm or passion for life, but I came out of it knowing that I had to play by the rules that everyone else does. ... We lost everything. We had nothing. But we were able to come back and pick ourselves up off the floor and dust ourselves off. **TRD**

Photo by Michael Toolan

MARYANNE GILMARTIN

CEO | **FOREST CITY RATNER COMPANIES**

Gilmartin is overseeing Brooklyn's multibillion-dollar Atlantic Yards development, which includes Barclays Center. She also led the construction of the new 1.6 million-square-foot New York Times headquarters in Midtown. Before joining Forest City Ratner in 1994, she participated in the city's Urban Fellows Program and spent seven years at the Public Development Corporation — now the New York City Economic Development Corporation. *Interview by Candace Taylor*

"I slay the dragon every day and my husband is the quiet warrior."

What's your date of birth?
May 28, 1964.

Where did you grow up?
I was born in Queens. My father left when I was young. Rockaway Beach was his playground, and so we moved to my mother's preferred playground, Woodstock, N.Y.

How many siblings do you have?
Two sisters and two [half] brothers. I'm the second oldest.

How did your father's leaving affect you?
It cultivated a fierce sense of independence, and a determination to be a different kind of parent and a provider for my family. I think it also taught me that nobody will bring you happiness; you make it yourself.

What kind of kid were you?
I was the nurturer to the younger siblings. The fixer. And I was an exceptionally good student, a curious learner. School was predictable, focused and rewarding, whereas home life was a lot more chaotic.

Where did you go to college?
I was offered a generous scholarship and financial package by Fordham. We were broke at the time so I worked two jobs during my four years there: work-study and waiting tables at Jerry and Val's Seafood Café at 76th and Third Avenue. Everybody should have to wait tables at one point in their life. It teaches you how to multitask and treat people with dignity.

How did you meet your husband?
We met on campus the first week I was at Fordham. We were friends. I had a huge crush on him. But it didn't become a romance until our five-year reunion. We married in 1995, when I was about 30. I had a rule: I didn't want to be married before 30. I thought my 20s were meant to be lived as a single woman in the city.

Where did you live when you were single?
I lived in Brooklyn for quite a few years. I had an amazing apartment on Atlantic Avenue across from the prison, when they still did conjugal visits [laughs].

How do you get from your house in Westchester to Forest City's headquarters in Downtown Brooklyn every day?
I have a driver ... I used to laugh with Bruce [Ratner] when I was pregnant with each of my children that I would go into labor on the BQE and have to name one of them after an exit.

I read that your husband stays home with your kids.
I slay the dragon every day and my husband is the quiet warrior. He nurtures and cultivates our home life. It's the secret to my success in so many ways.

How did that come about?
He went into the police department and then got his law degree. After 9/11, we looked at our life and said we wanted to participate in as meaningful a way possible in raising our children. I had the better gig, so he was willing to give it a whirl. I like to say he couldn't pack a diaper bag in 2001. Now he's quite good.

How old are your kids?
Devin is 13, Aidan is 11, and Tess is 6.

How did you end up in development?
It was really serendipity and a little bit of air-conditioning. For the Urban Fellows Program, you interviewed with city commissioners. I toured the various agencies and was aghast at the conditions — desks in the hall, fairly deplorable buildings. But I arrived for my interview at the Public Development Corporation, and it was air-conditioned and carpeted. I thought, let me try public development.

What has been challenging for you personally about the opposition to Atlantic Yards?
It's a complicated project with lots of dimensions. And that's just hard work and I love that. I can't say I love the friction and the tension in a public setting. But it comes with the territory. I knew that and I accept that.

What do you think you're like as a boss?
I imagine at times I'm overbearing and exhausting. Hopefully at times, uplifting, funny and inspirational.

Why are you exhausting?
I'm passionate. I definitely do my finest work after 11 p.m. I sleep five hours a night. I keep a certain pace that I imagine can at times be challenging for those who work with me.

What do you do to relax?
Relaxation is the grass between my toes in my yard with my children underfoot. A game of Wiffle ball, a swim in the pool. I have two dogs, two fish and two birds.

I read that you taught aerobics. Is that true?
That would fall under the category of, if you want the job done you do it yourself. I had far too many workouts that were less than satisfying. So I taught myself how to teach. I was [New York Sports Clubs'] secret weapon when they needed a sub. If they had 60 people signed up for a class at Lincoln Center, they'd call me at 4 and I'd see if I could steal away. This was in the 1990s, pre-children.

Do your kids understand what a big deal Atlantic Yards is?
They used to be flummoxed by what I did. They wondered ... how could she leave every morning in a suit and build that building? When did she pick up her tool belt and how did she get so high up in the air? Whenever possible I include my children. For example, at the Atlantic Yards groundbreaking, both of my boys were there. I always say if I have to leave my children every day it better be good. And this has been quite good. **TRD**

August 2010

THE CLOSING

JEFF GREENE

REAL ESTATE INVESTOR

Greene, the billionaire investor, is best known for making hundreds of millions of dollars shorting subprime mortgage-backed securities before the 2008 financial crisis. But he's also a developer and property owner, with a portfolio of 3,000 residential units in Los Angeles. In 2013, he had plans for two New York City condo projects in the works: a 140,000-square-foot property at 100 Vandam Street, and a six-story building at 576 Broome Street. He's also tried his hand at politics. In 2010, Greene made an unsuccessful bid for a U.S. Senate seat in Florida, losing in the Democratic primary. *Interview by Katherine Clarke*

"For the most part, people who have worked for me tell me they don't like me much, but they learned a lot."

What's your date of birth?
December 10, 1954.

Where do you live?
We're in Palm Beach about eight months of the year. We're in the Hamptons two to three months a year, and we also have places in Beverly Hills and Malibu.

How did you meet you wife, Mei Sze?
We first met at a charity dinner and then we became reacquainted seven years ago in Sag Harbor, at a birthday party for Mike Tyson on my boat. We have two boys and a third on the way.

Mike Tyson was also the best man at your wedding. How do you know each other?
We met in Malibu 20 years ago. I know a lot of very colorful people from living in L.A. I consider him one of my best friends.

Sounds like you had a pretty crazy social life before getting married.
It's described by some people as crazier than it really was. I'd have a few big parties and they'd sometimes be a little crazy, and so people would assume that's what I did all the time. I wasn't going to parties every day — I was a serious adult, with a business career. I'd go to St. Bart's over New Year's in my boat and have one big party, and the next party would be Memorial Day weekend.

Do you still throw big parties?
Yeah, but now the average age [of the guests] is 2. It's all Elmo and Ferris wheels.

Where did you grow up?
Worcester, Massachusetts. My dad had a textile machinery business, [but] he lost his livelihood in the late 1960s because the textile industry moved to the South. My mother, who had been a stay-at-home mom, ended up having to work as a waitress to make ends meet. In my junior year of high school, they moved to West Palm Beach and bought a company that made rubber stamps. I stayed in Massachusetts with a great-aunt to finish up school.

Did you make trouble for your aunt?
No. I was really nerdy and played trumpet in the high school band. I thought the cool thing was getting into a good college.

Where did you go to college?
John Hopkins University. I finished a four-year degree in two-and-a-half years. I was working three jobs, teaching Hebrew school and working as a busboy and a waiter.

What did you do when you graduated?
I lived on the road for almost three years selling circus tickets. I had a Pontiac Grand Am with a bar across the back seat with my clothes hanging on it. I'd pull into, like, Bluefield, West Virginia, or Dubuque, Iowa, check in to the local Motel 6 or Econo Lodge, and be there for a week or two running these telemarketing operations. It was a very lonely life. But I saved up $100,000, which was a lot in the mid-1970s.

How did you get into real estate?
I decided to go to Harvard Business School, and I wasn't sure where to live, so I took all this cash I'd saved and bought a three-unit building, in Somerville, Massachusetts. The idea was that I would live in one unit and rent the other two to cover the costs. It worked out so well that I started buying more. By the time I got my MBA, I had 18 properties and my $100,000 was worth over $1 million. I was running around showing the apartments and collecting the rents.

After business school, you moved to California and got into real estate there.
Around 1983, I bought an eight-unit building in Brentwood for $510,000. ... By 1991, I had about a $110 million portfolio, and my net worth was probably $35 or $40 million. I was feeling pretty pleased with myself. I was 36 years old and I had a house up in Bel Air and one in Malibu, on the beach. I was a single bachelor with a Mercedes and a Ferrari in the garage. Then, all of a sudden, the market crashed. I spent the next three years trying to dig out from under the mess.

What made you start investing in mortgage-backed securities in the mid-2000s, where you were betting against them?
I was sitting on a billion-dollar real estate portfolio and thinking, What if the market dips again? I really felt like these prices couldn't go on forever, and I thought, there's got to be something I can do to protect myself in the event of another slowdown.

How much did you actually make from those trades?
In the $800 million range.

You're known as a very tough boss, and you've been nicknamed "Mean Jeff Greene." Is that an accurate characterization?
I don't think I'm mean. I put a lot of pressure on myself to do well, and I put the same pressure on the people around me. For the most part, people who have worked for me tell me they didn't like me much, but they learned a lot. I'm very proud of that. It would be worse if they said, 'Boy, he was a sweet guy, but I learned nothing.' **TRD**

JONATHAN TISCH

CO-CHAIRMAN | LOEWS CORPORATION

Loews — the company that Tisch's grandparents started back in the 1940s — is now worth in excess of $50 billion, with interests in off-shore drilling, insurance and commercial real estate with a major focus on hospitality. The Tisch family owns 50 percent of the New York Giants. Tisch, the son of late business mogul Robert Tisch, is also chairman of Loews Hotels; the subsidiary owns and operates hotels in more than a dozen major cities in the United States and Canada. Among its properties is the Loews Regency Hotel at 540 Park Avenue, where real estate executives have long gathered for their "power breakfast." Tisch is also a co-founder of Walnut Hill Media, which invests in movies and TV projects. *Interview by Katherine Clarke*

"When you look back at the games, you realize how much could have gone wrong, but it went right."

What's your date of birth?
December 7, 1953. Pearl Harbor Day.

Where were you born?
Atlantic City, N.J. I spent my early years in New Jersey.

What was your childhood like? Were you aware that your dad and uncle were creating a business empire?
Certainly, my siblings and cousins and I were very much aware. My uncle Larry was always referred to as "the inside Tisch" and my father was "the outside Tisch." Larry was a financial genius and my father was the one who knew everybody. ... Today I run the corporation with my two cousins, Andrew and Jim. But there are seven of us — three on my side and four on my cousins' sides. We were virtually raised as one family.

Did you ever consider staying out of the family business?
I didn't go into Loews for many years. I graduated from Tufts University in 1976 and I was hired by WBZ, then Boston's NBC station. I was a cinematographer and editor. I spent three years there, producing sports, public affairs and children's shows, and was nominated for three local Emmy Awards. I didn't win any of them. I've since been nominated for two more and didn't win those either. I'm 0 for 5. I'm the Susan Lucci of my generation.

Didn't you also have a TV show?
I had my own show for seven years [called "Beyond the Boardroom with Jonathan Tisch"]. It was the only show where CEOs were interviewed by other CEOs. I did 52 interviews in seven years.

Were you ever stonewalled by a CEO?
I'm not sure that they always gave me the answers I was hoping for. Hopefully I came back with another way of trying to get the information.

How long have you been married to your wife Lizzie?
Five and a half years. She has a business that introduces new designers to clients in New York City. She's very knowledgeable about the up-and-comers of Paris and London. She's very attuned to what people are wearing.

How many kids do you have?
I have two kids in college from my first marriage and a step-daughter. I first got married in 1988. My ex-wife [Laura] and I are very close.

Your first wedding was a big society affair with guests like Barbara Walters. Did you go for something smaller this time around?
I'm not answering that.

Your family owns a stake in the Giants. What's it like when they win the Super Bowl?
They've won twice in the last five years. It's a truly remarkable experience. In both of our wins, the game wasn't decided until the final seconds. When you look back at the games, you realize how much could have gone wrong, but it went right. It tells you a lot about life. For my father, a kid growing up starting with not a lot in Brooklyn, to be able to buy half of his hometown NFL franchise, it was wonderful. Until he passed away seven years ago, it brought him so much pleasure to go out to Giants Stadium on a Sunday and stand on the field.

You're renovating the Loews Regency. Are you attached to that property?
It's certainly a labor of love. The power breakfast there goes back more than 30 years to when the federal government was turning its back on New York and the city was about to go broke. The leaders of the day — including my father, Lew Rudin, Felix Rohatyn and others — would gather to talk about how to save New York. My father lived at the Regency, so they had breakfast downstairs.

There was a story awhile back speculating on whether or not New York hot shots will return for the breakfast after the renovation. Are you worried that they'll find another spot?
My feeling is not only will they come back, but they will be so pleased with what they see that the fact that we inconvenienced them for 10 months will be a distant memory.

Speaking of power breakfast, are you a morning person?
I'm usually up by 5:30. I only sleep about five hours a night. Most days I'm at SoulCycle by 6 or 7 a.m.

What are your hotel pet peeves?
I don't think that people should be obsequious when they offer service. Don't shout in my face that you're giving me service.

What's been your biggest personal gaffe?
Probably some of the dates I went on. The people I dated probably thought it was their biggest gaffe.

Who are your friends in the industry?
Billy Rudin [son of Lew Rudin] is a dear friend, Jeff Wilpon, whose family owns the Mets, and Jeff Blau at the Related Companies. I'm also fortunate to know Rob Speyer.

What's your biggest vice?
French fries from Balthazar and Pastis. **TRD**

May 2013

JAMES KUHN

PRESIDENT | **NEWMARK GRUBB KNIGHT FRANK**

Kuhn's tenure as president of one of New York's largest commercial brokerages began in 1992, when he joined Newmark & Company, after 15 years of owning real estate with legendary investor Bernard Mendik, with whom he acquired 6,000 apartments and more than 11 million square feet of office space. In 2011, Newmark was acquired for $63 million by global financial services firm BGC Partners, which bought brokerage Grubb & Ellis the next year and merged the two companies. During his career, Kuhn has been an advisor, broker or principal in more than $4 billion of transactions. *Interview by Katherine Clarke*

"My father never really made much money in real estate, until he came to work for me."

What's your date of birth?
May 17, 1948.

You grew up in New York, right?
I grew up in Stuy Town. It was a great place to grow up because everyone there was the child of a war veteran. There was no class structure and nobody had a lot of money. I went to a public school on 10th Street and First Avenue.

Your dad was a war veteran?
Yes, he flew B-17s in World War II.

What did he do after he came back from the war?
He worked for the IRS chasing tax evaders, and then went into real estate — in the movie-theater-site-location business. Eventually, he came to work with me.

What were you like as a kid?
I looked like Howdy Doody. I had asthma, curly red hair, freckles and big ears.

You were a fencer in high school?
I was a fencer in high school and college, and then in the veteran's division. I was seventh in the country up until about 10 years ago. I'm retired now.

You're also a musician?
Yes, it all started when I was eight and my parents bought us a piano. I had a high school band called Jimmy and the Jelly Beans. It was a band of four redheads. We played mostly in churches and temples. When I got out of grad school, I tried to become a songwriter, but I had too many student loans to pay back.

You're in a band now with NGKF managing director Billy Mendelson, called Square Feeet? Where do you play?
We play about once a month, sometimes at the Red Lion [in the West Village] or Prohibition [on the Upper West Side]. It's me, Billy and three other guys. We've been together 12 years. We're a classic rock cover band, and I play keyboards.

Where did you go to college?
Syracuse for undergraduate and graduate. I was an aerospace engineering major initially, but that didn't work out too well. I switched over to business and got an MBA. My dad said I could do anything but real estate.

Why was that?
He never really made much money in real estate, until he came to work for me.

Where do you live?
On 73rd Street between Lexington and Park, in a townhouse I bought in 1987. I have a summer house in Quogue on the ocean. I bought the land in 1983.

How long have you been married to your wife, Marjorie?
It will be 30 years this coming March. She was a student in a class [I taught] at NYU. We didn't start going out until after she'd finished the class.

How many kids do you have?
Three. My oldest son, Joey, is a brilliant filmmaker. My daughter, Carly, works as a producer for the "Chelsea Lately" show in L.A. My youngest son, Jake, just graduated from Duke with a major in Japanese. He's interning for a music producer.

When did you decide to get into real estate?
When I got out of grad school in 1972, there was a recession. The only job I got was in the mortgage department at Metropolitan Life Insurance Company foreclosing on New York City landlords. I made $12,000 a year.

Didn't you try to foreclose on Harry Helmsley?
Yes, at 1 Penn Plaza, but my superiors didn't think it was a good idea. It was okay; I didn't get fired.

How did you meet Bernie Mendik?
He was one of the other landlords I tried to foreclose on. He decided to hire me instead. He and his partner Larry Silverstein were splitting up, and he needed someone to do acquisitions for him.

How did you end up joining Newmark?
I knew Barry [Gosin] and Jeff [Gural]. They had started a fledgling brokerage company, and they wanted me to run it, so I started here as president and COO in 1992.

How are the three of you different?
Barry is serious, Jeff is laid back, I am emotional. People like Barry after the first meeting, people like me after the second meeting, people like Jeff before they meet him. Barry is Neil Diamond, Jeff is Lou Reed, I am Billy Joel.

Do you often put your foot in your mouth?
People will tell you I'm a 'tell-it-like-it-is' kind of guy.

What are your bad habits?
I watch much too much TV. My wife says I'm always plugged in. I like "Sons of Anarchy" and "The Good Wife."

Are you a tough boss?
You never have to guess where you stand with me, and you may not always like what I tell you, but I'm fair and loyal.

Who are your closest industry friends outside of NGKF?
Mike Fascitelli [formerly of Vornado] and Jeff Levine [of Douglaston Development] are some of my closest friends in the business.

Do you make as much money as you'd like to?
I don't put much value on possessions. I drive a Jeep Wrangler and I wear a $50 watch. The reason I make less than I'd like is because I'd like to give a lot more away. **TRD**

ROBERT IVANHOE

CO-CHAIRMAN | **GREENBERG TRAURIG**

As the head of Greenberg Traurig's real estate practice in New York, Ivanhoe has handled a slew of high-profile deals during his career, including MetLife's record 2006 sale of Stuyvesant Town to Tishman Speyer for $5.4 billion. In 2013, he represented the Chetrit Group in its $1.1 billion acquisition of the Sony Building at 550 Madison Avenue. *Interview by Katherine Clarke*

"Sometimes I crash on the couch in my office when things get really bad. It's not a very comfortable couch."

What's your date of birth?
April 29, 1953.

What were you like as a kid growing up in Great Neck?
I was very into sports. I was quite shy. I didn't start to excel in school until I was in junior high school. I don't think I was that interested.

What did your parents do?
My mother was a housewife. My father and uncle were in the aluminum extrusion and window manufacturing business making windows and doors for high-rise apartment buildings.

Did you ever want to join the family business?
I always had it in the back of my mind. My father called me when he and his partners were considering selling, when I was in college, and he asked me my feelings about taking it over one day. [But] I was a sophomore in college and I wasn't ready to make that commitment.

How did his decision to sell impact you?
That changed my direction. I thought I better start thinking about what I wanted to do with my career and my life.

Where do you live now?
In Greenwich. I've lived there for 24 years. It's rather bucolic. I like that as a contrast to my everyday life [in the city]. I commute by train. I often do document review on the way home. It's the longest stretch of uninterrupted time I get most days.

Do you have any other homes?
We have a home in Park City, Utah, which we've had for about five years. I took up skiing at the ripe old age of 47, which a lot of people thought was crazy. But I was in very good shape for someone my age.

You don't keep a place in the city?
My daughter lives in the city. I've crashed at her place once in two years. Sometimes I crash on the couch in my office when things get really bad. It's not a very comfortable couch. A few months ago, we handled the [$250 million] sale of the Monterey for Related and I was here a few nights until 3 or 4 in the morning.

How long have you been married to your wife, Anne?
This month, it will be 30 years. We met on a blind date set up by my cousin. I don't know that I'd ever been on any other blind dates.

How did you get started in real estate?
I worked two summers for [Glenwood Management's] Leonard Litwin as a renting agent. He was a big customer of my father's, and has been an incredible mentor to me. He is one of the most incredible human beings I've known in my life.

What's the best advice he ever gave you?
When I was graduating law school, I wanted to take a job in the federal government, in Washington, D.C., but he told me not to accept any offers until I went and met with him when I was home that Thanksgiving. He said to me, 'I've known you your whole life and I see the potential that you have. While I admire and respect the fact that you want to go work for the government to do good in the world, it's not well-suited to you.'

What did he advise you to do instead?
He said I should come work for his firm, or for the law firm he used. Then he set up an interview for me at the firm, Dreyer & Traub. I stayed there until the firm dissolved in 1995.

What was the first big case you worked on?
Donald Trump's purchase of the site that became Trump Tower in 1978 or 1979.

You tried to invest with Bernie Madoff before he got busted. Why did he turn you down?
The investment I was going to make at that time would have been very small, and I was shut down very quickly. I was told he's not going to take that kind of investment from a lawyer. Now, it seems obvious what that meant.

Will you finish your career at Greenberg Traurig?
I've been thinking about that a lot lately. I'm in good physical shape and I think I could do this a lot longer if I wanted to, but there are other things I'd like to do. I see myself traveling a lot more and maybe taking on more of an advisory [role] to certain clients, but not necessarily in a purely legal capacity.

What are your hobbies?
I play golf. My index is 6.8. It used to be a lot better. I was as low as a 2 at one point.

I read that you often play golf with Stephen Green of SL Green. Is he a good partner?
I've played with him many times. He used to be a championship squash player, but took up golf at about 50. He was a beginner when we got paired at a REBNY outing. I didn't play that well, but he was so in awe of me because I was a single-digit golfer. He became kind of enthralled and took to the game with tremendous determination.

How would you like to be remembered when you die?
As a man who was thoughtful, a good listener, and of high integrity in all aspects of life, as well as a good husband, father and friend. **TRD**

December 2013

DOUG STEINER

PRESIDENT | STEINER EQUITIES GROUP

Steiner wears multiple professional hats: His Steiner Equities Group, which was founded by his father, specializes in office, industrial and retail development nationwide. He is also head of Steiner NYC, the development firm behind an upcoming 52-story rental building in Downtown Brooklyn, among other projects. And notably, he's chairman of Brooklyn-based Steiner Studios, the largest film and TV production complex on the East Coast. In 2012, the studio announced plans to drastically expand its 300,000-square-foot facility; some 170,000 square feet of new soundstages are in the works. "Spider-Man," "Sex and the City" and "Boardwalk Empire" are just a few of the productions that have filmed at Steiner Studios. *Interview by Katherine Clarke*

"Sometimes I go for a big real estate meeting in a Midtown building and they think I'm the bike messenger."

What's your date of birth?
1960. I don't want to give you my exact date of birth. Then you're going to ask me for my passwords. I'm paranoid.

Where did you grow up?
South Orange, N.J.

Do you still live in New Jersey?
I raised my kids in New Jersey, so I used to split my time between Short Hills, N.J., and New York City. My kids have moved on now, so I'm fully in New York.

Where in the city do you live?
I'm moving to Williamsburg in six to nine months. I'm going to get rid of [my place in the East Village]. I'm also getting ready to sell my home in Short Hills. I'm looking forward to living in one place. I want all my kids to have a room and feel like they have a home.

Do you have any other homes?
I have a place in Cape Cod. I've been going to the same town there for 24 years, and I finally bought a house there in the fall.

What were you like as a kid?
Painfully shy. I always felt — and still sort of feel — like an outsider.

Where did you go to college?
Stanford. My degree is in English and creative writing. I didn't give much thought to picking a major, but there were a lot of books I thought I had to read to feel educated. In hindsight, I probably should have majored in something else; I don't like literary criticism and that's most of what being an English major is.

Steiner NYC was founded by your father in 1996. Did you go straight into the family business after college?
When I graduated, I moved to Paris to become a novelist, but I figured out that I liked reading a lot more than writing. I was living a trustafarian's life, supported by my father. After about six months, I was just dying to start working. I came back and started to work [in the family business] the next day.

Do you still use your French from time to time?
Pas du tout [not at all].

Have you ever had a job outside of the family business?
I worked as a gardener in college for a while, and I was the editor of Stanford's humor magazine, the Stanford Chaparral. It's like the Harvard Lampoon, but very funny. I also worked for Cushman & Wakefield in Oakland one summer.

What's it like to work so closely with your dad?
When it's good, it's great. When it's bad, it's really bad. We got along fantastically for many years, and there was a little rough spot with Steiner Studios opening and me dividing my attention between the real estate and the studios. The studios were really my baby. But we've gotten back to our old thing, and I can rely on him for anything, and he can rely on me for anything.

You got divorced in 2000. Do you still have a friendly relationship with your ex-wife?
I got married in '88 and separated in '99. It was a five-and-a-half-year divorce. It was grueling, [but] I get along fine with my ex.

How old are your kids?
My kids are 22, 18 and almost 17. Two boys and a girl. My son George, the 22-year-old, started his own business called TheHockeyNetwork.com. My son Neil just started at Middlebury College and my daughter Isabel is at boarding school. We named the commissary at Steiner Studios after her, Café Isabel.

Are you dating anyone?
Pass.

What are your hobbies?
Photography. I like taking pictures of the urban, industrial landscape. I also play poker once a month with my high school friends. It ranges from Indian No Peekie to Seven Card Stud to Guts. I don't know if you've played Indian No Peekie — you don't look at your cards, you just hold them up like a headdress and you're laughing at everyone else.

Are you a film buff?
I like a great film like I like a good novel. My dream someday would be to write a novel and make it into a movie and direct it.

I heard you also collect art.
I like weird, disturbing or strange art. I have art by Gary Panter, Suzan Pitt and Jane Dickson. I get a lot of pleasure from looking at it. But I don't spend a lot of money on art. I'm cheap.

Do you still get starstruck when you run into celebrities at Steiner Studios?
Rarely. But I recently saw Paul Simon at a political function and I was totally starstruck. I left him alone. I try to stay out of celebrities' way — they come to Steiner Studios so they don't have to meet people like me.

You're well-known in the industry for dressing casually. Do you not like suits?
I try to avoid wearing suits or blazers. I like to be comfortable. Sometimes I go for a big real estate meeting in a Midtown building and they think I'm the bike messenger, which is totally okay with me. **TRD**

DOTTIE HERMAN

CEO | **DOUGLAS ELLIMAN**

Herman began her career as a real estate broker on Long Island, and purchased Prudential Long Island Realty in 1989. After expanding the company to the Hamptons, she purchased longtime Manhattan brokerage Douglas Elliman for nearly $72 million with her business partner, Howard Lorber, in 2003. The company, New York's largest residential brokerage, now has more than 70 offices in New York City, Long Island, Westchester, the East End, South Florida and Southern California. Through a partnership with Knight Frank Residential, Douglas Elliman expanded its network to 43 countries across six continents.

Interview by Candace Taylor

"In business, anything you decide to do should be put in writing. Even with friends."

What's your date of birth?
I'm not telling. I'm not putting that on the tape.

Where did you grow up?
Franklin Square, Long Island.

Where do you live now?
In the city I live on Central Park South. On the Island, I live on the North Shore. And I have a place in the Hamptons.

Do you own or rent in the city?
I own, and I bought at the peak of the market. I knew I was paying a lot, but there weren't many apartments available and I just went with it.

When you buy property, who do you use as a broker?
I actually used one of my brokers [Howard Margolis]. The listing was from a competitor. By the time the transaction was done, she was with me.

Of all those homes, which one is your favorite?
I love them all differently. I guess the home in the Hamptons is special because I always dreamed of owning a home there. I purchased it when we were going through a pretty bad recession in the early '90s. At the time, people said, 'Why would you buy in the Hamptons? Look what's happened!'

Is it on the water?
No. I couldn't afford on the water. If I could have, I would have.

How many children do you have?
I have a daughter, [Christine]. She's 32. She lives on the Island now.

How long have you been married [to second husband Jay Herman] and how did you meet him?
I've been married ... a long time. He's an attorney. I met him socially. I was in my 20s, I was out with friends.

How often do you see each other?
We don't see each other much, especially not during the week. It's worked for us; both of us were serious about our careers from the day we met. Any relationship takes compromises. I don't think there's a perfect formula for marriage. If it works for both of you, that's what counts.

What time do you go to bed and wake up?
I get up at 5:30. I work out at 6:15. I have a trainer and I work out four days a week if I can. I'm not a sleeper. You can talk to anyone who works for me; they get e-mails from me at 1 a.m.

When you were young, your family was involved in a car accident that killed your mother. How has that impacted you?
Because my mom died when I was 10 and I was the oldest, I think that I really fended for myself more than most kids do. I kind of grew up quickly. I've often wondered what it would have been like if my mother hadn't died.

When you started in real estate, you were a divorced single mom. What were some of the challenges you faced?
I didn't have the money for a nanny. I had to rely on family and neighbors. At the time, most mothers didn't work. My daughter would say, 'Everyone else's mom is home.' But in certain ways I was a role model for the kids.

What was one of the mistakes you've made in your career?
There was a deal where somebody shook my hand and said, 'I'm giving you my word.' I was hesitant, but I was working with another broker who said, 'Oh, just take it.' And he broke it. So I learned that in business, anything you decide to do should be put in writing. Even with friends.

Before you bought Douglas Elliman, you had a successful company on Long Island. Why did you decide to begin a risky and expensive venture in New York City?
I could have sold. I was offered a decent price. But I wasn't done. There was no company that was from Manhattan to Montauk. But it wasn't about the money. I did it because it was my vision.

Did you encounter snobbery from other agents?
I wouldn't know what other people said. I can just tell you that I had really good experiences with all the brokers and with all the owners.

How do you get back and forth to Long Island?
I have a car. I love driving, but not in the city.

What kind of car do you drive?
I've had a Mercedes SL for I don't know how many years. It's a convertible. When it's nice out, I can put the top down and I can listen to my music. A lot of my best thoughts come when I'm driving.

Tell me about your office. Is that a photo of Bill Clinton?
Yes, I had a fundraiser for Hillary at my house. You see the big shoe in the background? My house in the Hamptons has a shoe theme. I love shoes. That's what people give me when they don't know what to get. **TRD**

December 2009

YAIR LEVY

REAL ESTATE DEVELOPER

Levy is a developer who rose to prominence through several high-profile condo conversions during the boom, including the Sheffield and 225 Rector Place. But Levy's roughly $400 million Manhattan real estate empire unraveled during the recession amid financial troubles. In 2011, a state Supreme Court judge found that Levy was using the reserve fund at Rector Place for personal expenses and ordered him to pay $7.4 million in restitution. He was permanently banned from selling condos in New York. Levy, who has denied that he stole from the fund, has since sought to get back into NYC real estate. In 2013, he bought several four-story row houses in Tin Pan Alley on West 28th Street. *Interview by Katherine Clarke*

"Money for me is not everything. What bothers me is they use my name and lie about me stealing money."

What's your date of birth?
November 5, 1949.

What's your hometown?
Tel Aviv.

Why did you leave Tel Aviv?
I had ambition.

Where do you live now?
Right by Lincoln Center, in a condo.

What's your vice?
I smoke a cigar about once a week.

What were you like as a kid?
I was one of six — three boys and three girls. Since I was a little boy, for some reason all I thought about was business. I was thinking about how to make money all the time. I used to sell all different types of items after school, like flowers and notebooks. I would buy flowers from the wholesaler and then sell them door-to-door after school when I was about eight. I left high school when I was 13 to help improve my family's quality of life.

What did your parents do?
My mom used to make custom evening dresses and my father was a real estate broker.

Weren't you a diamond cutter at one point?
I had all different kinds of businesses. But when my businesses weren't doing well, I used to work as a diamond cutter. I had a boutique shop, selling men's clothes, that opened when I was 19. When the store wasn't doing well, I would go in the morning and work on the diamonds. It was sure money. You're paid by the diamond.

How did you end up moving to New York?
I had started my own line making men's sweaters and had a brother who owned some clothing shops in the Village at that time. I smelled the opportunity in the United States. I thought I'd come to the United States and open my clothing line here. We decided to open a ladies line called Cactus. We opened a store on 58th and Lexington in 1974 and two stores on 34th Street. We sold all over the country: in Bloomingdale's, Macy's and Neiman Marcus.

How long have you been married?
Since I was 22. Sony [Sosana] and I grew up in the same area. When I had the shop [in Israel], she used to come by.

Do you have kids?
I have two daughters. One is 39 and one is 40. Both of them are residential brokers. They used to work for Douglas Elliman. Now they work for [the brokerage] Homestate Properties. I have six grandchildren.

How did you get into real estate?
I always had real estate mixed with my fashion. We paid all cash for our building on 58th and Lexington. At some point, I began to feel like I could do better in real estate. I'd had enough with the fashion. I sold my stake in the label to my brother [in 1997].

You made headlines with the bankruptcy at the Sheffield a few years ago.
The Sheffield was one of the most exciting buildings I bought. Then I brought in partners, Kent Swig and Serge Hoyda. We got Kent Swig to manage the building and he went way over budget. My plan was to go in and out, and sell quickly as-is. He kept getting fancier and fancier. He thought the market was going to stay forever, but he took way too long and the market collapsed.

There were infamous reports of you pummeling him with an ice bucket over the dispute.
We had a meeting about the Sheffield, and he started screaming and fighting with my lawyer. He stood up, and I said, 'Sit down.' He came at me and I grabbed the ice bucket to protect myself. He's a much younger man — younger by 10 years. He got wet and I dropped the bucket. He tried to use it for publicity and make me out to be the bad guy.

The Attorney General banned you from selling condos for allegedly stealing money from the reserve fund at Battery Park City's Rector Square. What's your response to that?
They used me for publicity by doing this before the election. Money for me is not everything. What bothers me is that they use my name and lie about me stealing money when it's not true. They refused to look into documents I prepared to prove everything I was saying. I've been a New Yorker for 43 years. I've never had any problem with anyone besides Kent. I felt it was an embarrassment.

How do you feel about the ban?
This country is a very big country. Nothing can stop me doing from business. I don't have to do condos.

What's your goal in this round of real estate investment?
My family is investing in income-producing deals and no development. The goal is to be involved in trophy-type buildings.

What's the biggest lesson you've taken away from this saga?
I won't listen to a lawyer again. **TRD**

July 2014

Photo by Marc Scrivo

ROBERT LAPIDUS

PRESIDENT | **L&L HOLDINGS**

Lapidus co-founded his company with David Levinson in 2000. L&L's portfolio includes trophy properties like the Metropolitan Tower at 142 West 57th Street and 150 Fifth Avenue, an office and retail building. The firm is also developing a 650,000-square-foot office tower at 425 Park Avenue designed by starchitect Sir Norman Foster. An attorney by training, Lapidus attended the University of Pennsylvania and Benjamin N. Cardozo School of Law and worked as a real estate lawyer before changing careers. *Interview by Katherine Clarke*

"My dad worked six days a week and we sort of lived hand to mouth. That wasn't the existence I wanted."

What is your full name?
Robert Tod Lapidus.

What's your date of birth?
February 12, 1961. I was born on Abraham Lincoln's birthday, and I'm named after Abraham Lincoln's eldest son, Robert Todd Lincoln, but my father didn't like the two Ds.

Where did you grow up?
On Long Island, in a town named Bellmore in Nassau County. It was a great suburban upbringing — we played outside until dark every day, and the door was never locked.

What did your parents do?
My dad was an optometrist, and my mom went back to school to become an optometric technician. They worked together for many years.

Did you ever think of going into the optometry business?
My dad worked six days a week and we sort of lived hand to mouth. That wasn't the existence I wanted.

What were you like as a kid?
My mother thought I was perfect, but I was probably a bit of a wise-ass. Once in eighth grade, the teacher told my mother, 'Your son is very smart, but he thinks he's smarter than I am.' My mother said, 'That's because he is.'

Where do you live now?
I live in Tenafly, N.J. We've been there for about 13 years. But now that our children are grown up, we'll probably move back into the city. We also have a place in Bridgehampton.

How old are your kids?
Alexandra, my daughter, just graduated from Lehigh University. My son, Brian, is at the University of Michigan. Alexandra wants to get into the real estate business.

What's your house in Bridgehampton like?
We live next to [Hamptons developer] Joe Farrell's "Sandcastle" house. Joe built my house first, about five years ago, and then his. Mine is a small little house compared to his, but it has pretty much every amenity you can imagine. You never have to leave.

Farrell has rented his house to a number of celebrities. Do you have any good celebrity gossip?
Not really. Jay-Z and Beyoncé were next door last year for a month. They were very quiet. One night at three or four in the morning, one of their guests buzzed on my door by mistake because we share a driveway. I didn't see Madonna at all when she stayed.

How long have you been married to your wife, Carol?
We just had our 30th wedding anniversary. We had a big party with about 200 people at our house in Bridgehampton. I met my wife when I was 19. The day I met her, I told my dad, 'I met the girl I'm going to marry today.' I just knew. We met through a mutual friend on the beach — I was a cabana boy at the beach club in Atlantic Beach [on Long Island]. So my wife married the help, basically [laughs].

What was it like being a cabana boy?
I got paid a salary of $87 a week, but I got $600 a week in tips because I hustled. Hustle pays off. It helped me pay for my wife's engagement ring.

How did you end up getting into real estate?
I worked for a law firm in New Jersey called Wolff & Samson. I represented a lot of people in the real estate business, and I said, 'I could do that.' When I left my law firm, I went to work as a real estate lawyer for my landlord, a big public company called Bellemead Development Corporation. I learned the business while I was there, and when I had the opportunity to move over to the business side, I did.

How did you and David Levinson decide to start L&L together?
David was a top broker, and we had very similar philosophies. We both wanted to go out on our own, so we held hands and jumped off a cliff together.

How are you and David different?
He's much more formal. I'm most comfortable in a Grateful Dead T-shirt and shorts, and he's very dapper and dresses very elegantly.

What's the most interesting deal you've ever worked on?
The building we're working on now, 425 Park, has definitely had the highest highs and the lowest lows. It's a once-in-a lifetime opportunity to build a new office tower on Park Avenue. The frustrating thing was that our partner was [the now-defunct] Lehman Brothers. That brought a lot of angst and uncertainty.

What car do you drive?
I drive a Maserati convertible. It's black with tan leather. It's my fun little fantasy car.

What are your hobbies?
I like sports. David and I both have an ownership interest in the Yankees. We acquired it about seven years ago. I don't collect art, so I thought, 'What the hell?' **TRD**

BILL RUDIN

CEO | **RUDIN MANAGEMENT COMPANY**

Rudin is CEO of a dynastic real estate firm started by his grandfather, Samuel Rudin, in 1925, and previously run by his father, Lew Rudin, and his uncle, Jack Rudin. The firm's portfolio is comprised of 10 million square feet of commercial space at buildings such as 3 Times Square, 345 Park Avenue and 80 Pine Street, as well as 20 luxury apartment buildings, including 1085 Park Avenue and 945 Fifth Avenue. The company's current projects include the Greenwich Lane, a collection of 200 condominium units across five buildings at the former site of St. Vincent's Hospital in the West Village. *Interview by Katherine Clarke*

"You could walk from the Four Seasons to the 21 Club on 52nd Street, and the world would pass by."

What's your date of birth?
April 20, 1955.

What were you like as a kid growing up in the city?
I was not the greatest student in the world. I loved sports and I had a lot of friends.

At what age did you get started in the business?
There's a picture of me in the late 1950s. My dad and my grandfather took me down to 80 Pine Street, where they were excavating the site. That was my first trip to a construction site.

Did you always want to be in real estate?
There was a moment after I graduated from college where I worked in the film industry. I was a production assistant for a couple of movies, like "The Deep" with Jacqueline Bisset, Robert Shaw and Nick Nolte. My stepfather was in the movie business [so he helped get me the job]. I then realized that the real estate business was where my heart was.

When did you join the family company?
I had worked for the company on and off over summers. One of my first jobs was in the mail room, and then I worked for the building manager at 345 Park Avenue.

Your dad was a huge New York personality. What was it like to grow up with such a well-known father?
It was always fascinating. He would hold court on Sundays at P.J. Clarke's, and it would be a revolving door of people in politics, entertainment and sports. We were invited once to dinner at Gracie Mansion with John and Mary Lindsay when I was 14. That was pretty cool.

Your father was very civically involved, starting with the fiscal crisis.
He understood early on that our real estate was tied into the health of the city. My grandfather didn't want him to get so engaged. He wanted him to focus on the business. But my father said, 'Pops, what I'm doing is our business.'

They named the street your office is on "Lew Rudin Way." What would he think of that?
That was his favorite corner. He would say, "You could walk from the Four Seasons to the 21 Club on 52nd Street, and the world would pass you by."

You won a New York Emmy Award for a documentary you helped make about your dad. How did that happen?
My dad wanted to do an oral history. We started to do interviews on tape. Then, he got ill. There were probably five or six hours of audio. Each one, you could hear him getting a little weaker. When he passed away, it took me six months to listen to the tapes. It was just unbelievable, the things he talked about, but it wasn't enough to tell his story. So I used that and other interviews for the documentary.

Where did you go to school?
I went to Dalton and the University of Arizona for two years. Then I came back to NYU.

How did you meet your wife, Ophelia?
At NYU, in Finance 101. It was September 1977. I knew she was taking an evening course, so I arranged to be walking near the building she'd be coming out of with one of my dogs so I could bump into her.

Do you have grandchildren?
Yes. My daughter Samantha is married, with an 18-month-old daughter named Elle. My son Michael got married last June.

Where do you live?
In one of our buildings on the Upper East Side.

Do you have any other homes?
We have a home in Bridgehampton. We love it out there.

What do you do for exercise?
I rollerblade in the morning. I try to get in two lower loops of Central Park. I get all my pads on and my helmet and use that time to think about things I need to do, or strategize on a deal we're working on. Ophelia and I swim a lot together, too.

What's your vice?
Eating too much, probably, whether it be J.G. Melon's hamburgers or Mezzaluna pizzas.

Your sister Beth DeWoody is a well-known art collector. Do you also collect?
Yes, we like the sculptor Ugo Rondinone, we have a couple of [pieces by sculptor] Anish Kapoor and [painter] David Hockney, but we're nowhere near my sister's level.

You're a dog lover, right?
I've had a dog in my life since I was 14 years old. That's probably one of the reasons my wife fell in love with me, because of my brown standard poodle, Smitty.

You have to be pretty comfortable with your masculinity to have a poodle.
He was a big poodle. I was not a small-poodle person until after Smitty II passed away. Ophelia and I have two dogs, Sebastian and Biriba. **TRD**

March 2014

ZIEL FELDMAN

FOUNDER | **HFZ CAPITAL GROUP**

Feldman is the founder of investment and development company HFZ and the chairman of Polar Investments. A graduate of Queens College and Cardozo Law School, Feldman has bought, sold and developed over 10,000 residential units over the course of his career. Prior to launching HFZ in 2005, he was a principal at the national development firm Property Markets Group. As of 2014, HFZ was one of the most active developers in New York, with projects including the Marquand at 11 East 68th Street on the Upper East Side, 305 East 51st Street in Turtle Bay and the high-profile One Madison Park condo in Flatiron. *Interview by Katherine Clarke*

"I grew up in Kew Gardens, where [thanks to the cemeteries] there are more dead people than live people."

What's your date of birth?
May 28, 1958.

Where did you grow up?
I grew up in Kew Gardens, Queens, where [thanks to the cemeteries] there are more dead people than live people. It's a nice suburban community, but kind of claustrophobic.

What did your parents do?
My dad was in the textile business, and my mom was a homemaker. My dad was born in Germany, and my mom was born in pre-Palestine. My dad came to the U.S. in 1939 and my mom came in 1952. They still live in Queens.

Do you have family members who lived through the Holocaust?
My dad escaped Hitler — he was about 12 when he fled. But my father-in-law, who is Hungarian, was one of the youngest survivors of Auschwitz.

How did you meet your wife?
I met her through the Jewish singles scene back in the 1980s, in Miami during Passover. It turned out that her father and my parents, as refugees, met in school. I believe her parents were actually at my circumcision.

What drew you to each other?
What drew her to me is obvious! [laughs]. I found her inner beauty even more striking than her outer beauty. She's extremely personable and can make conversation with a hat rack. We have three kids.

Where do you live?
I now live in Manhattan at one of our buildings at 11 East 68th Street, which is currently under construction. But we still have a home in Englewood, N.J., which has been on the market for sale. We also have a home in Bridgehampton, where we spend a lot of time.

Why are you selling your Englewood home, which I heard is designed to look like a French chateau?
I built it in 2000. When my youngest daughter was about to go to college, we decided to move back to the city, where we lived for about 15 years when we were first married.

How did you get into real estate?
I graduated from law school in 1983 and got a job in a small [real estate] legal practice. When the market collapsed, I could have become a bankruptcy lawyer to help my clients who went bankrupt, but instead I formed a real estate company called Property Markets Group, which I co-founded with Kevin Maloney.

You worked a little with Extell Development's Gary Barnett during that time.
I was introduced to Gary through a family member. He [Barnett] lived in Belgium and was in the diamond business with his wife's family. He wanted to bring investors to New York in the early 1990s. We bought a lot together, including the Belnord in 1994. We were partners for a number of years and then at a certain point he moved to New York and started doing his own stuff.

Why did you decide to leave PMG and launch HFZ?
Kevin's interests had moved to Florida and it was time for me to be on my own.

What's been your biggest career mistake?
I was involved in investing in a rock and roll amusement park in Myrtle Beach. Our timing was a little off. We finished it under budget and early, but it opened in the summer of 2008, which was the worst time to open up. Most people drive to Myrtle Beach, and gas prices were at a record high. It was very hard to attract people. It went bankrupt and was sold.

Did you at least get to try out the rides yourself?
Yes. They had a Led Zeppelin roller-coaster ride, set to "Whole Lotta Love." We had a Moody Blues "Nights in White Satin" roller-coaster ride.

Are you a rock and roll fan?
I like Bruce Springsteen and Simon & Garfunkel. The Rolling Stones are wonderful.

Have you ever played an instrument?
Years ago, I went to accordion lessons, which is kind of embarrassing. I guess my mother wasn't cool. I played the accordion without the monkey. **TRD**

KEN HORN

PRESIDENT | **ALCHEMY PROPERTIES**

Founded by Horn in 1990, Alchemy has purchased or developed more than 2 million square feet of real estate. The company's focus has been on condominium and multifamily residences in Manhattan and Brooklyn. Most notably Horn and his partners Joel Breitkopf and Gerald Davis are transforming the top 30 floors of the Woolworth building into 40 luxury condominiums. The trio acquired the upper portions of the iconic building for $68 million in 2012. Alchemy has also been behind such residential projects as the Isis at 303 East 77th Street and the 35XV condo at 35 West 15th Street. *Interview by Katherine Clarke*

"Lawyers make the rules while other people play the game. I thought it would be more fun to play."

What's your date of birth?
September 28, 1956.

Where did you grow up?
In Crown Heights and then in Flatbush, Brooklyn. Growing up in Brooklyn in the late 1960s and 1970s was wonderful.

What was it like?
On my street alone, there were probably 15 kids my age. We'd play football and baseball in the street. All the parents worked — my mother was a teacher and my dad was an accountant — but every single parent on the street looked after every kid. If I misbehaved, another parent would step in and drag me home by the ear.

Does your family still live in Brooklyn?
My dad still lives there. My mother developed brain cancer in her late thirties and passed away when she was 48. My brother passed away at 35 from AIDS. He was in the first wave of people who died in the city.

How have their deaths affected you?
I learned that no matter how bad things may get, at times there are always much worse scenarios.

Where do you live now?
I live in Scarsdale, in Westchester County, and I have a home in Manhattan, at the Isis.

Have you tried to move your dad closer to you?
He's never moving.

Tell me about your apartment at the Isis.
[Interior designer] Benjamin Noriega-Ortiz designed it. We wanted something that was wildly lavish and colorful. We didn't want it to look like your grandmother's house.

How long have you been married to your wife, Marjorie?
It will be 30 years in October. We got married in our early 20s. We had three kids by the time we were 31.

How did you meet?
I was an attorney at a law firm and she was a paralegal there. She claims she'd been flirting with me, but I was very proper and would not date anyone I worked with. Then she came to me and said, 'I just got a new job. Now we can go out on a date.'

Who is the boss at home?
My wife is very good at moving me in the right direction, let's put it that way. I never feel like I'm being bossed, but we always end up doing what Marjorie wants to do.

Tell me about your kids.
Alex is 26. He is working in commercial real estate. Katie is 24. She works at Alchemy in the PR department. My youngest, Jed, just graduated from college this month.

How did you go from real estate attorney to developer?
I had my law job for three years, at the firm now known as Bryan Cave, and then I started a gelato company. I didn't like being a lawyer. Lawyers make the rules while other people play the game. I thought it would be more fun to play.

Where did the gelato idea come from?
I went to Italy with Margie and learned to make gelato, and then I raised the money I needed to open my first gelateria [named Gran Gelato] on Third Avenue and 90th Street. My father-in-law used to call me the Good Humor man. He was none too happy that his daughter married a Fifth Avenue lawyer who was now becoming an ice cream guy.

Was the store successful?
Within a year, we had two gelaterias in New York and two franchises in Long Island. We were written up as the best gelato in New York. I was just 26 years old.

Why did you leave the gelato business?
Someone came to us and wanted to buy us. We got all our money back and we had a note [from the seller that said] that he was going to give us additional monies, but he vanished. He ran away with a 19-year-old scooper.

What did you do next?
I interviewed at a law firm and the partner interviewing me said, 'You don't want to be a lawyer, but I've got a client you'd be perfect for.' His client was Steve Shalom, owner of 2,300 apartments in Queens. I worked for him for five years. He taught me the business. I followed him around like a little chicken.

When did you start Alchemy?
In 1990, when the market was terrible. We began doing workouts for banks in defaulted co-op and condominium buildings. We would come in and figure out a way for the bank to recover its money. Once we recovered the money for the banks, we [had the option of buying] those units.

Have you always wanted to own the Woolworth Building?
No, but if someone said to me 15 years ago that I would be in a position to own the upper portion of the Woolworth Building, I would have said, 'What, are you crazy?' We've had a lot of luck. My dad, who is retired, was taking a course on the architectural history of New York City and they were discussing the Woolworth Building. The professor kept saying, 'The rumors are that someone is going to be going in and potentially making it residential.' Of course, my dad knew it was us, but he couldn't say anything. **TRD**

June 2013

THE CLOSING

| 41

DAVID CHILDS

CHAIRMAN EMERITUS | **SKIDMORE, OWINGS & MERRILL**

Childs is best known for designing the 1,776-foot-tall One World Trade Center, the centerpiece of the rebuilding effort in Lower Manhattan. He has also designed such notable New York buildings as the Time Warner Center at Columbus Circle, Worldwide Plaza and the New York Mercantile Exchange. In addition, he has worked on the National Mall master plan and Constitution Gardens in Washington, D.C. Childs has served as the chairman of the National Capital Planning Commission, the federal agency charged with overseeing development projects in the nation's capital, and as the chairman of the Commission of Fine Arts in Washington, both Presidential appointments. *Interview by Lauren Elkies*

"It was very meaningful to us, and cathartic in a way, to be working on a project that we saw destroyed."

What's your date of birth?

April Fools' Day, 1941. My mother always said she did everything to try and not have me that day, but I always thought it was great because people remembered it ... Seventy is old. But actually it's kinda nice.

Did you have a party for your 70th birthday?

No, but for many, many years I've been involved with the American Academy in Rome, a great institution for scholars, artists, sculptors and architects to study in Rome. One of the things I always wanted to do was go over there for a longer visit — rather than race over there for a meeting and come back, since architects usually go to China for an afternoon. One of my fellow academy trustees had actually renovated an old abbey in Tuscany, so I took his place for a week and took our three children and our six grandchildren.

Where did you grow up?

I was born in Princeton, N.J. My father was a professor of classics and he was drafted, so to speak, in the second World War because people who spoke ancient Latin and Greek were deemed to be good at cryptology. So I grew up in Princeton for a little bit and then in Washington. Then I pretty much grew up outside New York City, in Bedford Village, N.Y., from fifth grade on.

You majored in zoology at Yale University before switching to architecture. Why zoology?

I came from a family of scientists, medical mostly. I've always loved the sciences and I went away to an all-boys school in New England for high school. In this school you were suspect if you were interested in the arts, if you know what I mean. I say that with a smile, so be careful how you say that.

How did you and your wife of 49 years meet?

I was asked to be one of her escorts at a party. Girls in those days had to have two escorts to take them to a party.

Where do you live?

I'm on 86th Street, right near the park and the Egyptian art collection of the Metropolitan Museum of Art.

Do you have any other homes?

My children [all in their 40s] have a small place in the Adirondacks. We'd been going up there since they were born, renting a place, but there was a small little piece of land — well, 'small' up there is 60 acres — for sale in 1984 for nothing. And with some savings that they had gotten from their grandparents, they bought this piece of land. And then over time they built [sleeping] cabins. The nine buildings combined is 2,000 feet. But the property is unbelievable. You go up there to the top of the mountain, and you see these 6 million acres in the Adirondack Park, and you suddenly realize that all these things we do every day are not really that important.

What do you do in your free time?

Lots of things. I'm a great climber. When I was young, I used to do technical climbing of mountains. Now I do long Adirondacks hikes. I travel a lot. I'm a pretty diverse reader.

What's your favorite restaurant in New York City?

The Gotham Bar and Grill. The chef is still doing his thing there. He hasn't gone and opened an empire, flying around.

Who's been the toughest developer to work with?

It'd be hard for me to say, and if I could say, I wouldn't tell you.

What year did you start at SOM?

I began with SOM in 1971. But right before that, I went to work in Washington, D.C. — my first job — for Nat Owings, founder of the firm, and [Senator Daniel] Pat Moynihan, who were heads of the Pennsylvania Avenue Commission in Washington, to redesign Pennsylvania Avenue.

I read that you've said that you and architect Daniel Libeskind had a blowup at one point over your design for One WTC, but Libeskind denied it. How did you work it out and what's your relationship like now?

It is excellent and it's always been excellent. For the press, the story is much more interesting if there is a to-do. There really wasn't.

There were reports that some schematics went missing when Libeskind's employees were working in your offices. [The Libeskind employees allegedly wanted to bring the design to then-Governor Pataki to show him that Childs was ignoring his design.]

I wasn't there. It was 2 o'clock in the morning. I don't know what happened. There was a fuss the next morning. By noon it was all over. And, of course, it's been talked about for 10 years.

Does One World Trade Center achieve what you hoped it would?

It does achieve many of the very largest goals originally set for it, which have to do with being in the New York tradition, a marker in the sky for the most important building down there, which is the memorial. It's interesting, the void is the most important matter there. ... It gives form to Downtown again. It's also the answering gesture to the other great Downtown of this city, which is Midtown. ... And, of course, being two or three blocks away from the site here, we watched it and were very affected by it. We lost an employee. It was very meaningful to us, and cathartic in a way, to be working on a project that we saw destroyed. **TRD**

Photo by Marc Scrivo

HENRY ELGHANAYAN

CEO | **ROCKROSE DEVELOPMENT**

Elghanayan leads the Manhattan investment and development firm he founded back in 1970. Over the span of four decades, Rockrose has developed 10,000 residential units and has developed or acquired over 3 million square feet of commercial space. When the brothers Elghanayan split the family business in 2009, Henry kept the Rockrose name, and his brothers, K. Thomas and Frederick Elghanayan, left to form TF Cornerstone. The company has $1 billion invested in the Court Square area of Long Island City, where it built a 700-unit rental tower called the Linc LIC. Rockrose is also planning a large residential and commercial development near Hudson Yards. *Interview by Katherine Clarke*

"I have an unnaturally optimistic view on life — it's a sickness."

What's your full name?
Henry Elghanayan. Henry is my middle name. My first name is actually Houchang.

What's your date of birth?
August 2, 1940.

Your family moved here from Iran. Have you ever been there since?
I was there once before the [1979 Iranian] Revolution, on a business trip.

How come you haven't been back?
I can't. We're Jewish and that doesn't work there so well since the Revolution.

Why did your family originally move here?
When I was five years old, my father — who was in the import-export business — traveled to New York for the first time. He landed at the airport in the middle of the night, took a taxi into the city and was amazed when the cabbie stopped at all the red lights even though there wasn't any traffic. He was so impressed by the civility and orderliness of the American system that he made an on-the-spot decision to emigrate. Shortly after, our family flew to New York and moved to a house he bought on Rockrose Place in Forest Hills, Queens — hence the company name.

Where did you go to college?
I went to Hamilton College, Columbia Business School and then to law school at NYU. I was a matrimonial attorney initially, unfortunately. It was a rather unpleasant experience. Often the litigants aren't really looking for justice — they're looking for revenge. I decided I couldn't do it anymore and I switched to a law firm that happened to do real estate.

Is that how you got interested in owning your own real estate firm?
I was working very hard for all these real estate clients and I could see they were making a lot of money. I naively said to myself, 'I'm doing all the work, and they're making all the money.' So I switched to real estate.

What was your first property acquisition?
It was a five-story brownstone at 31 West 16th Street. I bought it for practically nothing because it had a lot of tenants in it. On Saturdays and Sundays, I would have an attaché case full of greenbacks and would go to each apartment to talk to the tenants. I would bring them flowers and gifts and make friends with them. Bit by bit I convinced them to move out. I carried the hundred dollar bills with me so that when they said they were willing to leave, I could give them the money.

Did you get them all out?
I got everyone out. The last one was an elderly lady who lived on the fifth floor. I carried all her boxes down five flights of stairs, packed her into my Ford convertible, and took her to the new apartment.

You've been married to your wife, Nancy, for 45 years. How did you meet?
When I was in law school, I worked weekends as a rental real estate agent, and she rented an apartment from us. After we went on that first date, it never ended. We're still on that first date.

Tell me about your kids. You have three?
My oldest son, Adam, teaches psychology at Princeton. Justin [president of Rockrose] is my second son. My third son, Ben, is a law student at Harvard. I consider them all brighter than me. I also have two grandkids.

Why did you initiate the 2009 division of the company?
I looked to the future and said, 'There's going to be some conflict as to who the ultimate successor would be.' I wanted to sidestep that whole thing. I didn't want that whole confrontation going on when I was gone. [My brothers] were a bit upset at the time. I think they've accepted it now.

Are you on good terms now?
There's some tension, but if you think of all the divisions that have happened in the real estate industry, this was a rather smooth one.

Do you need to have a certain amount of ego to be a successful developer in New York City?
You must not only have an ego, you must have a super-optimistic view of life. I have an unnaturally optimistic view on life — it's a sickness. If you understood the real dangers involved in doing a project, you would never do one.

Who have been your mentors?
I don't know if I'd call him a mentor, but Bernie Spitzer, Eliot Spitzer's father. When I first started my career, he was in business doing what I wanted to be doing, so I watched him very carefully and copied some of the things he did. I eventually got to meet him and we became tennis partners.

I read that you collect art. Which artists do you particularly like?
Toulouse-Lautrec, and I have a few Matisses. I wish I could do more of it, but we're so busy.

How do you measure success?
I won't have really made it until I can come to work in sandals. That's tongue-in-cheek to some extent, but it's true also. **TRD**

April 2013

LESLIE WOHLMAN HIMMEL

MANAGING PARTNER | **HIMMEL + MERINGOFF PROPERTIES**

Himmel founded the real estate investment company with Stephen Meringoff in 1985. The firm operates a portfolio of some 2 million square feet of Manhattan commercial real estate, valued at more than $750 million. Its properties include the 480,000-square-foot office building at 521 West 57th Street, as well as 401 Park Avenue South, a 12-story office and retail building. Before launching the firm, Himmel worked at the national real estate syndicator Integrated Resources. *Interview by Katherine Clarke*

"I asked, 'What's your greatest accomplishment?' He paused and then said, 'What are you doing tonight?'"

What's your full name?
Leslie Ellen Wohlman Himmel. Wohlman is my maiden name and Himmel was my married name with my first husband. I got remarried five years ago to Alan Shuch, but I didn't take his name. I just use it for making restaurant reservations.

What's your date of birth?
March 6, 1954.

Where did you grow up?
In White Plains. I went to a rough public high school, right around that Martin Luther King period. Every day, people were beaten up. I was in the minority as a Jewish Caucasian. I didn't get hit because I was a cheerleader and everyone liked me. My older brother went to private school at Horace Mann. They gave me the choice to go there too, but I liked my friends and I wanted to be on the [White Plains] tennis team. I promised that if they let me stay in public school, I'd still end up at a top college. I went to the University of Pennsylvania and then Harvard Business School.

What did your father do?
My dad had his own accounting firm and taught me from an early age the importance of numbers and entrepreneurship. There was a lot of math talk in my house.

When did you get married?
I married Jeffrey Himmel in 1984. We were married for about 22 years and divorced in 2006. I married Alan in 2008. He's a retired partner from Goldman Sachs.

How did you and Alan meet?
We were fixed up. We went out to dinner to a restaurant called Fiamma. All of a sudden it was midnight and the tables around us were empty. We'd been there for four and a half hours.

Did you go on a lot of bad dates before you met Alan?
It was a period in my life where I went way too much on a carousel. When I got divorced, I said, 'I'm not going to feel sorry for myself. I'm going to go out and have fun.' And I did. It was quantity, not quality. I went on a lot of dates, but Alan was by far the standout of the group.

Where do you live?
I live at 15 Central Park West. I used to see A-Rod in the gym but I couldn't quite compete with his athletic prowess.

Do you have any other homes?
My husband has a home in Nantucket, so we go there on weekends.

How many kids do you have?
Two. Andrea is 27 and David is 25.

What was your first job?
When I was about eight, my brother and I used to go door-to-door selling seeds to grow vegetables and flowers. I was the salesperson, because I had a great smile.

How did you get into real estate?
I didn't know what I wanted. Before I went to Harvard, I worked for Mobil for six months. In my summers off from Harvard, I worked for an investment bank. After business school, I worked for Clairol. At that time, I was dating someone whose family owned a lot of real estate. He used to say, 'It's a waste of your talent to be selling hair color.' I wasn't selling hair color — I was doing strategic marketing for Clairol — but that comment made me think about getting into real estate. I interviewed at Integrated Resources and they gave me the lowest-rung position there, running the appraisals and engineering studies for their acquisitions. I was eventually promoted to acquisitions.

Why did you leave Integrated Resources?
I knew I wanted to have my own business one day. I met Steven Meringoff in a continuing-education real estate class at NYU. [The late mogul] Harry Helmsley was speaking in the class. He asked if anyone had any questions and I raised my hand. I said, 'What's your greatest accomplishment?' He paused, and then said, "What are you doing tonight?' That night, Steve introduced himself to me. He thought, 'If Harry Helmsley is hitting on her, she must be someone worth knowing.' I ran into Steve again years later, when I went to his office on behalf of Integrated, trying to buy the tax position of his real estate. He looked at me and said, 'Why are you there?' At that moment, we started talking about being partners.

What is Harry Helmsley like, and did you ever meet his wife Leona, the notorious "Queen of Mean"?
My first year working with Steve, I went away to Barbados. We were staying at Sandy Lane [a luxury resort], and went into the dining room for dinner and who was there? Harry and Leona. We ended up befriending them and having lunch and dinner with them the entire week. Harry told me stories of how he built his empire. I was never in Leona's line of fire, so I never saw her fury.

What are your hobbies?
I'm addicted to exercise. Tennis, yoga, Rollerblading, skiing. I have a racing bike. I'm passionate about my friends. Mary Ann Tighe has been a close friend since 1988, when we bought 411 Lafayette Street and hired her as the exclusive leasing agent.

Do you make as much money as you'd like to make?
Every time I've reached the next bar, it seems like that bar is too low. **TRD**

November 2013

THE CLOSING

SETH PINSKY

PRESIDENT | **NYC ECONOMIC DEVELOPMENT CORPORATION**

At the helm of the EDC under Mayor Michael Bloomberg, Pinsky worked on projects like the $2 billion Cornell NYC Tech applied sciences campus on Roosevelt Island, the redevelopment of Willets Point and the new Yankees and Mets stadiums. A graduate of Columbia College and Harvard Law School, Pinsky previously worked as an attorney in the real estate practice at Cleary Gottlieb Steen & Hamilton before joining the EDC. He also served as director of Mayor Bloomberg's post-Hurricane Sandy Special Initiative for Rebuilding and Resiliency. (In September 2013, he left government service to become an executive vice president at RXR Realty.) *Interview by Leigh Kamping-Carder*

"I was celebrating my 30th birthday when the World Trade Center was attacked."

What's your date of birth?
September 11, 1971. I was celebrating my 30th birthday when the World Trade Center was attacked. At some point, somebody remembered that it was my birthday and gave me a cupcake with a candle in it.

September 11 also inspired you to go into the public sector.
I would sit in my office [at Cleary Gottlieb] and watch the recovery efforts at Ground Zero. They would put the remains onto a golf cart, which had a stretcher on the back, and then they would cover it with an American flag and everyone would stop working. They would line the ramp out of the pit and would salute as the golf cart went up. And watching this, over time I said to myself, 'I talked a good game about wanting to go and do public service. If I'm ever going to do it, now is the time to do it.'

Where did you grow up?
Until I was 5 years old, my family lived in Great Neck on Long Island. Then we moved to New Jersey, and then when I was 10, we moved to Minneapolis.

Why did you move so much?
My father is a rabbi, so he moved to different congregations, and we followed. But from the minute that we crossed the St. Croix River into Minnesota, I knew that as soon as it was my decision, I was moving back to the East Coast.

Are you religious?
This is dangerous. Can I plead the Fifth on this? I am religious in my own way. ... I don't eat pork, I don't eat shellfish. I belong to a synagogue; I attend that synagogue from time to time.

How did you end up at the EDC?
In early 2003, I was talking to [Maria Gotsch, the president and CEO of the New York City Investment Fund] and she said, 'Well, have you ever thought about EDC?' And my response was, 'No, because I've never heard of EDC.' So she put me in touch with some people here and that was finally what got me into public service.

You became EDC president when you were 36 years old. Has anyone called you too young for the job?
People may have thought that. Nobody said that to me.

Last July, you married Angela Sung, a senior vice president at the Real Estate Board of New York. Do you always talk about real estate?
No, we try not to talk too much about work. I certainly am very careful about things that we're working on that involve REBNY members, and I think she's very careful about things that she's working on that involve city matters. We both overlap with a lot of the same people, which makes it interesting.

You went to Sudan and Egypt for your honeymoon, but she wanted to go to Hawaii.
Yes, she still wants to go to Hawaii! Our deal is that we alternate trips, and the honeymoon happened to be a "Seth trip." That being said, we worked in a number of more typical honeymoon-like elements to our vacation, including a Nile cruise and a couple of nights at a Red Sea resort.

You've also traveled to Iran, Colombia, Armenia, Moscow and through central Asia. It sounds like the "Seth trips" can be difficult.
Yeah, they're often not relaxing [laughs]. One night on our honeymoon, when we were in a waterproof — and, therefore, very hot — tent in the middle of the desert at about one in the morning, we had sand blowing into our tent. I think that was where maybe Angela had reached the limit of her tolerance.

Where do you live now?
We live in Park Slope. We're in the process of moving to another apartment in Park Slope. We're going to totally change scenery and move about a block and a half away.

Do you own any other homes?
No, we don't. We'll be lucky if we can afford our new home.

Do you have kids?
No. We're expecting [at the end of November]. I haven't told a lot of people, so this is my way of letting everyone know.

Do you know if it's a boy or a girl?
No. My preference would be not to find out. Angela's preference would be to find out. And, as I've come to learn very quickly, in a tie, the mother's vote is the one that counts. So we'll find out in a couple weeks.

What are your other hobbies?
I really enjoy classical music, listening to it, going to concerts. I enjoy photography — taking photos and going to photography exhibits as well.

When Bloomberg's term ends in 2013, are you out of a job?
The tradition is that the mayor appoints the president of the EDC. So my expectation is that at the end of the mayor's term that the next mayor will want to appoint someone else. **TRD**

July 2012

OFER YARDENI

CO-CHAIRMAN & CEO | **STONEHENGE PARTNERS**

The Manhattan-based real estate company that Yardeni co-founded in the early 1990s owns and manages more than two dozen residential buildings and commercial properties in New York valued at some $2.2 billion. The company is transforming 555 Sixth Avenue, a former staff-housing site at St. Vincent's Hospital, into a 180-unit luxury residential building with ground-floor retail. In 2013, in a big-ticket deal, Stonehenge agreed to sell the Olivia, a residential and commercial tower at 315 West 33rd Street, to SL Green for $386 million. *Interview by Katherine Clarke*

"Very early, I realized real estate in New York is like the celebrity in L.A. We are consumed by it."

What's your date of birth?
March 6, 1960. I'm a Pisces.

Do you believe in star signs?
Absolutely. Pisces is the only sign that has two animals; it's two fish. For me, it's about being able to move and go with the flow [like a fish]. When I meet people, I always ask them when they were born.

Where did you grow up?
In Israel in a town called Bat Yam. It's on the Mediterranean, south of Tel Aviv. It's like Queens to Manhattan.

What did your father do?
He was a steelworker. If you asked my kids, they would say, 'You were poor,' but growing up, I felt I was the richest boy in the world. I did not miss anything. I had my ocean. My mother made me cakes and the best food. We felt we were the happiest, best family in the world. I talk to my dad once or twice a day still. He lives in Israel. My mother passed away.

Why did you decide to move to the United States?
I was studying history at Tel Aviv University. When I was getting ready to graduate, I realized that I would have to work, but I wasn't ready. I was watching the movie "Animal House," and I saw the life of American students on campus. I said, 'That's where I want to go.' I came to study Middle Eastern Studies at NYU. I thought I would just come to the United States and have some fun and then go back to Israel and become a teacher or a professor.

You were in the Israeli army. What was that like?
I was in the army for three years. I think that it was the best thing that could have happened to me at that moment of my life. It took a kid like me — I don't know if I was mischievous, but I was a contrarian — and showed me discipline. A lot of things that I have today are because of the training I got in the army. It put me in line.

How did you get into real estate?
I was single in New York and every woman that I met, her parents were in real estate. Very early, I realized real estate in New York is like the celebrity in L.A. We are consumed by it. People wake up in the morning and talk about real estate. When they have sex, they talk about real estate. Even if you have only a cheap apartment, you talk about real estate.

How did you get your first real estate job?
I started taking business courses at NYU, and it came easy to me. I was introduced to a broker at LB Kaye. I went in to interview with a woman. It was almost like we were dancing the tango. It was a sexual flirtation. She gave me the job, and I became a broker at the firm. I met my wife [who was an assistant to the brokers] there. We got married in 1989.

Where do you live?
On Long Island, in Upper Brookville. It's 30 miles from Manhattan. I've lived there 16 or 17 years.

Do you have any other homes?
We have a place in the city in one of our buildings, the Olivia, which was named after my daughter. We rarely stay there because we love our bed at home. I also have a place in Beaver Creek, Colorado. It's in the Ritz-Carlton.

How many children do you have?
I have three beautiful kids. Max is almost 21, Josh is finishing high school and Olivia is 14.

How did you meet your Stonehenge partner, Joel Seiden?
I met him when I was a broker. I brought a buyer to a deal and he was the seller. He was a big owner in New Jersey. One year later, I was walking down the street and I ran into him. He was coming out of his Rolls-Royce. He said, 'Hey, Ofer, what are you doing?' I said, 'I'm going to open my own company.' He said, 'Let's do it together.'

What was your first acquisition?
I bought the note on 240 West 72nd Street for $400,000 [in 1995]. It was a small building that was being foreclosed on. I kept it for a long time, but decided to sell in 2003. I wanted to show everybody that worked in my organization that you don't fall in love with real estate. I didn't want to be too attached. I sold the building for $3.5 million, which was a great return. But I must admit that the day after I sold it, I called the buyer and asked if he'd sell it back to me.

You were one of Rabbi Yoshiyahu Pinto's well-known followers. What was that relationship like?
I loved the rabbi dearly. Other than my wife and my partner Joel, he was the person who helped me be where I am. He helped me become a better husband, a better father and a better leader in my community and in my company. In my early 40s, when I was making so much money, I started to think I was God's gift. The rabbi was able to show me that the most important thing in my life was my wife, and the reason I succeeded was because of my wife.

How do you feel about his arrest?
Sometimes there are things that happen and we don't understand them when they happen. What we see right now is only a chapter. The truth will come and everybody will understand. I was sad to hear the stories, but inside I believe in the rabbi.

Who are your heroes?
Michael Jordan and Madonna. Michael Jordan was able to achieve the highest levels in basketball. Madonna is my age and look how she was able to transform herself from one style to another style to another style. Thank God I never met them. If I met them, I would see all their flaws and realize they're the same as you and I. **TRD**

February 2013

THE CLOSING

BILLY MACKLOWE

CEO | **WILLIAM MACKLOWE COMPANY**

Macklowe founded the William Macklowe Company in 2010 after splitting from his father Harry's company, Macklowe Properties. Macklowe's departure as CEO, after 17 years at the firm, came after his father famously lost his prized possession, the GM Building, along with a $7 billion Midtown portfolio — a collapse that became synonymous with the real estate bust.

After several years of focusing on renovating office space with his new firm, Billy Macklowe has begun inching onto his father's turf — with plans to build luxury residential condos at the site of the iconic Greenwich Village bowling alley Bowlmor — as well as other purchases including 386 Park Avenue South and 636 Sixth Avenue. *Interview by Lauren Elkies*

"A bill is something one pays. I am Billy — always have been, always will be."

What's your full name?
William Samson Macklowe.

What's your date of birth?
April 22, 1968.

Where did you grow up?
At 82nd and Fifth. We also have a house in Sagaponack, Long Island.

What were you like as a kid growing up in New York City?
still think I'm a kid. I was active, athletic, I think social. I grew up sailing so I spent a lot of time on the water.

Does your family still sail?
My parents do. I sold my boat, courtesy of my wife, three years ago. But we've replaced the sailing with surfing.

Are you a good surfer?
For a weekend warrior, I think I can hold my own.

How did you and your wife [Julie Macklowe] meet?
On a blind date through a friend, eight days after my 35th birthday.

Were you married previously?
I had a rookie marriage many, many years ago. It was for less than a year.

What's it like being married to a socialite [a fixture on the city and Hamptons social scenes]?
Julie's considered a socialite, but I think she's a far cry from that. She's a powerhouse of a woman. She had a great 12-year career in finance. She ran her own hedge fund [Macklowe Asset Management, which she closed in October 2010], trading consumer retail. Most recently she raised a bunch of money to launch her own skin care company.

Do you feel like you have to attend a lot of society affairs with her?
Oh, I don't go. Julie and I have an understanding.

What kind of understanding?
I don't need to go to all these things. She's the face of her brand. There's a lot of entertaining that I do for business. But really, we have a handful of events that have real meaning and those are the ones that I go to with Julie.

How do you compare as a dad to your father?
My dad was a great father. I spent a lot of time with my parents growing up on the boat. My dad spent a lot of time building a business. I think the way business happens today is different. Unless I need to be in a conference room negotiating or out raising money, if I want to come home and see my daughter [Zoë], I can.

So you get to see her more than your dad saw you as a child?
Yes. My dad worked hard and built a big empire.

There was an article in the Wall Street Journal where you lambasted your father.
I think the article you are referring to was in 2008 and there has been enough written about it on both sides.

What's your relationship been like since then?
Great. He's a very good grandparent. Both my parents spend a lot of time with my daughter. We have holiday meals. We have family brunches, stuff like that. I don't think it's anything dissimilar to what it was in the past — other than he has his company and I have mine.

Why did you choose a company name that is so similar to your dad's?
Tishman Speyer and Vornado were already taken.

Do you think you can fill your dad's shoes?
I don't think it's a question of filling my dad's shoes. I'm building a business and I just want to be successful, be a good steward of institutional capital and to have fun doing it.

Why did you decide to get into real estate?
Peter Martins' dance company rejected my application [joking]. I've always liked real estate. It was something I had always been around. I worked on the real estate side of banking at Manufacturers Hanover Trust before I joined my family's business. That was my business school.

Why did you leave Macklowe Properties?
Dad always had the experience of starting his own company. I wanted that moment of starting my own company.

Your sister Liz was married to Kent Swig [president of Swig Equities]. What's your relationship like with your former brother-in-law?
Never had one then and don't have one now. Do you know the difference between in-laws and outlaws? Outlaws are wanted.

Did you get your sense of humor from your father?
I like dialogue and banter. My humor is a blend of the two of them. My dad's humor is more on the schtick side of life [Harry can be seen telling jokes at oldjewstellingjokes.com] and my mom has more of a caustic wit.

Why are you so sensitive about being called Bill?
A bill is something one pays. I am Billy — always have been, always will be. **TRD**

Photo by Max Dwork

LARRY SILVERSTEIN

CHAIRMAN | **SILVERSTEIN PROPERTIES**

In July 2001, Silverstein closed on the then-largest real estate transaction in New York City's history: a $3.25 billion, 99-year leasehold on the Port Authority's 10.6 million-square-foot World Trade Center site. Seven weeks later, the buildings were destroyed in the Sept. 11 terrorist attacks, and since then Silverstein has been largely focused on rebuilding the Lower Manhattan skyline. An alumnus of New York University, Silverstein is the founder and chairman emeritus of New York University's Schack Institute of Real Estate and a former vice chairman of the university's Board of Trustees. *Interview by Sarabeth Sanders*

"Life is very unpredictable, and very terminal, and serendipitous. I'm a fatalist, clearly."

What's your date of birth?
The 30th of May, 1931.

You were born and raised in Bedford-Stuyvesant. Have you been back there recently?
Yes. I had dinner at … what's that famous restaurant near the Williamsburg Bridge? Peter Luger's. I had a dinner at Peter Luger's and then I suggested to my wife, 'Let's see if we can find where I used to live.' I couldn't find it. The neighborhood has changed completely. It's unrecognizable. The quality of the housing and so forth, the shops, everything about it is much better.

What kind of house did you live in growing up?
We lived on the seventh floor of a seven-story walk-up.

Wow. Were you an athletic kid?
[Laughs] I remember the ice man bringing up the ice for the ice box because we didn't have a refrigerator. I remember walking up those steps — my God, that was a hike. And the ceiling had a tendency to sort of fall. Everything used to leak.

Where do you live now?
Not in the same conditions. Now we live on Park and 59th.

Do you have any other homes?
No.

But you do have boats.
Yeah.

Last we heard, you were building a new yacht to replace your 131-foot boat, Silver Shalis. Have you taken it out for a spin yet?
Oh, yes. It's a lot of fun.

Is it true that it cost more than $30 million?
That's irrelevant.

Your father was also in the real estate business. What did you learn from him?
During the summers I'd leave NYU and work for my father. He was a leasing broker of loft space in the rags, woolens and remnants district in Lower Manhattan. Today you'd call it Soho. The rentals at that time were maybe 40 cents a foot, 50 cents a foot, 60 cents a square foot. It was all secondary, tertiary real estate. It was a difficult existence, but it showed me the value of a dollar. It showed me the art of negotiating.

Your daughter, Lisa, and your son, Roger, both work for Silverstein Properties. What kind of boss are you?
I think a dramatic, impossible, unpredictable, tyrannical individual who constantly changes his mind and moves off in different directions without predictability. Just a wonderful, wonderful experience to work with.

Do you have any plans to retire?
At the moment, my focus is on completing the World Trade Center, and my sense is that will be done by 2015, 2016. At that juncture, I'll be 85, and assuming that I'm still in good health and have some energy, what I'm going to do is … I don't have a clue.

You closed on your deal at the World Trade Center weeks before 9/11. Do you ever wish you had lost the bidding?
It's funny but I don't recall the focus [of my thoughts at that time], other than the disaster, and the magnitude of the problems we were facing as a result of it. And the loss of life was horrendous. We lost four of our people, four of our employees who had six children among them.

For years during the rebuilding negotiations, public opinion wasn't exactly on your side. Did that bother you?
Did it bother me? Did it rankle me? Of course. You can't escape that. But it became obvious to me early on that it was important to focus on rebuilding. The first thing we decided was to rebuild 7 World Trade Center. We went into the ground in '02. Everybody said it was gonna be a disaster, we'd never lease it, we'd never finance it, and so forth. Thank God they were all wrong. By May of '06 we finished building and suddenly people began to look at this thing and say, 'Hey, maybe he's not the problem. Maybe the problem lies elsewhere.' And that's when things began to change in our favor, significantly.

You were almost killed by a drunk driver shortly before your bid for the World Trade Center was due. And you would have been in the Twin Towers on 9/11 if not for a doctor's appointment that morning. How do you feel about fate?
Life is very unpredictable, and very terminal, and serendipitous. I'm a fatalist, clearly. When I was hit by a drunk driver while I was crossing 57th Street, I thought I was going to die. The pain was horrendous. He broke my pelvis in 12 places. That kind of thing you can never fully recover from, so as I get older I feel it more intensely. That's life.

You told *The Real Deal* in 2004 that you spend 20 to 21 hours a day, seven days a week, either thinking about or working on the WTC projects. Have things calmed down at all?
To some degree. But it's been consuming. It's been the focus of my business life … [laughs] … well, my life.

What's your work schedule like now? Do you still wake up at 3 a.m. worrying about the rebuilding?
Well, not necessarily 3 a.m. Sometimes 2 o'clock, sometimes 4 o'clock. It varies. **TRD**

September 2011

Photo by Marc Scrive

JEFFREY GURAL

CHAIRMAN | **NEWMARK GRUBB KNIGHT FRANK**

Gural has headed the full-service commercial real estate firm since 1978 with business partner Barry Gosin. During their tenure, the New York-based company expanded nationally, and in 2006 formed a strategic partnership with London-based real estate firm Knight Frank. Gural is the son of the late Newmark chairman Aaron Gural, and is also the owner of New Jersey's Meadowlands Racetrack and the chairman of American Racing and Entertainment, which owns two upstate racetrack/casinos. BGC Partners acquired Newmark in 2011 and Grubb & Ellis the following year to form Newmark Grubb Knight Frank. *Interview by Leigh Kamping-Carder*

"I think I'm more known for being a nice guy than I am for being a brilliant real estate person."

What's your date of birth?
July 6, 1942.

Where do you live?
The El Dorado [at 300 Central Park West]. I exercise in the park every day when the weather's nice. By exercise, that means walking fast, not running. My running days are over.

Where did you grow up?
On Long Island, in a town called Woodmere.

What's different since BGC Partners acquired Newmark Knight Frank?
For me, it's had very little impact because my focus has always been on the buildings Newmark Holdings owns [which includes about 8 million square feet of office space in Manhattan] and charities and politics. But everything's different working for a public company. Before, if there was a decision to be made, I'd just make it — rightly or wrongly. Now, when you're part of a public company, there's a whole process involved. But I'm 70 years old, so it was really time to make a change, and I think it enabled the company to grow.

What's the biggest mistake you've made since joining the family business?
Barry and I owned one building — 521 West 23rd Street — and we sold it for a $1 million profit. We were so happy because, in the late '70s, West 23rd between 10th and 11th avenues was no great spot. Recently, my granddaughter wanted to take a walk on the High Line, and when I got to the end and went down the stairs, the stairs emptied out right in front of the building. Now that building's got to be worth a fortune.

How did you meet your wife?
I went to Rensselaer Polytechnic Institute in Troy, N.Y., which is a [mostly] male school, and she went to Russell Sage, which is an all-girls school, and they're about three miles apart. It was fairly common for Rensselaer guys to date girls from Russell Sage. Back then, when you graduated from college, you either got married or you broke up. We've been married for 47 years, so it was a good decision.

How many kids do you have?
Three kids and six grandchildren. I like the grandchildren better than the kids.

You are a major financial backer of the Democratic Party, including President Barack Obama. Why?
Right now, wealthy Americans are doing fine and everybody else is struggling. I don't think the system is fair.

How did you get involved in politics?
I was always pretty much a liberal. But I never was involved until my daughter's friend was a fund-raiser for John Kerry when he ran for President. I got to meet him, and then I became good friends with Nancy Pelosi. Over time, I've met just about every major politician on the Democratic side.

Obama?
Yeah.

What was that like?
He's a charming guy. He actually called me over Christmas to thank me for helping out.

How did you know it was actually him?
They tell you in advance that he's going to call. And then they say: 'This is the White House operator, please hold for the President.' It's a thrill.

What are your hobbies?
I'm involved in the standardbred horse-racing business. I own two standardbred breeding farms and I own three racetracks.

How did you get interested in that?
I grew up near Roseville raceway, and I started going to the track when I was in high school. That was actually a cool thing to do back then.

How would you describe yourself?
A nice guy, basically. My business philosophy is to be nice. I never understood why people get a reputation for being difficult, and they look at that as the way to be successful. But I can tell you I'm successful by being nice and charitable. I think I'm more known for being a nice guy and a charitable guy than I am for being a brilliant real estate person. But that's okay.

How did you get to be the chairman, then?
Nepotism. I had the intelligence to recognize it would be easier to go into a business that was family-owned than to try to be a hero. Not that I don't totally respect people who didn't have a leg up. ... I think that I proved myself to the employees [at Newmark] by working hard. If you work hard, people will accept the fact that, 'Yeah, okay, his father was one of the owners of the company, but he didn't just go on vacation.' **TRD**

October 2012

Photo by Hugh Hartshorne

STEVEN SPINOLA

PRESIDENT | **THE REAL ESTATE BOARD OF NEW YORK**

Spinola is the longest-serving president of the Real Estate Board of New York, the powerful 12,000-member trade association that represents the industry before numerous legislative and regulatory bodies. REBNY, the body which Spinola led starting in 1986, has lobbied in Washington for myriad issues such as the first-time homebuyer tax credit. The organization, which helped push for luxury decontrol of rent-stabilized apartments in the past, has also lobbied against proposals to extend the reach of rent regulations at the state level. REBNY was founded in 1896. (After this interview, in mid-2014, Spinola announced he would step down from his position the following year.) *Interview by Candace Taylor*

"I'm very proud of the people who lead our industry. And that's about as sentimental as I'm going to get."

What's your date of birth?
January 13, 1949.

Where were you born?
In Greenpoint, Brooklyn.

Where do you live now?
I live in Garden City, Long Island.

How long have you been married [to Eileen Spinola, REBNY's senior vice president of brokerage services and education]?
I gotta be careful here. We were married in December of '71. It's going to be 38 years this year.

Do you have children?
Two daughters, ages 27 and 32.

You and your wife work together. Are you her boss?
Yes, technically.

Who is the boss at home?
My dog.

What are your hours like at REBNY?
I'm not going to pretend I work all hours of the night. I don't. I prefer to go home to eat. Most of the time I can get the job done during the day, and thanks to BlackBerrys and phones and computers you're reachable. However, there are events that I have to go to. If I have to go to Albany then you know it's gonna be a long day. When rent regulations were up 12 or 14 years ago, I went up there for one day and ended up staying for a week. ... When Albany is in session it may be anything. Two years ago, when we were negotiating for an extension of the 421a tax abatement program, I was up in Albany till 1 in the morning negotiating the language. There are days when you go into the wee hours. And then there are days like yesterday, when we had a golf outing.

What did you do before coming to REBNY?
I ran the city's Economic Development Corporation [from 1983 to 1986], which was then called the Public Development Corporation. In doing that, I did deals. So the South Street Seaport, I negotiated, and Metrotech in Brooklyn was a deal that I helped put together, and the redevelopment of 42nd Street. My experience for the job was negotiating deals and understanding what government is capable of and how they think.

How did you get into that?
Well, during school at City College, I was a shoe salesman at the 34th Street Bootery, which I don't think is there anymore. ... But after college my first job was working for the NYC Off-Track Betting Corporation. I did community relations for them.

Are you a gambler?
If I walk into a casino, I might spend $50 playing around with a few machines, but no, it's not something for me. Much of what I did at OTB had nothing to do with gambling.

Is there a professional gaffe or mistake you've made in your career that you regret?
I've made mistakes and stupid decisions, because everybody does that, but nothing that has haunted me. At PDC, we were offered a $100,000 bribe, and we reported it, and the person was going to jail. A reporter said, 'Well, I guess this proves that PDC can't be bribed,' and I jokingly said, 'It's just that $100,000 isn't enough.' The public relations guy yelled at me.

Who is your closest friend in New York City real estate?
That's a dangerous question because of all my 12,000 members. The late Bernie Mendik served as my chairman for almost 10 years. He was more than a chairman to me. He was a friend, and he was someone who showed me every element of the industry.

When we write stories about REBNY, we sometimes get comments from members complaining that REBNY doesn't do enough for them. What's your response?
I would welcome them to send me a note or call and tell me what they'd like me to do. You might also just get their comments that we just care about the bigger firms. The answer is it's just not true. We handle arbitration and ethics complaints and I will tell you that as often as not, the smaller firm will win.

Who is your favorite celebrity and why?
I happen to like Bruce Willis movies a great deal, and it's not just the violent ones. I'm not saying he's the greatest actor in the world, but he's very good. ... I don't collect autographs, although I do have a Yogi Berra autograph and a few other people in baseball.

Who's your baseball team?
I don't want to upset Fred Wilpon [the owner of the Mets]. My wife's a bigger Mets fan and I just grew up as a Yankees fan. It's tough to break that. Fred gave me a wonderful Mets jacket with my name on the back for my 20th anniversary at REBNY. I don't know if that means I have to now go in the bullpen and warm up for him.

Twenty-plus years. Are you going to retire anytime soon?
Well, I don't think so. I still wake up in the morning, most mornings, and want to come in to work. When I sit in a room with our Board of Governors and I look around the room, I'm very proud of the people who lead our industry. And that's about as sentimental as I'm going to get. **TRD**

October 2009

RICHARD MEIER

MANAGING PARTNER | **RICHARD MEIER & PARTNERS**

In 1984, Meier became the youngest-ever recipient of the Pritzker Architecture Prize — the field's highest honor. The noted Modernist architect, perhaps best known for the Getty Center museum in Los Angeles, has also designed 173 and 176 Perry Street in Manhattan and On Prospect Park in Brooklyn locally. Newer projects include two luxury residential towers in Bogota, Colombia and Teachers Village in Newark, a mixed-use complex with charter schools and middle- and lower-income housing. *Interview by Candace Taylor*

"You have to give people freedom to do what they do best and hope that they do it well."

What's your date of birth?
The 12th of October, 1934.

Where did you grow up?
In Maplewood, N.J.

Where do you live now?
Manhattan. I live in a building that was built the year I was born, 1934. It's a conventional apartment that I made into a loft.

Do you have children?
I have two. The oldest [Joseph], lives in Washington, D.C. The youngest [furniture designer Ana Meier] got married in September, at my house in East Hampton.

What's the status of your project in Newark?
Hopefully, in a year we'll start construction.

Do you have a particular emotional connection to that project?
I love that you don't have to get on an airplane to get to the site. I feel very strong ties to Newark, growing up in New Jersey. For us, it's a very, very significant project.

I read that one of your influences was the burger chain White Castle.
I don't know if you'd call it an influence. I remember as a young person going to White Castle, and I liked the white metal panel.

Your trademark is using white.
Well, it didn't come from White Castle. [laughs]

How did it develop?
Well, I read a lot about Frank Lloyd Wright when I was young, and he always talked about organic architecture, that there was a relationship between the interior and exterior space of a building. In the first house I designed, I created walls which began on the inside of the living room and extended into the garden. When it was completed, I observed that the outside of that brick wall had moss on it, it changed colors when it rained, and the inside never changed. I said, "You know, you have to think of architecture as manmade. It doesn't change with the weather or with the seasons, it's inert." So you may as well paint it white to reflect back the colors of nature.

You must get sick of explaining that.
Yes.

What is your greatest professional accomplishment?
The Getty has 5,000 visitors a day, almost the same as when it opened 10 years ago. So it's remarkable; people keep going there and going back there.

Is there anything you regret, any mistakes you've made in your career?
If so, I've blocked it out.

What do you do in your free time?
I've been doing collages for 40 years. I've made individual collages, and I also do them in books with blank pages. I've completed 150 books.

How did you start doing that?
I was on the airplane a lot. I carried a box with glue and scraps of paper, and did them on the trips between New York and Los Angeles to pass the time away.

You carry glue with you when you travel?
Well, I used to use rubber cement. I remember I was on a trip and I had to change planes in Kansas City. And they went through my box, took out the rubber cement and they said, 'This is flammable; we have to take it away.' I said, "What do you mean you're taking my glue away?' They said, 'You can have it back when you come back to Kansas City.' I said, 'Don't worry, I'm never coming back to Kansas City.' What I use now is not flammable. [Takes out a glue stick.] They can't take this away from me.

Making collages on planes must be difficult with all the security now.
I can't take scissors, so I cut the paper before I leave.

I noticed your bracelet — is that from Turkey?
Yes, it's an evil eye [intended to ward off curses]. I've just worn it for years. It's like the copper bracelets I wear — it doesn't hurt, and maybe it helps.

What is the significance of the copper bracelets?
Well, the copper is supposed to be good for your bones. It keeps you from getting something, I don't know — rheumatism. It's very good for you, I recommend it.

What kind of boss are you?
Terrific. [laughs] You have to give people freedom to do what they do best and hope that they do it well. And if they don't, well, then you have to make a decision.

What do you make of the criticism of the house you're building for [English actor] Rowan Atkinson? Critics have said it looks like a space-age petrol station.
This is a very conservative part of England, Oxfordshire, so there are no modern houses. There are very few modern houses in England at all. So it's a real event, and everyone has a comment.

How do you want to be remembered as an architect?
As an architect, I'd like to be remembered for the quality of the work. But ultimately, I'd like to be remembered as a good dad. **TRD**

STEVEN POZYCKI

FOUNDER & CEO | **SJP PROPERTIES**

Pozycki heads SJP, which made a bold move into the New York market when it built 11 Times Square, a 40-story, 1.2-million-square-foot speculative glass office-and-retail tower. The building hit the market in the midst of the recession but later filled up with tenants including Microsoft; SJP also moved its own corporate offices into the building in 2014. The New Jersey-based company has developed over 25 million square feet of residential and commercial property since 1981. SJP completed Panasonic Corp.'s 340,000-square-foot North American headquarters in Newark and is building the Modern, a pair of 47-story glass residential buildings in Fort Lee. *Interview by E.B. Solomont*

"Bruce moved in with the band. Clarence Clemons would come down every night and say, 'Hey, are you guys drinking tonight?'"

What's your date of birth?
November 25, 1949.

Where do you live?
In Far Hills, N.J. But I'm moving into a [condo] on the Upper West Side soon.

Why are you moving?
My daughter [Kate, who's married to SJP vice president Enrique Alonso] and granddaughter are here. This is also a strategic move professionally. It gives me the opportunity to be closer to the action in New York City, while still being close to New Jersey.

Do you have other homes?
We have a house at the beach on the East End of Long Island. During the summer of freshman year of college, my coach got me a job as a Jones Beach lifeguard. I was from New Jersey, I didn't really know where Jones Beach was, but I wound up enjoying the island.

Was that your first job?
I delivered newspapers when I was a real little kid, and I had a roofing job. I worked for a bunch of masons, mixing mud and carrying bricks around a lot of construction jobs, delivering pizzas at night. Almost any job you can imagine.

What were you like as a kid?
I was a hyperactive kid. I wasn't much of a student. I liked to entertain in class; I thought that's what you should do when you get there, get a couple of laughs.

How did you meet your wife, Elaine?
We met senior year in college at a party.

You went to Monmouth University, where you lived down the hall from Bruce Springsteen.
Brighton Avenue, where the apartment was located, was a very inexpensive place to live; the bathroom was in the hall. Bruce moved in with the whole band. They would get up around 3 o'clock in the afternoon and go over to this greasy spoon, Harry's, across the street, and then they'd play music till the wee hours of the night.

How well did you know each other? Did you keep in touch?
Casually. We didn't really keep in touch, but [saxophonist] Clarence [Clemons] would come down every night and say, 'Hey, are you guys drinking tonight?' We'd say, 'No, Clarence,' and he'd say, 'Well, are you chipping in?'

What did you do after graduation?
I got a license to sell houses in college — I just went and got one with a friend. When I graduated, I focused on getting a job in real estate, but at an institutional level where I could get more exposure and experience than selling houses on the corner. As I graduated I started working at MetLife in their real estate department and then at Equitable Life Assurance Society.

When did you form SJP?
When Equitable was moving to Atlanta in the 1980s, I wanted to stay in the New York area, so I went with Lincoln Property Company, the national commercial and residential real estate firm, and became their partner in the Northeast. In the '90s, they were in financial trouble, so I bought them out and have been in business ever since. We only concentrate on the Metropolitan area. We think we can do better things for people if we do it in a tighter geographical area.

What are your hobbies?
Anything on the water — scuba diving, swimming. I play a little golf with friends and do mountain biking. I started scuba diving about four years ago. It's another world. The colors are spectacular.

Were you always athletic?
I swam in high school, and my first year in college I played soccer and pole vaulted for a little bit. I was playing soccer and saw these kids in the field flying over the top of this bar and thought it looked pretty cool. It's harder than it looks.

When did you start swimming?
I had polio when I was in second grade. My mother got me into swimming, which was pretty smart. I wasn't walking for a while and we had to get the legs going again.

Do you have any vices?
I smoke cigars. I was in the construction business my whole life. Most of the guys on the job were smoking cigars, so I started smoking cigars in my late teens.

What kind of car do you drive?
A Range Rover. I'm on sites all day, and when I drive through, I like to have that kind of vehicle.

Your son-in-law, daughter and wife work with you. Was it always real estate at the dinner table?
It was. My daughter started out as an inner-city school teacher. I was shocked to hear she'd like to try real estate. I questioned it, to make sure she'd like it. But it's an interesting business. You meet people from all walks of life. No day is the same. **TRD**

Photo by Marc Scrive

BARBARA FOX

FOUNDER | **FOX RESIDENTIAL GROUP**

The boutique brokerage that Fox founded in 1989 handles high-end real estate in Manhattan and Brooklyn. Fox — who in the past has sold homes to celebrities like the late legendary newsman Walter Cronkite and the actor Robert Redford — also had a hand in the 2012 sale of Yankees slugger Alex Rodriguez's Upper West Side apartment. Before starting her own firm, she created a residential division of the now-defunct Cross & Brown Residential Company. *Interview by Lauren Elkies*

"I wouldn't do 'Million Dollar Listing.' Did you see it? It's embarrassing."

What's your date of birth?
January 17. Nobody needs to know the year. My mother-in-law, who is 104, says that 'age is a number, and hers is unlisted.'

Where did you grow up?
Rocky Mount, N.C. — it's a small Southern town of 6,000 people. The town consisted of a lot of tobacco farmers. My family was in the furniture business. It was a fantastic place to grow up. But I did terribly in school, and I never knew why. The reason, I later found out, was I had attention deficit [disorder], which I still have but have learned to live with it.

Do you take medication for it?
No. I figure I've lived this long without medication, so I don't need it.

Where do you live now?
180 East 79th Street.

Do you have any other homes?
We have a weekend house in Easton, Connecticut. I fenced in six acres, so it's a dog heaven.

Why did you go into real estate?
I really wanted to do something where no one could control how much money I could make. And I had real estate in my blood. When my father sold his business he became a real estate investor. He bought properties in our town and rented them out.

How long have you been married to your husband James Freund?
Twenty-seven years. He's a retired partner at Skadden, Arps.

How did you end up in New York?
When I separated from my first husband, my sister lived here. I had always wanted to live in New York. My mom had lived here when she was younger. We used to come here all the time on vacation. We came to see the Beatles the first time they were in New York.

Where was your first New York City apartment?
500 East 85th Street. My rent was $300 a month.

Do you have kids?
No kids. I have four dogs and two cats. They're my kids. I have two step-children in their 40s. At the point where I was deciding whether I should have a child, my mother — God bless her, this is a terrible thing — said, 'If I had to do it over, I probably wouldn't have kids.' I said, 'Thanks a lot.' She was a career woman, too, and it was very hard to juggle things.

Your first real estate job was working for legendary broker Alice Mason. What was that like?
I only worked there for a few months. But Alice was a wonderful teacher.

Did you ever attend her famous dinner parties?
She never invited the competition, and by the time she started having those I was at another firm, Whitbread-Nolan [which was bought by Douglas Elliman].

What was your first celebrity client sale?
Ralph Lauren. I called his office and his secretary said he was busy. I said I read in an article that his wife [Ricky] was expecting their third child and I had a couple of apartments for him to look at. He got on the phone. A couple of years later, I sold them an apartment on the Upper East Side. From Ralph and Ricky I got a bunch of referrals. I think Ricky referred Robert Redford.

Have you been approached about being on "Selling New York" or "Million Dollar Listing New York"?
Michele Kleier [president and co-chairman of Kleier Residential] got me on "Selling New York." I did a segment with her. I wouldn't do "Million Dollar Listing." Did you see it? It's embarrassing. I mean, the whole thing with [Ryan Serhant] shaving the arms. I even think "Selling New York" is embarrassing.

What are your hobbies?
I love to ski. I love tennis. I do stone sculpting.

What attracted you to stone sculpting?
Frustration, because you beat the crap out of the rock. It gets out so much of your inner angst. It's very, very cathartic.

You're the founder of WOOF NYC Dog Rescue. Why are you so passionate about animal rescue?
Humans can speak for their needs. Dogs can't. Cats can't. I really feel what's happening in the shelter system in New York right now is so sad and so pathetic, like how many dogs are put down who are totally adoptable.

What kinds of dogs do you personally own?
They're all mixes, except for one who's a bichon frisé. I did a DNA test on all of them to see what they were a mix of.

Your vet bill must be insane.
I probably spend $200 a month on insurance for the dogs. And I spend almost $400 to bathe them every other week.

What's your greatest fear?
If something happened to my husband and me, I really worry I wouldn't be able to keep my animals together. I made a provision for that in my will, that they have to stay together. **TRD**

ARTHUR MIRANTE II

PRINCIPAL & TRI-STATE PRESIDENT | **AVISON YOUNG**

An attorney by trade, Mirante joined the Canadian commercial brokerage Avison Young in 2012 after 41 years at Cushman & Wakefield. At Cushman, he became the firm's first non-broker CEO at age 40. In his 20 years as chief executive of Cushman, he oversaw the firm's expansion from 60 offices in the U.S. to 173 offices globally, and grew revenues tenfold, from $100 million to $1 billion. He stepped down as CEO in 2004 to become a broker and Cushman's president of Global Development. He's been involved in many megadeals, including the record $1.8 billion acquisition of 666 Fifth Avenue in 2007 and the $1.72 billion sale of 200 Park Avenue in 2005. *Interview by Leigh Kamping-Carder*

"Most of the other guys in my high school class went on to be electricians, carpenters."

What's your date of birth?
August 25, 1943.

Where do you live?
On East 76th Street, right on FDR Drive. We also have a home in Sharon, Connecticut.

Where did you grow up?
Right across the river in North Bergen, N.J. I was lucky to get a football scholarship to Holy Cross College in Massachusetts. It got me out of the neighborhood. Most of the other guys in my high school class went on to be electricians, carpenters; they went to work in the shipyards. We were in a [lower middle-class] economic situation, so absent an athletic scholarship, I don't know if I would have gone to college.

What were your parents like?
They were very loving. My father was a refrigeration mechanic. I am Arthur J. Mirante II. They didn't want me to be called 'junior,' so they put the 'second' on my birth certificate. I never used it until my father went bankrupt. He used his savings to get a patent on an invention he had, an automobile engine run by Freon gas. But the gas then became illegal because of the environmental fumes it gives off. I had to start using 'the second' to get a charge card when I was in college. Otherwise the application would come back and say, 'You're bankrupt.'

I heard that you played pro football for a day.
Yes. For the Newark Bears [a now-defunct minor league team]. I had a contract, $75 a game. After the first game, I ran back a few kickoffs and I said, 'I don't think I want to do this anymore.'

Why?
No. 1, I wasn't good enough to be in the NFL. No. 2, getting your brains beat in is kind of a difficult way to make a living.

What did you do instead?
My [now ex-] wife got pregnant, and I went to St. John's University Law School during the day, and worked at night. I worked in the jails up in the Bronx, in what was known as Fort Apache, for the probation department. When I wasn't interviewing prisoners to see if they qualified for parole or not, I could study.

What did that teach you?
It taught me not to commit any crimes. [Laughs]

How did you get into real estate?
I was an attorney practicing for a firm called Albanese & Albanese [founded by real estate attorney and developer Vincent Albanese]. I applied for a job as a lawyer at several of the big real estate companies. About six months after I applied for the job, I got hired by Cushman & Wakefield in 1971.

You were appointed CEO in 1984. How did you get that job?
I was very young and unprepared when [then-general counsel George Lees] had a stroke. I was the only lawyer in the firm, and our then-president Jim Peters came to me and said, 'I know you're not ready for this, but you're going to be our general counsel.' Then there came a time when [former CEO Stephen Siegel] asked me to please undertake the oversight and management in the New York area. When Siegel left, I became CEO.

Why did you leave Cushman for a firm that's been described as a start-up, at least in New York City?
Well, it's not like I've been jumping around! It's 41 years at the same company. The single reason is the opportunity that Avison Young offered me to build a brand-new business from the bottom up, here in the New York tri-state area. I wouldn't have moved to another giant firm.

Was there a catalyst, or a moment when you decided to do that?
No. The moment was when I got a call and I said, 'What's the name of the company?'

What are the best and worst parts of the new firm?
The best part is the excitement and energy. The worst is that I miss my friends at Cushman & Wakefield.

What is your proudest real estate transaction?
Helping the Alvin Ailey dance company [where I am a board member] find a permanent home. Two years earlier, we had just avoided bankruptcy. We now have a building on 55th Street and Ninth Avenue.

Are you married?
I'm on my second marriage. My first marriage was 20-plus years, the second is 18 years. I have a 17-year-old from my current marriage, two adult children in their 40s and six grandchildren. I'm very lucky.

Where's your wife from?
She grew up on the Caribbean island of St. Vincent and the Grenadines, so we used to go down a minimum of once a year. We even bought some land on this wonderful island called Bequia.

What makes a successful marriage?
Oy. I think it's all about one word: sacrifice. It's very hard, I think, to live with one person, be monogamous, because of all the stresses that life has. A lot of times, you don't figure that out until your second marriage. **TRD**

STUART SAFT

PARTNER | DEWEY & LEBOEUF

Prior to Dewey & LeBoeuf's 2012 bankruptcy and collapse, Saft chaired the law firm's global real estate department — the position he held at the time of this interview. During the course of his career, Saft, who is one of the country's leading commercial and residential real estate lawyers, has represented developers such as Swig Equities at the Sheffield, the Feil Organization at the Apthorp and the Moinian Group at the W Downtown Hotel and Residences. In addition, Saft is the author of books on commercial real estate law. (In May 2012, Saft became a partner at the law firm Holland & Knight, chairing its New York real estate practice. *Interview by Lauren Elkies*

I believe that you have to separate your right to disagree with your government from your obligation to serve."

What's your date of birth?
February 17, 1947.

Where did you grow up?
In Brooklyn, and then I moved to Rosedale, Queens.

Where do you live now?
1040 Park.

How did you meet your wife, Stephanie?
We met at the beginning of our freshman year in college and got married while I was in law school.

When did you know you wanted to be an attorney?
I didn't. When I was in college [at Hofstra University], I didn't spend a great deal of time focusing on my studies, but I was very involved in student government and the anti-war movement. This was as Vietnam was heating up. I had been elected president of the student senate around the time that all the college campuses were being shut down due to protesters. I went to the president of the university and I said, 'Why don't we look into the causes of the war and what can be done about it?' We had a conference at Hofstra. Governor Rockefeller came, Fulbright came, Jacob Javits was there. Shortly after that, I was talking to the president of the university and he said, 'Maybe you should go to law school.'

If you were anti-war, why did you join the Reserve Officers' Training Corps as a freshman in college?
Because it was an easy way to pay my tuition. Little did I know there was going to be a war. I also believed that I could protest the war, but I had an obligation to serve my country if I was required to do so. I know that sounds crazy, but I have always believed that you have to separate your right to disagree with your government from your obligation as a citizen to serve. ... But when I was accepted at Columbia Law School, I got a three-year deferment. While I was waiting to go on to active duty, I developed hepatitis from bad seafood. The Army then wouldn't take me for a year until I was fully healed. By the time I went on to active duty, I was a captain, because I got promotions in ROTC.

You got promotions without having to do anything?
It's funny you should say that. My father enlisted in the Army right after Pearl Harbor, and landed on Normandy beach on D-Day, liberated concentration camps, was at the Battle of the Bulge and they made him bury his dog tags because they had a J on it for Jew and the Germans killed the Jewish soldiers. So, he comes down to [an Army base in Virginia] to visit me, and I go to the airport to meet him. By the time he left the Army, he was a master sergeant and he had all of these medals. But I was a higher-ranking captain. So we're walking through the airport and this old sergeant comes walking past me and salutes me and I salute him back and my father just stopped, looked at the sergeant, looked at me, and you knew he was thinking, 'That's the end of the United States as a world power. Either that or everything I ever thought about officers has to be true.'

Who are the top three real estate attorneys in the city?
Jay Neveloff at Kramer Levin, Leonard Boxer at Stroock and Jonathan Mechanic at Fried Frank.

How much do you charge an hour?
My standard rate is $925 an hour.

In March, you responded to news reports of financial and personnel trouble at your firm by assuring clients that the real estate practice was largely unaffected. Is that still the case?
The real estate practice was never affected by either the partners who were asked to leave or the partners who left on their own. There was more of a hubbub in the press than in our offices. I don't understand why an internal dispute among partners in a privately owned partnership caused such press.

Are you on Facebook or Twitter?
I don't Twit. I don't Face.

You took home the trophy for Best Overall Debate Performance at *The Real Deal*'s forum at Lincoln Center last year. What was the experience like for you?
I thought it might be interesting to do, and then as we got closer to it, I said, 'I must be out of my mind debating Adam Leitman Bailey' — who is a litigator. I'm a transactional lawyer. So I was in complete and utter panic because I figured that Adam was just going to tear me apart. But backstage I watched the other debates so I could get an understanding of what was going to happen. ... I'm going to give away my big secret now: I saw what the moderator was doing. He would pick one person in each debate and give him a really hard time. I figured he was going to come after me because I was defending the developers. So by the time I walked out onstage, I was very calm. And I knew that I had to deal with that up front and directly, and I did. I was very pleased with my performance because I had such low expectations going into it. **TRD**

April 2012

THE CLOSING

| 69

MICHAEL SHVO

CHIEF EXECUTIVE | **SHVO**

Michael Shvo, the "bad boy" broker of the last real estate boom, burst onto the development scene in 2013 with three Manhattan projects. The move was a departure for the 42-year-old, who was Douglas Elliman's top-producing agent in 2003, before leaving to start the Shvo Group in 2004. He became known for celebrity-studded launch parties before a semi-retirement during the recession. In May 2013, Shvo re-emerged as a developer, snapping up a Getty gas station parcel in Chelsea for a record $800 per buildable square foot and installing a buzzed-about art installation called "Sheep Station." He's also developing condos in Soho and in the Financial District *Interview by E.B. Solomont*

"I would hope I have critics. If everyone thinks it's OK, then there's truly no value to the creation."

You once owned 30 apartments. Where do you live now?
Throughout the years, I've owned and sold properties. Our home is at the Time Warner Center. We own a home in Water Mill, where we spend weekends in the summer.

What were you like as a kid?
was a dreamer. At a very early age, I came from Israel to New York and saw this great skyline. That's when I had the notion that when I'm old enough, I'd actually come to New York and be part of this great city.

What did your parents do?
They were both organic chemists and taught at Yale and Stanford, clearly not on the business side, definitely not on the real estate side.

So what sparked your passion for real estate?
I was six years old when I moved to New York. I was coming from a city, [Arsuf, north of Tel Aviv,] where the tallest building was a few stories high. Seeing all these great buildings — the Empire State Building, the Chrysler Building — blew my mind.

When you moved back to New York, in 1995, you managed a fleet of taxis. How did you go from there to top broker — and now a developer?
I moved here with $3,000. At the time, I was living down on Mercer Street and the building's rental agent said, 'You know, you should be a broker.' She introduced me to Yuval Greenblatt [now at Elliman]. I became a real estate broker, starting really from nothing.

How has the business changed since you got into it?
Brokers [15 years ago] were really sellers of information. Today you have to compete with the Internet. A lot of these guys doing the reality shows, they've asked me what I think. I always say, make sure that you monetize this exposure because this thing doesn't last.

Why haven't you done a reality show?
I am a private person. TV is all about the drama, and in life you try not to have drama.

You met your wife, Seren Ceylan Shvo, in Istanbul in 2009. How?
I was there to introduce my best friend, who is a big developer in Istanbul, to a couple of big hotel brands. My wife was his girlfriend's best friend. A few months later, she moved to the States. I guess she liked me enough to stay.

How do you feel about being known as the 'bad boy' of real estate?
I can't tell you why people think one thing or the other of me. When you change the status quo, there are people that like it and people that don't like it. I would hope I have critics. If everyone thinks it's OK, then there's truly no value to the creation.

You used to carry multiple phones. Do you still?
I carry two iPhones. I use one to speak and the other is to type emails.

During the recession, you kept a low profile. Was it intentional? What were you focused on?
In December of '07, I was asked to give a lecture to the advisory board of Hilton Hotels about the status of the real estate market. My team was preparing this huge presentation for me, and they showed me a shot of a garbage bag with the Louis Vuitton monogram on it. I [thought], 'Something is out of control here, this can't continue.' I decided to retire. Six months later, Lehman collapsed. I spent four years collecting art, met my wife, got married and dabbled in a little bit of real estate.

Tell me about your art.
It is really divided into three major categories: In the city we have an extensive collection of pop art, so Andy Warhol, Tom Wesselmann, Jean-Michel Basquiat, Alexander Calder, great monumental pieces. In the Hamptons, we have a collection of American heritage color field painters, so Frank Stella, Kenneth Noland, Tim Davis, Samuel Morse. And we are one of the larger collectors in the world of [artist duo] Francois-Xavier and Claude Lalanne, with over 100 of their works.

You've got three Manhattan projects planned right now. Does it feel risky to have them all going at once?
The risky move is to try to hit the market at the right time. The way to minimize risk is to build product that doesn't exist.

What's your relationship been like with Elliman Chair Howard Lorber since leaving the company? I heard he invested in 125 Greenwich.
Howard and I have always had a great relationship. We see each other almost daily at Cipriani.

What do you consider your proudest accomplishment?
Finding my wife.

What's your greatest disappointment?
That my father is not alive to see what I'm doing.

What's your ideal weekend?
Going to listen to my favorite performer, Antonis Remos. He's the greatest pop musician in Greece. His performances start at 1 a.m. and go until 7 a.m.

What would you like people to say about you in 20 years?
I think in 20 years, it would be great if people said, 'I want to live in a Shvo building.' **TRD**

October 2014

JOHN CATSIMATIDIS
PRESIDENT | **RED APPLE GROUP AND GRISTEDES FOODS**

Catsimatidis sits at the helm of Manhattan's largest supermarket chain, Red Apple Group and Gristedes Foods. Red Apple — with hundreds of millions of dollars in real estate interests — has proposed to build three residential towers in Coney Island, and is developing its third residential building along Myrtle Avenue in Fort Greene. In addition, Catsimatidis has said he personally owns 300 properties in New York State and Pennsylvania. He also owns United Refining Corp, which processes and distributes oil in the U.S. Catsimatidis is also a prominent political fund-raiser and donor, who after this interview ran for New York City Mayor in 2013, but lost in the Republican primary. *Interview by Lauren Elkies*

"You're a prisoner of the ghetto till you escape. I escaped."

What's your date of birth?
September 7, class of 1948.

Where were you born?
The small island of Nisyros. It was part of the Turkish Empire till the early 1900s. Then it became part of Italy till 1947. And I was born there in 1948 [when it was part of Greece]. Six months later, my dad brought me to America.

What did your father do?
He worked for the Italian government on a lighthouse by himself for 16 years. Just to remember how hard he worked, I have a picture of the lighthouse on my BlackBerry. I took it from the yacht we charter. It's emotional.

Where'd you live when you came to America?
We moved into 512 West 135th Street, near my father's brothers. We were prisoners there for 20 years. You're a prisoner of the ghetto till you escape. I escaped.

Where do you live now?
On Fifth Avenue in the 60s, in a condo. I've been living there since my second marriage [in 1988].

Do you have any other homes?
A house in the Hamptons — East Quogue, on the beach. We also have old family homes in Greece.

What was your first job?
At the Sloan's Supermarket on 135th Street, but they didn't pay me. I was 14. They made me hustle behind the register and deliver groceries. I ended up buying the company.

Why did you drop out of NYU as an undergraduate?
I didn't drop out. I completed four full years. I was eight credits short of graduating.

Why not complete it?
A family friend was having problems with his uncle's grocery store on 100th Street. He said, 'You gotta take my position with my uncle.' I paid to buy him out.

Did not having a college degree hurt you?
It didn't hurt me. It didn't hurt Bill Gates. But I don't want my son [John Jr., 18, who starts at NYU this fall] to hear that. [Daughter Andrea, 21, has one semester left.]

What's the story with your pilot being held hostage?
We were in the airplane and jet leasing business. It was 1996. We were stuck with a bunch of 727s. The only place to sell them was Africa. We delivered the last plane [to West African millionaire Foutanga Dit Babani Sissoko], but they took away our pilot's passport in an attempt to reopen negotiations on the price. He wasn't really a hostage. He was in a luxury hotel with many women and lots of food.

So what'd you do?
Lowered the price.

Who's the most famous person you've flown in [one of your two] planes?
President Clinton uses them often.

Are you friends?
We're friends. Hillary [Rodham Clinton] came to my daughter's wedding. Bill was away.

Your daughter's husband is Christopher Cox, Richard Nixon's grandson. He's 11 years her senior, so were you upset when they first started dating?
No. The kid was such a nice kid.

How much did you spend on their June wedding at the Waldorf-Astoria?
In excess of $1 million.

You were planning to run for mayor as a Republican in 2009, but withdrew when Mayor Michael Bloomberg ran for a third term. What happened?
Bloomberg called me in and asked me to withdraw and use my influence to get him the nomination. I'm being urged to run now by the county chairs.

Do you plan on running?
I am urging Police Commissioner Ray Kelly to run. If he doesn't run, I may.

Where do you buy your groceries?
At Gristedes — and I pay for them. We even — what's the word, schlep? — we schlep them out to the Hamptons.

Forbes recently ranked you No. 692 on its list of "The World's Billionaires" with a net worth of $1.8 billion. Is that enough, or do you aspire to climb up that list?
I don't care about the money. Like I tell my friends, if I wasn't in the supermarket business, I'd be higher up.

Your wife, Margo Vondersaar, is president of MCV Advertising and co-publisher of the Hellenic Times. She was your secretary when you first met as well, right?
Going back to 1972. There were rumors we were together [while I was married to my first wife].

Were you?
Sometimes.

You're a gun enthusiast. Ever drawn your weapon?
I captured one person 25 years ago. Three guys held up our store on 84th Street and York Avenue. The other two got away. **TRD**

August 2011

TARA STACOM

EXECUTIVE VICE CHAIRMAN | **CUSHMAN & WAKEFIELD**

Stacom has been with the city's largest privately held commercial real estate services firm since 1981, and has handled more than 40 million square feet of transactions. Her clients have included the Port Authority, the Durst Organization, SL Green and Blackstone. Stacom notably represented the Port Authority in the historic Condé Nast deal at One World Trade Center, where she is the co-leasing agent for the building along with Durst, an equity partner in the tower. In 2011, Stacom was awarded the Most Ingenious Deal of the Year award by REBNY for her work on World Trade Center leasing. Her sister Darcy Stacom is a top broker at CBRE. *Interview by Lauren Elkies*

"There's very little in life I'm not competitive about."

What's your full name?

Tara Irene Stacom. Hill of Tara in Ireland is what I was named after. It's where all the ancient queens of Ireland were buried. Mom liked short names that couldn't be shortened. Stacy. Darcy. Beau is B-e-a-u. Tara. There are six of us. And she was Claire.

So your mom passed on?

Yes. She died very quickly in a car accident at age 59. She was coming home from negotiating a leasing deal in Westchester [for Cushman & Wakefield] very late one night. She fell asleep and hit something.

What's your date of birth?

August 11, 1958.

Who's older — you or your sister Darcy [who does investment sales at the CBRE Group]?

I'm actually a year older. She came into the business a year before me, so people think she's older and I leave it that way as we get older.

Where do you live?

485 Park at 58th Street. I've been there for 20 years.

As long as you've been married [to second husband Arthur Diedrick]?

Exactly right. And we go to Connecticut on the weekends.

Doesn't Darcy have a home there as well?

She's in Easton and I'm in Litchfield. We're from Greenwich originally.

Do you have other homes?

In Naples, Florida, we have a condo on the beach. When we're visiting friends we look at real estate. In Naples, we toured and then went around again with an agent two hours later. I walked in and I said, 'I'll take it.' My husband said, 'We're not buying.' I said, 'Hey, I'm buying.' I said, 'Sell it to me lock, stock and everything in it.' We bought it with pots and pans, linens, towels.

How often are you and your husband in the city on the weekends?

My husband wrote in our marriage contract — I'm joking, obviously, but he means this sort of seriously — that he won't spend a weekend in the city. He likes to be in the country.

Is that why your marriage works?

Actually we hadn't spent a day apart in five years. The day he said, 'I really want to do this [state-appointed] political position and it requires me to live in the house in Connecticut,' I went, 'What?' We have the most phenomenal marriage and I could be with him every day of my life.

I know you don't have children, but if you did, would there have been room in your life for them?

I would have made the room, without question. But I wasn't confident I'd be able to pull it all off — a really great marriage, a really great career and terrific kids, and still have it all together. My husband had four kids and I wanted a really fabulous marriage this go-around.

Do you and Darcy compete with each other?

Darcy's in sales. I'm in leasing. We might fight over a piece of turkey if it's the last one — otherwise we're in different spheres of the industry. When we see each other it's Thanksgiving, it's Christmas, it's Easter and it's holiday time ... because we all don't get a lot of time together.

Did you ever work with your dad?

I did turn to him for One World Trade. Dad was the mastermind behind the Sears Tower. He was the agent that sold the land, that built the building, and he was the leasing agent. So when I wanted to figure out whether "Freedom Tower" was a name that was really going to help me lease One World Trade, I called Dad and I said, 'Dad, I think we need to change the name.' He was absolutely for it. He decided within a heartbeat it should be One World Trade Center.

Have you spent your entire career at Cushman?

Almost. I did sales at Time Inc. for one year out of college. Fourteen of us got hired in the recession in 1980 and 14 of us got laid off in '81.

How do you decompress?

Run. I love Bikram yoga. I love to go off and shoot birds. We're avid bird shooters. It's just fabulous. It gets you outdoors. I'm not a Bambi shooter. I just do the birds.

Do you do it competitively?

Oh, absolutely. There's very little in life I'm not competitive about.

Are you a health nut?

Are you kidding me? I'm the worst. Steak, fries, cheeseburgers, ice cream, candy every afternoon.

How are you and Darcy different?

I'm anal. I must do whatever I do 150 percent. If she's not interested, she won't. She can be quicker. It'll take me longer to figure something out and I won't give up till I've figured it out. As kids I was more studious; Darcy partied more. I was right attack wing in lacrosse and field hockey, and Darcy liked goalie. You have to be fearless to stand in a cage. I've got to outmaneuver, outrun and be very fast and artful in being the scorer on the team. **TRD**

January 2012

HAL FETNER

CEO | **DURST FETNER RESIDENTIAL**

Fetner heads one of the more active residential developers in Manhattan. The company, which formed in 2008 out of a partnership between Sidney Fetner Associates and the Durst Organization, is a residential owner and developer with thousands of existing and in-development units. The company's most notable project is a massive pyramid-like rental building on West 57th Street between 11th and 12th avenues, designed by starchitect Bjarke Ingels. (In early 2015, Fetner and Durst parted ways. His new firm, Fetner Properties, walked away from the 57th Street project but retains an interest in another joint development, 855 Sixth Avenue, a mixed-use building at West 30th Street.) *Interview by Lauren Elkies*

"I invited President Nixon to my bar mitzvah because I started getting interested in politics."

What's your date of birth?
December 7, 1960.

Where did you grow up?
Port Chester, N.Y.

Where do you live now?
Mount Kisco, and we keep a rental apartment here in the city on 94th Street and First Avenue in one of our properties, the Chesapeake.

Do you have any other homes?
We have a boat. Right now it's in Key Largo, Florida. In the summer, she's up here in Norwalk, Connecticut. It's a hand-me-down from my father. My sisters, mom and I share it. The boat was named Southern Star when my father bought it, and he joked that he was too cheap to change the name because all the towels were monogrammed.

Was he actually cheap?
My grandfather was a builder/developer in the Bronx and lost everything in the Depression. My father grew up very, very poor as a result. My father got into business building Mobil gas stations. From there, he grew the company. He was very tough on his kids. My sisters and I were raised to learn the value of a hard day's work and the value of a dollar.

Were you a good kid?
I would get into trouble — like at 15, being arrested for swimming in the Rye Patch Reservoir. I didn't serve time. My father thought it was funny until he found out it was a misdemeanor. They expunge it if you keep clean for six months.

Did you get into trouble again?
Not arrested, but I was taken to the police station for driving after hours with a junior driver's permit.

So you got into real estate because of your family?
Third generation. I always wanted to follow in my father's footsteps, but I had always wanted to go into public office. And so, even though I got into trouble as a younger kid, I then started modeling myself to be a better kid. I invited President Richard Nixon to my bar mitzvah because I started getting interested in politics.

I'm guessing Nixon declined your invitation?
Yes. I got the form letter that he was busy. But I then went to law school with the goal of never practicing — I wanted to run for public office. I ended up clerking for Joe Hynes, who at the time was a New York State special prosecutor.

What happened to the political dream?
My father became ill, literally, as I was finishing up law school. I knew I'd be taking over the family business.

How long have you been married to your wife, Nina?
Twenty-four years.

How did you two meet?
A blind date.

Do you have children?
Yes. My oldest, Samantha, is a junior at Syracuse University. My son, Alex, is a senior in high school. And Emma is in eighth grade.

What kinds of activities do you do with your kids?
I take each of my kids away alone. I try to do it every year, and when they all turn 16, I take them anywhere in the world they want that requires less than a seven-hour flight. My daughter picked London and my son picked Berlin.

How did you and Douglas [Durst, the company's chairman] meet?
Actually, my father and Seymour [Douglas' father] knew each other. I knew Jody [president of Durst Fetner and Douglas's cousin] better than I knew Douglas. Years ago, when they built 4 Times Square, I was fascinated with the green technology. Jody and I started a dialogue about how I can take some of what they're doing and incorporate it into some of my older apartment buildings. The Durst Organization never really did residential, but from there the whole conversation evolved into doing residential projects together.

How are sales going at 1212 Fifth Avenue?
Sales started last summer, and it's been unbelievable. Right this second, close to 20 percent is under contract.

Would you buy there?
My mom is actually thinking of buying there.

You like marathon running and triathlons.
I haven't done any in a while. I tore out my Achilles tendon three years ago, a few months after running in the New York City Marathon. I waited a year to do the surgery. I thought about running this year, but I just couldn't get motivated. I think I'm going to commit myself to next year. **TRD**

SCOTT RECHLER

CEO & CHAIRMAN | **RXR REALTY**

Rechler's multibillion-dollar private real estate firm, headquartered in Long Island, develops and owns Class A office and industrial space in the New York Tri-State area. Its properties include the 2.3 million-square-foot Starrett-Lehigh Building in Chelsea, which was purchased in 2011 for $920 million. Rechler previously served as CEO and chairman of Reckson Associates Realty, which he sold to SL Green Realty in January 2007 for roughly $6 billion in one of the largest public real estate management buyouts in REIT history. Rechler is also vice chairman of the board of commissioners of the Port Authority of New York & New Jersey

Interview by Lauren Elkies

"My son said, 'Dad, I think you're making a terrible mistake. I would never sell Reckson.'"

What's your date of birth?
November 4, 1967.

Where did you grow up?
Long Island. In Port Washington and Roslyn.

Where do you live now?
In Old Brookville, on the North Shore of Long Island.

Why not New York City?
My wife is a country girl from Arizona. We lived in New York City for a while and we figured the suburban life was more fitting.

Do you have any other homes?
Nope. I love my home. We have a pool, we have a tennis court and we're able to do a lot of stuff outdoors. I like to cook. I'm a big chef so I like to have a lot of dinner parties.

What's your culinary specialty?
I do everything. Italian's my favorite. I did a lot of studying in Italy on Tuscan food. I make pizzas from scratch. I do risottos. [Takes out his iPad and scrolls through pictures of dishes he prepared.]

Other than cooking, how do you have fun?
I like going to football games — I'm a big Giants fan. I do a lot of hiking and biking. For two weeks in August, my wife and kids [daughter, 18, and son, 14] and I go camping in Utah, stay outside, bathe in the lake and sleep on top of the houseboat under the stars. You're gone for two weeks and you see no one. We've been doing this for 21 years.

There's an amusing Indiana Jones story behind why you went to Clark University. Can you retell it?
I went there and there was this beautiful building that looked like one of the buildings from the Indiana Jones movies. It had the big stairwell, the big windows, that whole look. I met my wife there. My general counsel and partner, I met there. I was president of the student body and he was my treasurer.

For the Rechler clan, real estate has been a family affair.
My grandfather built the first planned industrial park in New York City. It was in Newtown Creek in Brooklyn in 1958. And then he went to Long Island to build industrial parks there. Then my father and uncle got into building office buildings in the suburbs with Reckson. I came into the business after my brother and my cousin, and we took the company public in 1995.

How many siblings do you have?
I've got two brothers and one half-brother named Bill. He's 15. My son and he go to school together. They have lunch and he calls him Uncle Bill. He looks like little Richie Rich.

Do you feel like he's your brother or your son?
I feel like he's my nephew. Sometimes I feel like he's my kid, like when I have to reprimand him. He's a good kid. He lives 10 minutes from my house. His mother just turned 50. I love her. I'm very close to her. I call her my evil stepmother [laughing]. My parents were divorced when I was like 3 or 4 years old.

Who'd you grow up with?
I was with my mom during the week and my dad during the weekends. That's why I cook, because we cooked for his dates. It was part of our fun.

Your son tried to persuade you not to sell Reckson. What did he say?
My partner and CFO came over and we were having a discussion the day before we were going to be launching this process of selling the company. So my CFO leaves and then I'm barbecuing that night and my son [who was nine or 10 at the time] comes out and he says, 'Dad, I think you're making a terrible mistake. I would never sell Reckson.' This is what he's telling me as tears are coming down my face. And then when we were going through the process it became a little tumultuous. It was my daughter's Bat Mitzvah the day that Carl Icahn announced he was putting in a bid to try to top SL Green's bid for the company. It was all over CNBC and there was all this craziness going on. And my son comes in and tells me, 'I told you; you shouldn't have tried to sell Reckson.'

What are you reading?
Right now I'm reading David Brooks' "The Social Animal." I'm also reading Thomas Friedman's new book, "That Used to Be Us." I typically read two books at once.

Are you religious?
I consider myself more spiritual than religious. I say a prayer every day and I think about spiritual stuff.

What prayer?
I pray for different things. It depends on what's going on in my life, like the health and wellness of my family, that people are safe. ... I have some specific prayers.

That you're not sharing.
That I'm not sharing. Some stuff has to be private. **TRD**

November 2011

Photo by Marc Scriv

JOE MOINIAN

FOUNDER | **MOINIAN GROUP**

Before venturing into real estate in 1982, Moinian founded the successful ladies' apparel company Billy Jack for Her. Today, the Moinian Group operates a 20 million-square-foot portfolio of assets across the U.S., valued at more than $10 billion. The firm's holdings include the W New York-Downtown Hotel & Residences and a stake in Chicago's Sears Tower. The Moinian Group is also developing an 1,100-unit residential tower at 605 West 42nd Street, adjacent to its Atelier condominium. *Interview by Candace Taylor*

"I did not take [the fight] personally. He made a business decision and I made another business decision."

What's your date of birth?
February 25, 1954.

Where are you from?
I was born in Tehran, the capital of Iran, and moved here to New York City when I was 17. I was the first one in the Moinian family to come here.

Where do you live now?
I live in 655 Park Avenue, and I have a house in Long Island, in the town of Quogue, on the water.

How long have you been married?
I have been married 29 years on May 29th. I met Nazee at an engagement party in The Waldorf Astoria hotel when I was 26.

What do you do when you spend time together as a family?
We get together with my whole family [which includes my five kids] at a minimum of once a week. Sometimes in my house, sometimes my sister's, sometimes my brother's. ... Big meal, nice discussion. My girls that still live with me, they get up in the morning on Friday and their first question is, 'Whose house are we going to tonight?' To them it's the biggest pleasure that they have for the whole week.

You are known as a dapper dresser. Who is your favorite designer?
I would have to say Prada and Tom Ford.

What is your greatest professional achievement?
I think I'm proudest of what we have done to develop and support the emerging neighborhoods in Manhattan. For example, we own and manage in excess of 5 million square feet in Lower Manhattan. Downtown is one of the markets that we have never given up on. Our W Hotel downtown is a tremendous success.

How did your deal with SL Green at 3 Columbus Circle come together?
I have been friends with Stephen Green and Marc Holliday and Andrew Mathias for many years. I have known Steve since before he went public. ... In the case of 3 Columbus Circle, they understood the value of the asset and the renovation that was nearly completed and they wanted to join me in executing our plans for the property, so this way we can create value and benefit a great deal as partners.

How did you react when Related's Stephen Ross said on CNBC that he'd purchased the building?
Three Columbus Circle is a very high-profile asset. And when Steve Ross went on CNBC to say he bought it, when he hadn't, well ... I would rather not do business in the media, but in this case I had no choice but to set the story straight [in the courts]. And the rest is history.

The Moinian Group sued Ross over that deal, alleging that he was trying to 'steal' the building. What is your relationship like with him now?
I did not take it personally. He made a business decision, and I made another business decision.

During the worst of the recession, were you ever really afraid you would lose the building, or others in your portfolio?
At times, I thought, 'This is the time for me to work harder.' So I worked harder. Our business is cyclical; sometimes we have to do more. We did what we had to do.

What other new projects are you working on?
We are working to restart construction on the development site on West 42nd Street, next door to the Atelier. That's a rental and it might have some housing for sale as well. I'm hoping to start construction very soon.

Who are your heroes?
Ayoub Moinian and Sarah Moinian — my parents. My father was in real estate back in Iran, and of course he has some investments with me.

Who is your mentor in the industry?
Certainly Larry Silverstein; we are very good friends. Jeff Gural, Mary Ann Tighe and Steve Siegel.

Did you go to them for advice during the downturn?
All the time. **TRD**

ROBERT K. FUTTERMAN

CHAIRMAN & CEO | **ROBERT K. FUTTERMAN & ASSOCIATES**

With offices in cities including New York, Las Vegas, Los Angeles, Miami and San Francisco, the retail firm of Robert K. Futterman & Associates has been responsible for nearly $20 billion in real estate transactions since its founding in 1998. Of late, the firm has been marketing retail space in buildings such as 250 Bowery and 855 Sixth Avenue. Futterman has personally been involved in transactions totaling some $10 billion, including Tommy Hilfiger's purchase in 2014 of the Raleigh Hotel in Miami Beach. *Interview by Candace Taylor*

"I'd ask for Harry Helmsley, I'd ask for Donald Trump. If they directed me somewhere else, then so be it."

What's your full name?
Robert Kenneth Futterman.

Why do you use the 'K'? I heard it's because there was a developer named Robert Futterman.
There was another Robert Futterman, but that's not why I use the 'K.' I grew up in the business admiring Edward S. Gordon [head of Edward S. Gordon Company]. I liked the E.S.G. — it was a person who became a brand.

When were you born?
December 14, 1958.

Where did you grow up?
Jericho, Long Island. Exit 40 off the L.I.E.

Where do you live now?
I have a home in Greenwich and an apartment in the city. I usually rent in the Hamptons in the summer.

Where do you spend most of your time?
I'm in the city every Monday, Tuesday and Wednesday night, and every Thursday night I go to Connecticut to be with my kids. I have two boys, ages 16 and 18.

How did you get into real estate?
I was interested in going into the music business. Concert promotion is what I did in college at the University of Maryland. But it was a weird time, it was 1981. MTV had just been created. Naysayers were saying that the live concert business would become obsolete, record companies were laying people off, and the compact disc was just invented. I got discouraged from finding a job in the music business. I didn't want to work on Wall Street. I liked the concept of real estate, that you could use your sales skills and at the same time get out of the office and meet people. I ended up interviewing at Garrick-Aug Associates, which was in the retail leasing business, and it really seemed perfect for me.

Why? Were you a big shopper?
I love to shop, and I love to walk the streets and get the exercise and update our maps and call people and always ask for the most important person at the company. I'd ask for Harry Helmsley, I'd ask for Donald Trump. If they directed me somewhere else, then so be it. But I had no fear of calling the top people.

Are you still into music now, and do you play instruments?
I play the guitar and sing. Right now I like the Decemberists and Mumford & Sons. I'm constantly finding new music.

You dropped out of college. How has that impacted your career?
It hasn't impacted my career. I was able to learn enough in college and enough in life to deal with anybody. I can deal with friends of mine who are Harvard MBAs; I can deal with the guy that owns the chain of local delicatessens.

What's your greatest achievement?
It's really going out on my own and starting the company. It will be 13 years in August. Pulling it off and making it successful — it took a lot of guts, and it paid off.

What's a mistake you've made in your career?
A lot of the mistakes are the deals I didn't do, the opportunities that slipped through my fingers. I've had some real successes, but there have been a couple of clunkers too. [laughs] ... Investing in some land in Las Vegas.

Prudential Douglas Elliman's Faith Hope Consolo has been called the Queen of Retail. Are you the king?
[Laughs] I would say [RKF Executive Vice President] Karen Bellantoni is the Queen of Retail. I don't think my ego would allow me to call myself king.

You're divorced. Are you dating?
I have a very serious girlfriend. Her name is Hollie Watman. She's a children's clothing designer.

How did you meet her?
She lived in my building. We lived in the building, the Porter House in Chelsea, for almost three years and never really talked to each other. Then I ran into her at the Soho House. And she recognized me, and said, 'Aren't you my neighbor?' And we've been going out ever since.

Are you going to get married again soon?
Well, we bought an apartment together [at 345 West 13th Street].

What do you do in your free time?
I play golf; I play basketball with my kids. My girlfriend has me going to fitness classes, Core Fusion. I'm such a good boyfriend. [Laughs]

You invested money with Bernie Madoff — what was the impact of that?
I didn't get hurt too bad.

Did you know Madoff personally?
No. My accountant recommended I invest some money. ... That was just one account. But it's a travesty; I feel completely taken advantage of. It's just disgusting. I think the SEC dropped the ball. It makes me angry. I have a hard time even reading all these articles. I change the channel if it's on TV. But I'm lucky it wasn't life-changing. I think the real travesty is the people who lost their life savings; that's who your heart breaks for.

Did you fire your accountant?
I switched accountants. **TRD**

April 2011

M A U R I C E   M A N N

FOUNDER | **MANN REALTY ASSOCIATES**

Mann, the owner of a large property management and residential development firm, is probably best known for partnering with Lev Leviev's Africa Israel USA to buy the Apthorp rental building in 2006 for $426 million. At the time, the deal was a record for the highest price paid per rental unit. The two firms planned to convert the storied Upper West Side tower to condos, but their relationship soured. Under pressure from Africa Israel, Mann agreed to step down as managing partner. Mann's firm is also behind the condo conversion of the rental building at 36 Gramercy Park East. Mann sits on the Rent Stabilization Association's Housing Court Reform Committee. *Interview by Leigh Kamping-Carde*

"It's a tragedy that a great iconic building was destroyed by greed."

What's your date of birth?
September 5, 1953.

Where did you grow up?
On the Jersey Shore. But I've been living in New York City since after graduate school. I spend summers in my home in East Hampton. I try to do my winters at my home in Fort Lauderdale. And I try to get to Paris a couple times a year.

Where do you live now?
I'm at the Laureate [at 2150 Broadway].

Have you ever been married?
No. I'm single.

What were you like as a kid?
Intense. Anal. OCD. Now, because I've gotten older, I'm just neurotic. I used to read a lot when I was younger. For my bar mitzvah, my father gave me a book called, "How I Turned $1,000 into Five Million in Real Estate in My Spare Time." I was fascinated with it. Dad had told me it was the greatest business in the world. He went on to explain things like depreciation and financing. I had no clue what he was talking about, but I listened. I recently gave the book to my nephew. I passed it on to him at his bar mitzvah.

What was your father like?
He was an importer and manufacturer of men's handkerchiefs and ties and hats. He had factories in Switzerland and Italy and Puerto Rico. He was a very humble man. Very good natured, very decent. Very, very honest.

What was your mother like?
My mother was very glamorous. She was Hollywood. And also, my mother was absolutely, without a doubt, one of the 100 greatest cooks.

What was her specialty?
We're Sephardic. Syrian Jews. So Mediterranean food.

What's your worst tenant story?
I was told that if tenants were not paying rent, you had to go and collect it. At that time, the upper part of the West Side — 110th Street — was nowhere near as built up as it is today. I went with someone who was basically a rent collector and knocked on the door. [The tenant] took the rent bill and ripped it up into 100 pieces, threw it in my face, slammed the door and said, 'I don't pay rent!' Without going into the details, we legally got that tenant out. It took about two years, but we got her out.

You're on the Rent Stabilization Association's Housing Court Reform Committee. What's wrong with housing court?
It's very socialistic, some would even say fascist. It's kind of a dictatorship down there.

What was a particularly bad experience dealing with the housing court system?
I had one case once where the judge adjourned my case [16 or 17 times] for no reason. I filed a formal complaint against [the judge] with the chief administrative judge, who ordered him to close his entire courtroom for one week while I had my trial. There was not one other case that judge heard until I had my trial. I ultimately won, but to have to go through that kind of energy and legal expense to collect $162 in unpaid rent — you can see the inequity there.

You haven't been back to the Apthorp in several years.
It's a tragedy that a great iconic building was destroyed by greed. [Africa Israel] threw me under the bus and shot themselves in the foot — that says it all.

How did that project fall apart?
We had received a preliminary condo approval, then Lehman Brothers exploded. Everyone thought the world was coming to an end. I didn't feel that way, but some of the partners did and asked me voluntarily to step aside and let them take over the management. I stepped aside only to find out within a matter of weeks that none of the contractual, legal obligations that they made were honored. That forced me into litigation with them. In the end, we litigated for a couple of years, and no one got anything — except the lawyers. No one stopped to think intellectually, 'What do we do? Do we cancel the condo plan and go back in at a later point and keep the building a rental for a few more years?' They never asked me. A lot of underhandedness, that's all I've got to say about it.

Do you regret getting involved with the Apthorp?
Oh, it's not what I did, it's what they did.

Do you regret partnering with them?
Oh, for sure. I regret trusting them and being betrayed. **TRD**

CHRIS SCHLANK

FOUNDER & CO-MANAGING PARTNER | **SAVANNA**

Schlank started a real estate private equity firm that has invested $2.3 billion in properties since 2006. He bought his first building while in grad school. He has personally overseen the acquisition and redevelopment of more than 65 real estate assets, comprising over 19 million square feet of space, the vast majority of which has been in New York City. He is also an assistant adjunct professor at Columbia University, where he teaches a seminar in real estate finance. *Interview by Katherine Clarke*

"My worst habit is saying things how I see them out loud. I'm trying to develop a filter."

What's your date of birth?
September 18, 1966.

You grew up in Manhattan. Which neighborhood?
On the Upper West Side in a brownstone on a dead-end block — 71st Street between West End and Riverside. We played soccer and baseball on the street without worrying about getting hit by cars.

What were you like as a kid?
I went to a [private] school called Collegiate on 78th and West End. It's the oldest school in the country. I was definitely not the smartest guy in the class. I was pretty shy and never got into too much trouble.

Where did you go to college?
The University of Pennsylvania. I was a French Studies major and an Urban Studies minor. I spent my junior year abroad in France, in 1986. What could be better than being 19 and living in Paris and having no worries? They were having student protests then over a hike in tuition costs. I remember going to class and there was tear gas everywhere. I still speak French today where I can. I have a good accent.

Where do you live now?
In Greenwich, Connecticut. I have three kids who are very sporty, so living in New York City became difficult. My oldest son, Johnny, is 16; my daughter, Julia, is going to be 15 in September; and my son Luke is 11. Johnny's sensitive and sweet like his daddy, Julia's a tough chick, and Luke is a surfer/skateboarder wild man.

Do you have other homes?
I have a house in Wainscott [in the Hamptons]. I have a boat, actually, a 26-foot regulator. I love to fish. Out there, it's striped bass and bluefish, pretty much.

What's the biggest fish you've ever caught?
When I went deep-sea fishing with my father in Cabo San Lucas, Mexico, in 1978, I caught a 150-pound marlin.

What do you drive?
A suburban gas-guzzler. All these guys I know in Connecticut have three different sports cars. I'm not a gadget guy.

If you were the mayor of New York, what is the first thing you would change about the city and what would you fight to keep the same?
First: I would lower taxes. Second: I would make quality education more accessible. The thing I would fight to keep is the diversity of the city.

How long have you been married?
Seventeen years. I met my wife, Joey, at a bar. We both went to Penn. She was a year older. She's an art consultant.

Why real estate?
I've been in real estate my whole life. My mom's a real estate broker. She had her own company, Joan Blackett Schlank Real Estate, for 20 years. At one point in the '80s, she had 30 people working for her. She still works a little bit, though she's almost 80. I grew up listening to her on the phone talking about co-op packages and how to get a dog into a building that didn't allow dogs. She worked from our kitchen for many years.

What did your dad do?
He was in advertising. He produced "Black Beauty" and "The Galloping Gourmet."

So how did you get started in the business?
After Penn, I worked for a nonprofit called West Side Federation for Senior Housing. In 1991, I went to the masters in real estate development program at Columbia. The first day of the program, I met the guy I started the business with, Jonathan Leitersdorf. He had a lot of money and didn't really want to work that hard. I had no money and wanted to work. While still in school, we bought our first building, 228 East 10th Street. It was a 24-unit, five-story walk-up. We bought the debt from Amalgamated Bank for $215,000.

How did you meet your business partner Nick Bienstock?
Nick and I first knew each other in high school. I think we might have dated some of the same women. I'm not sure. I founded Savanna in 1992 right out of Columbia [which was where Nick and I reconnected]. Nick joined in 1998.

What are your bad habits?
I've got a bad temper and I tend to talk too much. My worst habit is saying things how I see them out loud. I'm trying to develop a filter.

Do you exercise?
I do a great thing called gyrotonics. It's like three-dimensional Pilates. There's a machine that's called "the tower." It's like a medieval torture device. I do a one-on-one with a former ballerina at a studio on 71st Street.

You own the building that's home to Twitter's NYC headquarters. Are you big on social media?
No, I don't even know how to Tweet.

Do you make as much money as you'd like?
Right now? No. But I don't spend any time thinking about money.

Are you religious?
I don't believe in God, but I believe in a spirit that guides us. I believe that the world is round and in being nice to people because it comes around to bite you. **TRD**

August 2014

FAITH HOPE CONSOLO

CHAIRMAN | **DOUGLAS ELLIMAN RETAIL GROUP**

Well known for her ubiquitous marketing slogans, such as "To Find the Best Retail Space, You Need Faith," Consolo — the chair of Elliman's retail leasing and sales division — has brought many prominent retailers to Manhattan, including Cartier, Versace, Jimmy Choo, Manolo Blahnik, Giorgio Armani and Fendi. Before joining Elliman in 2005, she served as vice chairman of Garrick-Aug Worldwide for nearly 20 years, founding the firm's international division in 1987 and opening its European office in Paris. *Interview by Candace Taylor*

"I'm very sensitive. People don't know that. They think I'm tough, hard as nails. Ruthless. Can you believe that?"

What's your full name?

Faith Hope Consolo. That's my given name. My mother was very eccentric. The story was she almost died having me, so she said she had faith and now she has hope.

Consolo was your maiden name — but you've been married three times. Did you ever take a husband's last name?

Never. Because I never wanted to change the monogram on the luggage. In view of the number of times [I've been married], I think I made a smart decision.

Do you think you'd ever get married again?

Anything's possible — why not? I'm never without a boyfriend.

Who are you dating now?

Someone very well known from Wall Street.

What's your date of birth?

Oh my God, you're going to ask me? July 25, 1949. Just wait, somebody will write to you and say, 'Oh, that's not really her date of birth.'

Where did you grow up?

I was born in Ohio — Shaker Heights, the same town as Bruce Ratner.

Did you and Bruce know each other growing up?

No. We left there when I was 2 because my father died. So my mother moved us back East. I grew up in Westport, Connecticut.

Where do you live now?

Across from the Park, on Fifth Avenue in the 60s.

Do you have other homes?

In Westport, Connecticut, where I grew up — I still have that home. When I finally retire — who knows when that will be — I will buy something in Europe: Switzerland or France.

Your mother died, too?

Yes, when I was 12. She had a heart attack. I'm forming a foundation called Real Estate Has a Heart [for the American Heart Association]. I feel like it's payback time for Mommy.

How were you impacted by having both your parents die at a young age?

Not only wanting to survive, but always trying to find my way.

Elliman CEO Dottie Herman also lost her mother at a young age. Do you have a bond because of that?

We had a bond from day one. When I met her, in five minutes we were practically in tears. I came to Elliman because of Dottie. I felt she understood me personally and that's not easy to do, because I don't let that many people in, especially in this business. They see the façade and it's very difficult because when you negotiate for a living as I do, you don't want to appear vulnerable. I'm not letting those guys see me cry.

Did you ever consider having kids?

No. I never really wanted to have children. That might have been a result of my childhood, because I lost my parents and maybe I was afraid that either I wouldn't be around, or I wouldn't be the right mother.

Do you have other family?

No, I have no family left; I am truly an orphan. My last family [members were] killed in a plane crash about 10 years ago, my aunt and uncle. Terrible.

How have you coped with all this tragedy?

I think the key is not to dwell on it. You just have to go with it and not think, 'Oh me, the victim, look what happened to me.' Besides, if I cry a lot, I'll get lines around my eyes and then I'll have to go and do Botox and surgery like everyone else. And that won't work because I'm afraid of needles.

So you've never gotten anything done?

No. Probably should, but not yet.

What has been the greatest challenge or obstacle you've faced in your career?

At Garrick-Aug in the 1980s, being the only woman at the top. All of the partners and the senior-level executives were men. They all were very tough on me. I always felt that I had to keep proving myself.

Why do you think you've been the target of so much criticism over the years?

They like to say all these things: 'No, she didn't do that'; 'Oh, she's only big in her own mind.' I think if we had to take the plain answer, we could say it's jealousy.

What about shopping?

All the time. This is why I'm in the business: My accountant said we're going to turn a habit into a career. Bergdorf and Neiman and all the boutiques could tell you. American Express could tell you. They love me a lot. And not just New York. I walk into stores in Miami or Las Vegas. I'll find a pair of shoes or something, and I'll give them my credit card. And they'll say, 'Are you the real estate lady from New York?' I want to die!

Do you think you do too much press?

I know some people think it's overexposure, but I think the deals really drive the press. You make a deal with a new designer coming into New York, everybody cares, everybody wants to know about it. I've always publicized the stores. ... I know some people say, 'Oh, she gets all the press — she chases them.'

What is something that people don't know about you?

That I'm very sensitive. People don't know that. They think I'm tough, hard as nails, ruthless. Ruthless, can you believe that? **TRD**

January 2011

BRUCE MOSLER

GLOBAL BROKERAGE CHAIRMAN | **CUSHMAN & WAKEFIELD**

Mosler was the president and CEO of Cushman & Wakefield from 2005 until 2010, and now serves as the company's chairman of global brokerage — working with major tenants and investors on real estate matters. He has advised companies such as Brookfield Properties, Vornado, Cohen Brothers, JP Morgan Chase, NYU University Hospital, Citigroup and Madison Square Garden. He is currently spearheading office leasing for Brookfield's Manhattan West, a $4.5 billion development on the Far West Side of Manhattan. In the 1980s, he founded Riverbank Realty Company, which later merged with Galbreath New York. He joined Cushman & Wakefield as an executive vice president in 1997. *Interview by Candace Taylor*

"I think this is key to any person's success in life: To have a partner who gets it."

What's your date of birth?
October 16, 1957.

Where do you live?
We live on 62nd and Columbus. We have a home in East Hampton and a home in Williamsburg, Virginia, where my in-laws are.

Where did you grow up?
Born and raised in New York. I grew up in basically two locations, 1035 Fifth Avenue and 10 Gracie Square.

You spent two years as a teenager studying in Switzerland — why?
I think it's because my mother wanted to experience living in Europe [laughs]. I went to Le Rosey, a boarding school outside of Geneva. In retrospect it was a very good experience; at the time it was a difficult adjustment because I was uprooted.

Why didn't you join the family business, Mosler Safe?
You learn very quickly the benefits of a wonderful family business ... but you also learn about the challenges of a family business, which is family. I'm proud of the brand because Mosler safes sit in Fort Knox today. In the '70s they sold the business to American Standard. So there was no question coming out of college as to whether or not I needed to get a job. My father had a very interesting attitude. We butted heads early. He wanted me to go to Princeton.

Is that where he went?
Yes. I went to Duke and instantly fell in love with the campus. But it created significant stress in our relationship for a while. My father was a great friend and mentor but we diverged on a number of things. He made it clear very early that he felt his obligations to his children were to provide an education, provide a start, if possible, and the rest of his earnings were going to charitable causes.

So no inheritance?
He made it very clear early on that was not an expectation we should have.

So I guess it's a good thing you were successful.
It certainly put a fire in my belly. I was a terrible student. I wanted to work and earn a living as soon as possible.

Why were you a terrible student — did you just not try, or were you rebelling?
All of the above.

What was your first big real estate deal?
One of my first very big deals was with a client of mine today, Cohen Brothers, with Cahners Publishing, 475 Park Avenue South, about 66,000 feet. There's nothing quite like that feeling when you have the first one under your belt.

Is your switch to chairman of global brokerage a lateral move?
It's neither up, down or sideways; it's what I want to do in order to fully engage with the business that I think I'm best suited to do. I love brokerage.

You have two kids?
David and Charlotte. David is 16 and Charlotte is 12.

How did you meet your wife [Wendy Mosler]?
We met in college, and have been together since. We would have had kids earlier but we had challenges, and so we look at our kids as a blessing because it was not easy. I think older parents are better parents to some degree because they have more patience.

How old were you when you became a dad?
I was 37 when David was born. I was old. We were going to adopt.

How did you balance being a CEO with being a parent?
I coach David in the winter in the [Yorkville Youth Athletic Association basketball league]. As CEO, wherever I was in the world, I would get back on Friday to coach Saturday. When I was CEO, I clearly made a choice that it was business first and family was critical, but had to take a backseat. Now, business is still critical but my family is first. And that's a huge change.

How did your wife feel about business coming first?
I think this is key to any person's success in life: To have a partner who gets it. Wendy's a very independent person and she has her own career [as head of finance and acquisition for Miller Global]. And that is hugely important to someone who is going to put their business first for a period of time. I'm not saying she has done the same, because she hasn't. She's there for the kids' teacher/parent interviews. I am not. When I show up, they ask who I am. [Laughs] Sad, but it's part of the gig. As we look forward, I'm hoping they get to know me.

You're known for your love of fishing. Do you ever take the kids out fishing with you?
Yes, but they get seasick, so when I take them we go closer to shore, where it's calmer. When we're in Florida, it's easy because the fishing is so close. When I go from Montauk, we go 80 miles out.

You celebrated your 50th birthday in Philadelphia, when you were in the process of getting an advanced management degree from Wharton. What did you do to celebrate?
My wife brought down about 50 of my closest friends. Mike Fascitelli [CEO of Vornado] roasted me. It was a surprise, all engineered by Wendy after I said, 'Please just come down and we'll have dinner alone.' **TRD**

December 2010

SHARIF EL-GAMAL
CEO | **SOHO PROPERTIES**

El-Gamal became internationally known as the developer of Park51, a community center and Islamic prayer space planned two blocks from the World Trade Center site. The building — labeled the "ground zero mosque" by critics, a description that El-Gamal says is incorrect — sparked a worldwide firestorm. Opponents denounced it, saying that an Islamic center has no place so close to the site where so many died on Sept. 11. But supporters argued it promoted tolerance, and forcing it to move would go against America's commitment to freedom of religion. (In May 2014, after this interview, El-Gamal announced that he was planning to build luxury condos, as well as a three-story museum dedicated to Islam in place of the larger Islamic community center.) *Interview by Candace Taylor*

"I'm a college dropout. I've always been very restless."

What's your full name?
Sharif Mohamed El-Gamal. It's a capital 'E' — people have been spelling it with a lower-case 'e.'

Is it frustrating to see your name spelled wrong in the paper?
It is. But who would ever have expected that I would have gotten so much press for what I'm trying to do?

So you were surprised by the reaction to the project?
I can't believe that this is getting the amount of attention that it's getting. But I look at it as an opportunity on many different levels.

How so?
It's an opportunity to bring awareness about my religion, which is Islam; to bring awareness about my project and to get stakeholders, and to get people emotionally involved.

Let's back up. What is your birth date?
December 23, 1972.

Where did you grow up?
I was born in Methodist Hospital in Brooklyn, in Park Slope, which is much nicer now than when I was growing up there. I lived in Park Slope. I lived in Long Island and Manhattan. I'm a New Yorker.

But you also lived abroad.
I did. I went to American schools overseas, in Alexandria in Egypt, and Monrovia in Liberia.

Where did you go to college?
I'm a college dropout. I went to the New York Institute of Technology, to SUNY Farmingdale, to Pace University and a couple of others. I was not a disciplined student — I've always been very restless.

Did you go straight into real estate after college?
I didn't. While I was in college, I was selling stocks. I didn't love the business. I was very good at it, but it did not turn me on. Then I got into the restaurant industry — I was waiting tables and bartending.

Where did you work?
I worked at Serafina [on East 61st Street]. I tended bar at Michael Jordan's Steak House in Grand Central Station. They say in the restaurant industry that you get these golden handcuffs. I was making six figures waiting tables and bartending and having a very flexible life.

How did you get into real estate?
I just kind of realized that I needed to get serious about my life. I started out by renting apartments. However, I always wanted to sell buildings. I've always had a knack for being a closer — no matter what it was, whether it was asking a girl out to dinner or getting into a nightclub. I went to the commercial side and found a for-sale-by-owner. I ended up selling nine buildings that year [in 2001].

From there you got into development?
Then I segued into development and I founded Soho Properties in 2003. We've been very quiet and under the radar, and just making it happen.

Are you married?
I got married in 2005 to Rebekah. I have two daughters: Sarah, who is 3 and a half, and Jennah, who is 2.

Where do you live?
On the Upper West Side, and we spend time in East Hampton.

Were you religious growing up?
Holidays — that type of religiousness. But after 9/11, I really jumped into it and started understanding what Islam means.

What has been the most upsetting thing for you about the response to the project?
There has been a deception by the forces of evil — I'll just call it that — saying that this is the "ground zero mosque." One, it's not a mosque. Two, it's not at ground zero. There was a narrative that was built-in to provoke and sensationalize a topic that should have not gotten the attention that it got.

Would you like to set the record straight on anything?
I saw this as an opportunity to build a center to serve the Muslim community that needs a prayer space, but also at the same time to build a world-class community center like the Jewish Community Center or the 92nd Street Y, with robust programming and phenomenal athletic and recreational facilities.

How do you think [the Park51 project] will impact your future career as a developer?
I think the exposure is priceless. Everyone knows who I am. I'm looking for the next building that I'm going to buy. I want to buy one building before the end of this year, a trophy asset this time, up to $100 million.

Are you looking at distressed assets?
I don't think there's anything in distress in New York City. We're really focused south of 96th Street in Manhattan, not in the boroughs. I think the office market is where we want to focus.

What is something people don't know about you?
My mother, God rest her soul, was Polish Catholic. And I have more Jews for friends than Muslims.

Would you be open to opportunities outside of real estate — like being on a TV show?
I'm very focused on building my career in real estate. I think I need to make my first billion first. **TRD**

Photo by Michael Toola

PETER RIGUARDI

PRESIDENT | **JONES LANG LASALLE**

Riguardi heads up New York-area operations for the commercial brokerage firm Jones Lang LaSalle. Riguardi got his start at Williams Real Estate along with his father, Edward Riguardi, before the two left in 1989 to form Koeppel Tener Riguardi, which later became Colliers ABR. Peter, who was recruited to join Jones Lang in 2002, has completed transactions such as the Metropolitan Transportation Authority's 1.6 million-square-foot lease at 2 Broadway, which broke a record for the largest leasing transaction in city history, and Bank of America's 1.5 million-square-foot lease at One Bryant Park.

Interview by Candace Taylor

"When I'm with my sons, I can point out to them my connection with these beautiful skyscrapers."

What's your date of birth
April 10, 1961.

Where did you grow up?
Staten Island — in a place called Westerleigh, which is near the Staten Island Zoo.

Where do you live now?
In Rumson, New Jersey, home of Bruce Springsteen.

Are you a Springsteen fan?
Absolutely.

Have you ever met him?
I have. We belong to the same beach club and my 16-year-old son, Nick, and [Springsteen's] son Sam went to grammar school together. I've met him in that context — we're not friends or anything.

You have four sons. How old are they?
They're 23, 21, 16 and 14. We are big sports fans. When we're together we're talking sports, music and politics.

I hear you're a Mets fan. If you had to compare your style in real estate to a Mets player, whom would you pick?
Keith Hernandez, because I think this business has an art to it, I like to think about it a lot, and I like to try and win the game outside the lines and be as prepared as I can be for when I'm inside the lines.

You did your first deal as a college sophomore?
was an intern at Williams, and it was an 8,000-square-foot lease at 60 Hudson Street for a trading company. I bought a lot of beer at college when that commission check came.

When you went to Jones Lang LaSalle, your father joined you to serve as managing director. Was it weird that you were his boss?
My dad and I are father and son always, so it doesn't matter what the working relationship is. We definitely disagreed on things. We agreed on more things. My dad came from a different environment. His parents were immigrants from Italy. He was more conservative, and I was more of a risk-taker.

What are some of your proudest accomplishments?
I've done 100 leases of more than 100,000 square feet, and seven leases of more than 1 million square feet. Sometimes I'm embarrassed because I can't remember all the big deals. It is nice, particularly when I'm with my sons and I can drive up 42nd Street and I can point out to them my connection with these beautiful skyscrapers.

Will any of them go into the business?
My older son, Eddie, is working for a real estate investment company called Merchant Equities.

It must be tough for your wife, Linda, being the only woman.
It is. She's surrounded. And she is completely different; she was the valedictorian of our high school and college class. I was the guy copying the homework in the hallway right before class.

How did you meet?
We met in high school. I was on the stage crew working on a play, "The Glass Menagerie," and she was the lead in the play. I never noticed her until I was shining the lights on her.

You are working on leasing the former Goldman Sachs building at 85 Broad Street. How's that going?
We are really pleased with the activity. There is one tenant that has expressed interest in the whole building. We have three or four others that would occupy 25 to 33 percent. That building is so imposing — it's like the Death Star. There are some plans to make the building more inviting.

Do you know Fred Wilpon, Mets owner and head of Sterling Equities?
Fred Wilpon and my dad went to the same high school and knew each other as teenagers. When I was a young person in the business, I got to know Fred's son Jeff.

How do you like the new Citi Field?
I absolutely love it. And I had a tear in my eye when they tore down Shea — I grew up with it. But I've really enjoyed going to Citi Field, both with my family and as a great place to entertain clients. We have season tickets here at the firm for every major team — Mets, Yankees, Jets.

How do you approach challenges?
I love a quote from [race car driver] Mario Andretti: He said that in car racing, if you're comfortable with how you're driving, you're not driving fast enough. That's what I feel like. If I feel comfortable and not challenged, then I'm not pushing it hard enough.

Do you have one person in the industry that you're always competing with?
Mary Ann Tighe and Bob Alexander. It seems like those two are always fishing in the same pond. They're both really good at what they do.

What do you do in your free time?
I have a boat. It's just a powerboat. I call it a picnic boat. Fill it up with provisions and spend the day on it.

I see you've got a photo of Ronald Reagan. Is he a hero of yours?
I think for people my age, the U.S. was drifting a little. I'm not saying that all of his policies I agree with, but he got us back on course. I have a lot of respect for him. I just like having the picture. **TRD**

Photo by Marc Scri...

RICHARD MACK

CO-FOUNDER | **MACK REAL ESTATE GROUP**

Mack co-founded Mack Real Estate Group in 2013, which he runs with his father, William, and his brother, Stephen. The group was founded after Mack and his father sold their massive company, Area Property Partners, formerly known as Apollo Real Estate Advisors, earlier that year. Area's funds collectively invested in more than $70 billion of real estate ventures in 25 countries under the Macks. The company also co-developed the Time Warner Center with the Related Companies, and owned iconic office towers like 1290 Sixth Avenue. *Interview by Katherine Clarke*

"I was born on third base, but I've always tried to be respectful of the position I'm in."

What's your date of birth?
August 25, 1967.

What were you like as a kid growing up on Long Island?
I was pretty intense. Everything I did, I did hard. I've definitely mellowed a bit.

Are we talking studying hard or hard drugs?
I was doing some hard studying and had some hard playing, I guess. Soft drugs, not hard drugs [laughing].

Where did you go to college?
Wharton at the University of Pennsylvania. When I graduated, I went to the real estate group at Shearson Lehman Hutton, which became Lehman Brothers. It was a terrible time to be on Wall Street. I knew pretty early on that I was not long for that world. I was prepared for what was coming, so it wasn't a blow to my ego [when I was fired]. I didn't know anything, so I wasn't really of much value to anyone and I understood that.

Were you upset to be fired?
Luckily, I'd already sent out an application to Columbia Law School.

Did you go straight to Apollo after law school?
I started there two weeks after graduation. We were working 16- or 18-hour days. My wife, then my girlfriend, would call the office at 3 a.m. and be like, 'Why are you not home?' I'd have to put one of my colleagues on the phone to tell her, 'We are all still here.'

How did your family get into the business?
My grandfather was a demolition contractor. He demolished a number of high-profile New York sites, [clearing the way for buildings like] the United Nations and Peter Cooper Village. One of the outgrowths of that business was a lumber-and-brick yard in Queens. He ultimately decided to build a few buildings there. Then my dad got into building industrial and distribution centers near the Lincoln Tunnel, and that business grew into a large office development business, specializing in building corporate campuses.

When was Area started?
In the early 1990s, when the market was in a depression. Leon Black approached my father about buying junk bonds. ... They decided to start a real estate fund, and I was employee number three. What I presumed was just going to be one $500 million fund ended up turning into a real estate private equity business. Over the next 20 years, we raised about $14 billion in equity.

What's it like having a family in the industry?
What I'm very sure about is that I was born on third base, but I've always tried to be respectful of the position I'm in. Back in the early days, I worked harder than anybody because I felt I needed to.

Where do you live?
In a townhouse on 94th Street in Carnegie Hill. I bought the property as a development deal. I wanted to move to the suburbs, but my wife wanted to stay in the city.

You tried to sell off the whole thing at one point, right?
Before I was living there, it was for sale. Now it's not. But I've gotten more unsolicited calls from brokers and representatives of Russian oligarchs than I know what to do with. I always take the call because I'm interested in what number they're going to throw out.

How do you get to your Columbus Circle office?
I run sometimes and then shower at the [Equinox] gym in the basement. One time, I took my longboard to work. The young guys kept making fun of me as the skateboarding CEO.

Do you have other homes?
I have a home in Bedford, N.Y.

How did you meet your wife, Christine?
Through mutual friends. It was the reverse of a set-up. I was supposed to date her friend and she was supposed to date mine.

Do you get much time with your three boys?
Yes. We ski a lot in the winter. I'm taking them to Chamonix [in France] to do some off-piste in March.

What are your bad habits and vices?
I run late a lot. I'm pretty careful not to be late for fundraising meetings, though. I also like a good glass of wine, a good scotch and a good tequila, but I'm pretty disciplined.

Do you make as much money as you'd like to?
Yes.

What kind of a car do you drive?
I own a 15-year-old BMW M5. It was one of the first presents I ever bought myself. I mostly drive my wife's Escalade.

Are you close with your brother and his wife, Kelly Kennedy Mack [head of Corcoran Sunshine]?
Very close. We probably see each other every other Sunday for dinner. There's a lot of business discussed. **TRD**

ADRIENNE ALBERT

CEO | **THE MARKETING DIRECTORS**

Founded in 1980, the Marketing Directors, the residential real estate sales and marketing firm Albert leads, has served clients on projects from New York to California to Canada. She has been responsible for the marketing and sales of some $29 billion in properties. The firm's projects have included the Sheffield and the Battery Park City condos Liberty Luxe and Liberty Green, among countless others. Albert, who has a master of architecture degree from the Massachusetts Institute of Technology, was named a "Legend of Residential Marketing" by the National Association of Home Builders' National Sales and Marketing Council, and inducted into its Hall of Fame. *Interview by Candace Taylor*

"Women of my generation were in the golden age of women's lib, where you really thought you could do it all."

What's your date of bith?
February 26. Do you have to put the year? I'm a winter baby, but a summer girl.

Where are you from?
Brooklyn, and I lived there until I was about five. Then we moved out to the Island. I grew up in Great Neck.

You got a master's degree in architecture from MIT. Why didn't you become an architect?
Nobody would hire me. People thought a woman couldn't run a construction crew; I don't know why. This was 1976. I was offered a job as a receptionist in a tennis club even though I had been a partner with two other guys building tennis clubs. I was also offered a job drafting bathrooms in an architecture firm. Those were the two job offers.

How did you end up starting the Marketing Directors?
I met a guy who had an advertising business. I said, "I don't know anything about advertising." He said, "Don't worry, you'll learn." A year and a half later we were the largest real estate advertising agency in Toronto. It was essentially his business, so I moved on and opened a [real estate advertising] consultancy for a year while I tried to figure out what to do. Eventually the Marketing Directors was born.

You work with your son. What's that like?
have a wonderful son. He's our IT guy. His name is Matthew Brecher. Working together is the best. As your kids grow up, you don't get to see much of them. At least I get to see him.

How did you meet your husband [developer Oskar Brecher]?
He was at the business school at Harvard and I was at MIT. We like to tell people that we met at Central Square, which is halfway between the two. It's not true. We were set up by a mutual friend and went on a blind date.

Where do you live now?
live at 923 Fifth Avenue. It's a building my husband converted in the early '80s [which the Marketing Directors worked on].

You also have a place on Fire Island.
Yes, I've got sand between my toes. When I was in college I went to Fire Island for a weekend and I fell in love with it. Later, my husband and I were newly married and we were already not seeing a lot of each other. He's working hard, I'm working hard. And I said, This marriage isn't going to last unless we spend more time together ... so let's rent a house. That summer I became pregnant. So from about '84 on, we've been on Fire Island.

Why Fire Island and not the Hamptons?
It was the fastest place to get to from the city. And it's a great equalizer. Everybody walks around shoeless, in relatively old clothes. There is no scene. You don't know if somebody is the CEO of a major multinational firm, or if they're barely able to put two nickels together. And it doesn't seem to matter to anybody.

Why was the Marketing Directors founded in Canada?
I got my degree and moved to Toronto because my husband was working there. He's from Montreal.

What made you move the business to New York in 1982?
I wanted my son born on American soil. I am boringly patriotic — too many John Wayne movies as a child.

What advice do you have for working moms?
I think it's really tough to be a working mother. It was very, very tough for me. Women of my generation were in the golden age of women's lib, where you really thought you could do it all. Today's young women are different. They aren't trying to be all things to all people. I think that's a lot healthier.

What do you do for fun?
I play tennis — poorly. I'm a very good cook. I do a lot of cooking, mostly in the summer because that's when I have time, out at the beach. I paint a little bit, I do some watercolors. I try to ski. I ride horses. I love anything that has to do with a boat.

Do you have a boat?
No. Don't you know what a boat is? A hole in the water surrounded by wood into which you pour money. I don't have a boat but I love to rent a sailboat and go sailing for a week. I generally rent a captain and a cook.

I like your pedicure.
I just did this. Hot pink, for the summer. When you're in a corporate environment you really can't do too much. But you can have fun with your toenail color. So sometimes it's bright blue, and this time I said, "Let me try a bright pink."

But you're the boss. Can't you wear what you want?
No. We have an image and that is that we are professional and we will handle your $500 million sellout because we are serious people. So on those days I wear closed toes.

What kind of boss are you?
I'm afraid to guess. I'd like them to say I am a compassionate taskmaster. **TRD**

ROBERT A.M. STERN

FOUNDER | **ROBERT A.M. STERN ARCHITECTS**

A celebrated architect, Stern has been behind some of the most successful residential developments in New York. His architecture firm designed 15 Central Park West, the limestone condominium where total sales topped $2 billion — making it the most successful apartment building in New York history — and 18 Gramercy Park, where a penthouse went for $42 million, setting a record for Downtown Manhattan at the time. Other projects includ the Superior Ink on West 12th Street and 30 Park Place downtown, as well a Philadelphia's Comcast Center. Stern serves as dean of the Yale School c Architecture. He is the author of countless books on the subject, includin "New York 1880" and "New York 2000." *Interview by Candace Taylor*

"Architects are much more interesting than movie stars and what we do is much more enduring."

What's your date of birth?
I was born in 1939.

Where did you grow up?
Flatbush, Brooklyn.

Where do you live now?
Manhattan. I live in a building that we designed, the Chatham, so that's nice. I rent a loft in New Haven, and I have a weekend house in East Hampton.

Where do you spend most of your time?
I just go back and forth between New York and New Haven.

Which architects have inspired you?
Paul Rudolph was my teacher. I learned a tremendous amount from him. Robert Venturi was a teacher and mentor. Philip Johnson, Frank Gehry and Eero Saarinen ... I've learned from so many. Sometimes I learn what to do and sometimes I learn what not to do.

Which buildings do you admire in New York City?
There are many that I admire, but the nice thing about New York City is the space, the places between the buildings. There are many cities that you go to where you see a few buildings and you take your snapshots and you leave. But in New York, it's not the experience of the buildings, it's the experience of the spaces and places that they make.

Were you surprised at how much attention 15 Central Park West received?
Well, pleasantly surprised. I would have been even more surprised if it hadn't gotten attention because in my immodest way I do think it's a very beautiful building. And of course the public spaces within the building, the lobbies, the private dining room, the health club and all of that are pretty swell.

Why did you use limestone instead of brick?
Limestone takes the light very beautifully. A glass building may reflect the light at certain times, but oftentimes it just swallows it up and doesn't give much back. With a limestone building, whether it's sunny or cloudy, the building glows.

How do you feel about the retail in the building? For example, there's a Best Buy at 15 Central Park West.
Well, it's Broadway. The way we designed the retail is totally related to Broadway and the character of Broadway, though the detail of shop fronts is very fine. I've never been in a Best Buy; it looks nice to me. Every shop in New York cannot be Tiffany's.

When did you know you wanted to be an architect?
I kind of announced it when I was 13, 14, something like that. I always was busy playing with blocks, making drawings of hypothetical cities.

How do you feel about the term "starchitect"?
That architects have been given some kind of star status is nice. On the other hand, I don't think architects should be celebrated like movie stars. We're much more interesting than movie stars and much more important, and what we do is much more enduring. If you don't like the movie you're watching, you can turn it off or walk out of the theater or fall asleep. I do all of those things. But if it's a building and it's across the street from your window and it's an abomination, what are you going to do about it? Not much.

Do you get recognized while walking down the street?
People do recognize some of us, but I don't think they're confusing me with Brad Pitt.

How do you relax in your free time?
First of all, you're deciding that I have free time. I've spent my entire life trying to not have free time. When I'm not in the office I like to work on my writing. I like to travel, not for work but for pleasure. That's my greatest recreation.

What are some of your favorite places to travel?
London is a favorite. Paris is great, but my French is so terrible that I always feel I'm not getting the maximum out of it. Rome, I don't have any Italian so I blunder along in complete happy pleasure. This summer I'm going to Vienna. I haven't been there in 10 years. It's kind of on my B-list.

Tell me about your offices [at 460 West 34th Street]?
This is an industrial building on the West Side, built for the printing trades. It has high ceilings, big, muscular columns, and it's flooded with light on all sides. We keep it very open. There's virtually no office with a door.

Including yours?
Definitely not. People usually walk through. I don't mind that, and I don't like to pick up a phone and call. My preferred method of communication is a very refined shout. What do people do in offices with doors? They close the door and fall asleep or talk to their girlfriends.

Why don't you have a computer?
I don't even know how to turn a computer on and I don't want to. I use pen and paper, tracing paper, make sketches. That's the way I work. **TRD**

Photo by Ben Baker

BOB KNAKAL

CHAIRMAN | **MASSEY KNAKAL REALTY SERVICES**

The firm Knakal co-founded with Paul Massey in 1988 has grown to over 150 employees and four offices. It focuses mostly on brokering small- and mid-sized building sales. To date, Knakal has been personally involved in the sale of more than 1,300 properties with a market value of more than $10 billion. Among Knakal's notable transactions were the $179 million sale of seven buildings for Macklowe Properties, and the $138 million sale of Brooklyn's Vanderveer Estates, composed of 59 apartment buildings. In December 2014, Massey Knakal was acquired by Cushman & Wakefield in a $100 million deal. *Interview by Candace Taylor*

"This job is kind of like when you were a kid and you played a game of Monopoly that lasted for days."

Do you have a nickname?
People around the office generally call me B.K.

What's your date of birth?
May 5, 1962.

Where did you grow up?
I was born in Hackensack, N.J., and grew up in Maywood, N.J.

How would you describe your childhood?
It was very small-town-ish: Maywood only had a few thousand residents. We'd always be out with friends playing after school, and at six o'clock the fire department would blow the fire whistle. That was the signal for all the kids to go home because it was time for dinner.

How did you end up going to Wharton for college?
From the time I was in eighth grade, I wanted to be a stockbroker or an investment banker. I played baseball at Hackensack High School and the [coach's brother] was the baseball coach at Penn. So I was recruited to play baseball there. I thought the combination of playing ball at Penn and being able to enhance my business education would be a good combination.

Were you the star player?
Well, I was a pitcher, and I think I'm still number four on the all-time low ERA [earned run average] list. I think I had an ERA of under one my junior year.

Which of your deals are you most proud of?
I'll always be grateful to Harry Macklowe for hiring me to sell his portfolio of buildings. It was the largest transaction of my career on a sale-price basis.

What's Harry Macklowe like to work with?
I was amazed at the level to which he was familiar with his buildings. If we said, 'When did you renovate apartment 3C on East End Avenue?' he would know when it was renovated, and even would know what type of fixtures were in the kitchen. And he not only is very sharp, but he has an incredibly good sense of humor.

How did you meet your [second] wife, Cynthia?
She worked at my dentist's office. People at the office were very curious as to why I was making an appointment for a cleaning every two weeks. But it became obvious after a while.

How old is your daughter?
Sophie turned one Dec. 1.

Why did you wait so long to have kids?
For a long time I didn't think I wanted to have children, and work had always been the main focus of my life. I have always loved my job tremendously and viewed it as a vocation and a hobby all rolled into one. But now, I would like to spend all my time with my wife and daughter. So finding the balance between a professional life and a personal life is something that I work very hard at.

Do you ever get teased for living in Murray Hill?
Well, I'm very happy being in Murray Hill. The building that Steve Pozycki and Allen Goldman built [45 Park Avenue] is absolutely beautiful. And the fact that it's only four blocks from the office is a tremendous benefit. When Sophie first started walking, Cynthia called me and I was home in six minutes and got to see her walking for the first time.

The real estate press was always talking about your hair when it was longer. Why was everyone so obsessed with it?
I never understood the fascination with it. I just started to let it grow, and people curiously starting talking about it quite a bit. But then it was time to let it go.

Tell us about a mistake you've made in your career.
My first week in the business, one of the first people that I cold-called was Lou Brause from Brause Realty. Mr. Brause was nice enough to set up a meeting with me. I asked him where his office was, and he said, '52 Vanderbilt.' And I said, 'Where's that?' He said, 'You're in commercial real estate and you don't know where 52 Vanderbilt is?' But he was nice enough to keep the meeting.

One of the commenters on our site remarked that you have "balls of steel." Do you think that's warranted?
I'd like to think so. After closing over 1,000 transactions, you hope that you're doing something right. This job is kind of like when you were a kid and you played a game of Monopoly that lasted for days. This is like a big game of Monopoly.

As someone who talks to the press a lot, do you ever worry about becoming overexposed?
The audiences at many of my speeches or panels consist of different segments of the market with only very minor overlap. There are thousands of participants in New York's commercial real estate market, so there are always new people to speak to.

What's something people don't know about you?
I'm actually very handy as a carpenter. In college I had a business with a friend of mine building loft beds.

Maybe you can do that when you retire.
I don't think I'll ever retire from this business. The way technology is today, I may be able to do it from a beach in the Cayman Islands, but I don't think I'll ever retire. **TRD**

May 2010

ALICE F. MASON

FOUNDER | **ALICE F. MASON LTD.**

One of the city's legendary brokers, Mason ran her eponymous boutique real estate firm, which sold properties in the most exclusive buildings in Manhattan to the likes of Marilyn Monroe, Tommy Hilfiger and other celebrities, for over 40 years. Mason closed her Madison Avenue office in 2008. In addition to her long career in real estate, Mason is a well-known hostess. Guests at her famous dinner parties have included Walter Cronkite, Norman Mailer, Woody Allen and Jimmy Carter.

Interview by Candace Taylor

"Building by building, I got different people in. I basically changed New York."

Do you have a nickname?
Alice Mason.

Do you have a middle name?
No, but I have middle initial: F. I'm a numerologist and 22 is the most powerful number. I added the F so the name adds up to 22. But I also had a nickname, Fluffy, because people said that my mind was like a steel trap so no one could accuse me of being a bit of fluff.

How did you get into numerology?
Oh, I've been interested in that since the early '60s — astrology, numerology. I can never think of names, but I always remember the numbers.

What's your date of birth?
October 26, 1932.

You've been married three times?
Yes, briefly.

Would you get married again?
No, no, no. I haven't even been on a date in 30, 40 years. It just doesn't interest me. I love my privacy, my dogs, my books, my home, my pals. I think it's such a pleasure to live alone.

How many children do you have?
Just one, Dominique. I only wanted a girl and I only wanted her born on Sunday and I wanted her to be a Taurus, not Gemini. I got everything I wanted.

How did you get started in real estate?
I met Gladys Mills, founder of Gotham Realty. She got me my first apartment. She said, 'Why don't you come to work in real estate with me?' She worked with a lot of movie stars. Through Gladys I met all these movie people. Marilyn Monroe — I got her two different apartments.

Are you still working with real estate clients?
Yes, but very little now. I closed my office around a year ago. I have some clients that I work with because they're longtime friends. It's only Dominique and me and we're partners. She has a lot of clients. When I have clients she often takes them around.

How did you find this apartment [an eight-room spread at 150 East 72nd Street]?
I knew all the rental buildings and this was the only one I wanted to be in. When I got the apartment, in 1962, the rent was $400 a month. It went up legally whatever it could go up [according to rent-stabilization laws]. Now it's just under $2,000.

That's a pretty good deal.
Yes, isn't it? Wonderful. My social security pays my rent.

Did you ever think about buying?
No, no. I felt so lucky that I had this opportunity to rent. If this were a co-op, my maintenance would be so much more. This way I can have paintings.

Which of these paintings is your favorite?
I love that Pissarro. It's called "Mother and Baby."

Did any of your husbands ever live here with you?
No. Dominique's father lived in my last apartment. When she was nine in 1969, I married a Dutch diplomat. But I said he couldn't have a key to the apartment. I said I would marry him with some rules, and one was that we would only see each other two or three times a week, and he would keep his apartment and I would keep mine. Six months later, I knew I wanted a divorce.

How did you start hosting your famous dinner parties?
I thought, I'm going to have 20 people for a buffet and invite half movie stars and half [socialites]. They'd love to meet each other. So I had Marilyn Monroe and I had the Vanderbilts. I had a little one-bedroom apartment. I put the trays on the bed.

How did you start inviting politicians?
Actually Jimmy Carter was the first politician I ever met. I was sitting next to him at a dinner at '21' and he asked if I would support him. I said, 'I'm an astrologer so I'll look up your chart, and if you have energy in it I'll consider supporting you.' He had so much energy in his chart. When Carter was president I had a lot of people from Washington at my dinners, like the head of the CIA. I also had Peter Jennings, Barbara Walters and Tom Brokaw.

What made you decide last year to stop hosting them?
Oh, because I'm tired and I'm old. I stopped giving them every month around 2000. And then I gave them only twice a year.

Are you going to take up a new hobby?
No, not really, I'm just going to relax the rest of my life. When I turned 40 I made a list of everything that I didn't like, and decided I would never do it again. Exercise was on the top of the list.

How has real estate changed since you started?
When I started there were four managing agents and they only hired people in the social register, because they mainly worked in all those prewar buildings that were mainly WASP-y buildings. When I had Alfred Vanderbilt for a client, I called many buildings and they said, 'We would never take a Vanderbilt or an Astor — they're the 1880s, and we're the 1620s.'

What did you do?
I sold him an apartment at 31 East 79th Street, a penthouse. I knew a lot of different kinds of people, and I decided they all should be able to live in the same buildings. Building by building, I got different people in. I basically changed New York. That was my success in real estate. **TRD**

April 2010

HARALD GRANT

BROKER | SOTHEBY'S INTERNATIONAL REALTY

A top Hamptons broker, Grant has sold more than $1 billion in real estate, working with entertainment and business titans such as Pink Floyd's Roger Waters and Blackstone Group co-founder Peter Peterson. He joined the Southampton office of Sotheby's International Realty in 1987. Back in the day, Grant was a model who did several magazine covers and worked in Paris. *Interview by Leigh Kamping-Carder*

"I go up to Sag Harbor, I sit in my boat's cockpit, I put on Jimmy Buffett. And I'm in Never Never Land."

What's your date of birth?
April 13, 1951.

Where did you grow up?
I'm from Norway. I moved here when I was seven. To Bay Ridge.

Why did your parents move to the U.S.?
My father fought in World War II — he joined the [U.S.] Merchant Marines when he was 10 years old as a mess boy. Because he was a Norwegian citizen but fought in the American army, he was given U.S. citizenship.

After attending the University of Vermont, you worked as a model with Ford Models. What was that like?
I did a lot of work with Cybill Shepherd, with Susan Dey, and did magazine covers for Seventeen, Glamour, GQ, Simplicity — all that stuff. I lived in Paris, modeling for a year.

Then you sold computers for IBM. What did you do next?
From 1980 to 1985, I worked in New York in construction. Then at a black tie party, I met a young lady, Wendy Norris, who came from an upper-crust family. She had a horse farm in the Hamptons that needed someone [to help run it], so I retired from the construction business and married her.

How did you get into real estate?
Wendy's mother, Pat Patterson, was working for Sotheby's. And she got me an interview.

Is it difficult to work with ultra-wealthy clients?
It's very easy to work with them — because they want to cut to the chase. They don't have time to play games. These guys that are making this money, they're trading currencies in Europe at 5 o'clock in the morning. ... They'll call me at 6, 6:30: 'Hey, Harald, I'm on the computer, am I waking you?' And I say, 'No.' Meanwhile, I gotta wake up.

You're divorced now. Are you dating?
Oh, I'd love to find someone. My problem is, I don't have the time to look. ... Girls your age [late 20s] want to go out with me. I'm 60 years old. That's not age-appropriate. Not that I'm not attracted to girls 28, or 30, or 32. Don't get me wrong — there's a youthfulness, there's a vitality, and there's an innocence. ... Women who are 45 or 50, there's an anger-management deal. For my purposes, in order to go to these cocktail parties and socialize and have a significant other, she's gotta be age-appropriate. Because all these guys have wives. And I'm not going to walk in with some hot-looking girl like you who's 28. The guys are going to go, 'That's great,' but the wives are going, 'I'm not going to sell my house with him.'

Do you have any hobbies?
Sailing. I have a Hinckley 52 sailboat I keep here and in the Bahamas. My getaway is, I go up to Sag Harbor, I sit in my cockpit, I put on Jimmy Buffett and I have a Corona. And I'm in Never Never Land.

What was your biggest professional gaffe?
My biggest screw-up? I have a number of them. In 1988, I was with this very sophisticated French lady. We're in this house, we're walking around and I say, 'C'mon, you don't want to buy this house, it's got a small kitchen.' And she looks at me and goes, 'Don't ever assume something from somebody. Because I happen to like small kitchens.' I turn red as an apple. And she says, 'Learn to listen.'

What was the first deal that put you in the big leagues?
David Koch [the billionaire co-owner of Koch Industries]. 1990. I sold him the most expensive home in the Hamptons at that time, for $7.2 million.

How did you meet him?
He came to me through my mother-in-law. He's a 6-foot-6 guy, and I took him down to the basement of this house. Crawling around in the basement. He says, 'Harald, I don't have time for this.' He's got his G5 [Gulfstream V private jet] sitting at the airport. I'm crawling around to show him how the pilings weren't only put in loose sand — they were in cement blocks — to show him the strength of the home because it's on the beach. He's going, 'Harald, you're right. Nobody's ever taken me down here.' He liked the way I went into the nuts and bolts of the house.

You dress casually, often in shorts. How do clients react to that?
You have to be smart about it. I have a lot of repeat customers, and when you have repeat customers, you usually end up being friends. You can be somewhat more casual. Does that mean shorts and a polo shirt? Sure. When you're going on a presentation to acquire a listing, that's a special event, so you get dressed accordingly. That's when I wear appropriate attire for that moment. I wear a summer suit or a sport jacket.

Would you ever leave the Hamptons?
There's life beyond the Hamptons, but no. The grass is not always greener on the other side of the fence. **TRD**

August 2012

CHARLES COHEN

PRESIDENT | **COHEN BROTHERS REALTY CORPORATION**

Cohen Brothers owns and manages more than 12 million square feet of office space and design centers across the country, including 623 Fifth Avenue, 3 Park Avenue, and the Decoration & Design Building, also known as the D&D Building, at 979 Third Avenue. Cohen, whose family founded the company in the 1950s, was also the producer of the film "Frozen River," which in 2009 received Oscar nominations for best original screenplay and best actress. And in 2010, he formed Cohen Media Group to distribute French films in the U.S. *Interview by Candace Taylor*

"I'm actively involved in signing every check and negotiating every contract and signing every lease."

What's your date of birth?
February 8, 1952.

Where did you grow up and what were you like then?
In Harrison in Westchester County. In high school, I wrote and acted in plays, captained the tennis team and was also on the soccer and swim teams.

Where do you live now?
In Manhattan and in suburban Connecticut. In Manhattan, I live in a co-op apartment along 57th Street, just a short walk from my office, furnished in a French Directoire style.

You've developed a number of major design centers. What are the unique design elements of your homes?
In Connecticut, I have a movie theater modeled after the Paramount in Times Square in the 1930s. I wanted to do a home theater and when I started to develop that project back in the early '90s, I met a home theater designer who was able to take it one step further. I get caught up in the design of something, and follow it through to the nth degree.

How did you meet [second wife Clo Jacobs Cohen]?
Lady Caroline Wrey, a dynamic woman known as the "Martha Stewart of Britain," who had done some lectures at the D&D Building, threw a small dinner party in London for me and invited my future wife. I had told her I was a "softie" for women with English accents. Boy was I.

Do you have kids?
Yes. They range in age from 1 to 25. I have a 1-year-old boy, a 3-year old boy, a 21-year-old son and a 25-year-old daughter.

What is it like having a 1-year-old child at this point in your life?
It makes you feel great about being able to see the world through the eyes of a 1-year-old.

How did you end up in real estate?
I wanted to be a film director. I did some shorts when I was in high school and college. I went to law school because I thought that would give me a good practical background and profession. I thought I would start my law career as an entertainment attorney, but found the employment options in New York City very limiting. I had always been involved in real estate through my family, working summer jobs, and I guess just some osmosis. And it was a natural connection for me. I've been here now for over 30 years.

What lessons did you learn from your father about the business?
How to delegate responsibility and build strong relationships with your employees that enable your company to continue to grow.

How did you get involved in "Frozen River"?
The wife of someone I worked with developed the script based on a short she made, and asked if I could help with raising the financing for it. When I went out to look for some investors, it was very poorly received. I believed in it enough to take on most of the investment myself [and ultimately invested $340,000].

Did you ever think it would be Oscar-nominated?
I don't know, probably not. I'm just very happy, particularly happy for the filmmaker [Courtney Hunt], that she was able to begin a new career and to help take me along for part of that journey.

Are you looking at new movie projects?
Yes. There are some things I'm talking to people about right now. We'll see. But my day job is real estate, design centers.

What made you want to write the movie quiz book "Trivia Mania" in 1985?
At the time, no one had done anything like that. I thought I would try something different that married the passion I had for film with an opportunity to do something businesslike.

How did you come up with more than 1,000 pieces of trivia for the book?
I did it in the evenings every night for three to four weeks. A lot of it was from my own experience, but I did check some reference materials and did some other research. A thousand questions — that's a lot of questions.

Are you still pretty good at movie trivia?
I don't look at it as trivia. I look at it as facts. [laughs] One man's fact is another man's trivia, right?

Is it true that your employees are only allowed to wear white shirts?
It's light-colored shirts. Just not black shirts, and dark brown or navy blue shirts, because I think it looks less than professional.

Why?
I think the image we create for the people we want to do business with is very important. I'm not going to come into a business meeting in a pair of blue jeans and a T-shirt because that's not the image that I want to project. Do I do that on the weekends? Of course. But am I shaking hands with the bank representative or a financial institution that wants to lease a substantial amount of space? No.

What's something people don't know about you?
I'm actively involved in signing every check and negotiating every contract and signing every lease.

If you look back at your career, is there anything you wish you could do over again?
Probably all the things that didn't work out, but I try not to second-guess things. I believe in fate and destiny. **TRD**

THE CLOSING

| 109

Photo by Ben Baker

MARY ANN TIGHE

CEO | **CBRE GROUP**

The chief executive of CBRE's New York Tri-State Region has been involved in over 87 million square feet of commercial transactions, including Condé Nast's move to 4 Times Square — and that company's subsequent move to One World Trade Center — as well as the relocation of the New York Times to its new building on Eighth Avenue. In 2009, Tighe became the first woman to chair the Real Estate Board of New York, stepping down in 2013. After her mother and sister died of lung cancer, she and her family founded a nonprofit called Joan's Legacy Uniting Against Lung Cancer, which has raised millions to fight the disease. *Interview by Candace Taylor*

"I was a good girl. I had no idea that there was more opportunity in being a bad girl."

What's your full name?

I guess I consider my full name today Mary Ann Tighe Hidalgo.

You use Tighe as your last name professionally but you go by Hidalgo in your private life?

I have one son from my first marriage. I used to always want to go to school and be Aaron Tighe's mother. But now Aaron Tighe is a grown man, and I'm perfectly happy to be Mrs. Hidalgo.

What's your date of birth?

August 24, 1948.

Where do you live?

We own an apartment near the Metropolitan Museum of Art. And on the weekends, Southampton.

Where did you grow up?

In the South Bronx. I come from an Italian family. My mom was the secretary at the church rectory. My father managed a warehouse for Timken Roller Bearing Company.

What kind of student were you?

I was a great student. I was a good girl. I had no idea that there was more opportunity in being a bad girl.

What did you do before real estate?

My initial career was as an art historian. When I came out of undergrad, I was a fellow at the Smithsonian, and then I got my master's in art history. And then I got a job working for Joan Mondale when she and Vice President Mondale were in the White House. A year later I was made deputy chairman of the National Endowment for the Arts. I routinely went up to Congress and testified, defended our budget, defended the grants.

How did that prepare you for real estate?

If you've worked in the White House or testified before Congress before turning 30, it's hard to have people shake you up. What's somebody going to ask you that's scarier than having the Vice President of the United States ask you a question?

Did you take to real estate immediately?

My first 15 months on the job, I did zero deals. My first deal, when I finally did one, was 1,300 square feet. It was a very painful and shaky start.

What kind of mistakes did you make at first?

Sharing information. That was my single biggest mistake. I would come across an opportunity and would tell a colleague and be surprised that we were all of a sudden in competition for it.

Which deal are you most proud of?

The Condé Nast deal was transformational for Condé, but it also inaugurated the redevelopment of Times Square. In 1996 people still thought Times Square was sort of tawdry. One of the famous editors of Condé Nast said, 'Armani will never visit us there.' Armani, I have no doubt, has had his lunches in the Condé Nast cafeteria at 4 Times Square and has been happy to do so.

Do you ever get angry during negotiations?

I've mellowed with age, but remember, I'm Italian, and anyone will tell you that I'm a fairly intense personality. When I do get angry, it's typically not a small thing. ... I think that there is a certain shock element in having it come out of the mouth of a seemingly nice woman.

How did you meet your husband [plastic surgeon David Hidalgo]?

He was my student. I was teaching an art history class at Georgetown. He was looking to knock off his art history requirement that summer. He was the smartest boy in the class. He's five years younger than me.

Were you married at the time?

Yes. And I had an 8-month-old child. It's pretty shocking. In truth, I just thought this was some kind of aberration on my part and that life would return to normal. But from the moment David and I met, we've never been not involved with each other. It took seven years to get married because I was certain that I was never going to get married again and that we would just live together. But we've been married 30 years now.

What prompted you to speak to Oprah's O Magazine about having a facelift?

Wouldn't it be completely hypocritical of the wife of a plastic surgeon to say, 'Oh, I've never had anything done?' It would be such nonsense. We talk about plastic surgery at the dinner table. We talk about real estate and we talk about plastic surgery, among other things.

What was it like being operated on by your husband?

It was like being at home. It was nothing. I know my husband, I know his wonderful anesthesiologist, and I know his terrific team. These were all friends. What bad thing could happen?

How did you start Uniting Against Lung Cancer?

In '81, when Mom died, we said, 'How can this be?' She's never smoked a cigarette in her life. My sister Joan then was diagnosed in 2001. Both of them were diagnosed at stage 4 — that's very common in never-smokers. So 20 years later we asked, 'What are the new treatments?' And the answer was, nothing. At that moment, we knew we couldn't just allow this to go on. We're eight years into it now. Thanks to the wonderful Jeffrey Gural [chairman of Newmark Grubb Knight Frank], we have excellent, low-cost office space [at 27 Union Square West]. We've made 65 grants, and progress is being made in early detection and treatment. **TRD**

February 2010

DAVID LEVINSON

CHAIRMAN & CEO | **L&L HOLDING COMPANY**

The company Levinson co-founded in 2000 with Robert Lapidus has acquired more than 6 million square feet of commercial office space. Its holdings include 142 West 57th Street; 150 Fifth Avenue; 195 Broadway; 200 Fifth Avenue (the former International Toy Center); and 425 Park Avenue, which is being re-developed with a design by architect Sir Norman Foster. Before forming L&L, Levinson was the vice chairman of CB Richard Ellis. Levinson is also a partner in the New York Yankees. *Interview by Candace Taylor*

"When I came to New York City after college I was broke and lived on food stamps."

What's your date of birth?
I'm not at the mandatory retirement age.

Where were you born?
Brooklyn. But I grew up in Valley Stream, Long Island, and then went to college in Boston, at Northeastern University.

Where do you live now?
The Upper East Side. I have a townhouse.

Are you married?
I am married [to second wife Simone] and I have four children — 27 at the top end and 2 at the bottom end. There are three sons and, finally, a daughter, who turned two 10 days ago.

What did you do to celebrate?
We had 50 little kids and their parents over to the house. This house is party central. My wife was a very prominent special events planner, and the last thing she did before I got her to retire was Michael Douglas and Catherine Zeta-Jones' wedding. So she knows how to do events. If they weren't going on at my house, I wouldn't get invited to a lot of them [laughs].

What did your parents do for a living?
My father owned a toy store called Artcraft Hobby in Queens. I was the official toy tester. I was a great little salesman, because people would ask, 'What should I get my son?' and there I was. Here's a plaque, by the way, from the Toy Building. As a kid I used to go there every year for the toy show. It is a beautiful irony to have ended up owning this building.

How did the toy store influence your career?
I learned how to conduct business with people. One of the great things we used to do is on Christmas morning we would be at the store taking phone calls for all the people we sold presents to that couldn't build them or get them to operate, and we would spend the day going to people's houses setting up their electric trains and putting batteries into toys.

Did your dad impart any good advice that helps you in real estate?
He sold greeting cards also and, in those days, a Hallmark card was 10 cents. He pointed at the back of one and said, 'Son, do you know how many of these I have to sell to make a living?' He said to me, 'It's all about the zeros. Whatever you do in life, make sure there's just a lot of zeros to the left of the decimal point.' So when I went away to college I thought about real estate because it has a lot of zeros.

Do you have any other major investments outside of real estate?
I'm a partner in the New York Yankees — the World Champion New York Yankees [shows off his World Series ring].

How often do you go to games?
I probably go to 30 games a season. I bring the family. We were in the World Series parade. We spent the whole day with the team. I have these photographs of my son James [age 7] that will blow your mind. He's with every single player: Jeter, A-Rod, Teixeira, Damon and Yogi Berra. He's got a baseball signed by 30 players. When my daughter was born, her first article of clothing was a pink Yankees onesie.

How did you become a broker?
I started because I didn't have money to invest. When I came to New York City after college I was broke and lived on food stamps. I was literally a homeless person living on food stamps. I stayed with friends from time to time, but there were some times I stayed outside.

How did you get to the point of being homeless?
When I graduated from college, I was the largest landowner in Woodstock, N.Y. I was trying to build a ski resort. That was in the early '70s. There was an economic collapse and I lost everything. I came to New York and got a job as a leasing broker.

What aspects of your portfolio do you worry about now that we're in the recession?
We worry in good times and bad. That's one of the advantages of having been poor [laughs]. You never want to be poor again. Been there, done that. So you do everything you can to make sure that doesn't happen.

Tell me about your office. Why do you have that model ship?
I lived on a boat for seven years.

Was it a houseboat?
Well, it was big enough to live on — 25 tons. I lived on it six months out of the year in Sag Harbor. I was in between wives, so I needed a place to live out in the Hamptons. I started with the idea that it was really a floating condominium. And then I just fell in love with the idea of living on a boat and operating a boat. I became an expert, good enough to take it from Sag Harbor to the Bahamas several times. I have a small boat now, a 38-foot Hinckley.

Any funny stories from living on a boat?
Yes, but that's not for publication. **TRD**

IZAK SENBAHAR

PRESIDENT | **ALEXICO GROUP**

The development firm Senbahar heads has been behind such high-profile condo projects as the Grand Beekman on East 51st Street, 165 Charles Street, the Laurel on East 67th Street and the condo conversion of the Mark Hotel. Alexico was also able to jumpstart the once-stalled 60-story Herzog & de Meuron–designed Jenga-like residential condo rising at 56 Leonard Street in Tribeca. When completed, 56 Leonard will be the neighborhood's tallest building

Interview by Katherine Clarke

"I was always a bit of a rebel. That's why I came to the States. I thought, 'That's a country for rebels.'"

What's your date of birth?
March 21, 1959.

Where did you grow up?
Istanbul. I went to the French Lycée [a French-language school] until I was 17. Our background is Spanish, but my parents thought the French education was better. It's a city of east meets west — very James Bond-ish.

What were you like as a kid?
I was funny. I was the class clown at times.

What did your parents do?
My father had a factory for bras. That's a good business, no? It beats real estate. My mom took care of us.

When did you move to the United States?
In 1977, when I was 17. I went to the Catholic University in Washington, D.C., to become a mechanical engineer. After that, I went to NYU to do my master's in business. I was always a bit of a rebel. That's why I came to the States. I thought, "That's a country for rebels."

What was your first job out of NYU?
It was at Sucre et Denrées, the biggest French commodity trading company. I was at the precious metals desk. For a 23- or 24-year-old kid, to be trading a lot of volume, it was very exciting. It was all computer screens, paperwork and people screaming at each other. You had to be quick.

How did you first get into real estate?
I was about 26. An international construction company called Kiska, based in Istanbul, wanted to build a Manhattan high-rise. They wanted somebody local, and I was the only guy they knew. I said to them, 'I really don't know [anything about real estate],' and they said, 'We'll teach you.' It just fell on my lap, and I was scared. You can't find a job like that in the classifieds.

Why did you eventually leave Kiska?
They went into infrastructure work. I liked that, too, but it's more jazzy to build condos or hotels.

Where do you live?
On the Upper East Side on Fifth Avenue next to the Guggenheim.

Do you have any other homes?
I have a home in Water Mill, Long Island. I spend just the summers there. I'm a city person.

How many kids do you have?
Two. Alexi and Oliver. One is 18 and one is 16. Alexi is at SMU [Southern Methodist University] and the other one is in a boarding school. We're empty nesters.

Your wife, Sarah, is often called a socialite. Are you active on the social scene as well?
Not as much as her. She does a lot of charity work.

How did you meet Alexico co-founder Simon Elias?
In the gym. I used to live in 100 UN Plaza, and Simon and I were neighbors. He was in the hotel business and I was in construction and development. At first, we just told each other about our deals. At one point we said maybe we'd do a deal together. Then we did one and just kept doing it.

Is there a project from your career that stands out as being particularly meaningful?
The one I'm building now at 56 Leonard. It's going to be a landmark. It's sitting on an Anish Kapoor sculpture [integrated into the building's base]. I can't wait for it to go up.

That project stalled after the financial crisis. What was that time like for the company?
That was a tough time. We opened the sales office the day Lehman Brothers went down. We saw the recession coming, but we didn't think it was going to be that bad. After Lehman, our bankers wouldn't go forward with the construction loan. We also thought maybe it wasn't the right time to build, so we mothballed it until two years ago. In the last 18 months, we began talking to the banks again and we got a construction loan started.

You faced foreclosure suits at the Alex Hotel and the Flatotel after the recession. What was that like?
The recession hit us pretty hard. It looked like we were going to lose some [properties]. We learned from that to be more conservative. Deleveraging is a new word.

Do you have any hobbies?
I like drumming, percussion and bongos. I have drums at my house.

What do you read?
I read Dalai Lama books and anger management books. I'm short-tempered, so I have to work on it. I read a lot of things that teach me how to behave.

You don't seem like an angry person...
I am, trust me. I had an ulcer when I was 17. I'm a fair and polite person, I think, but I can't take it when other people are not fair and polite.

Do you have a strategy for dealing with your temper?
I usually say, 'I'm going to hang up now and I'll call you when I feel better.' **TRD**

March 2013

THE CLOSING

Photo by Max Dwor

MITCH RUDIN

CEO | **BROOKFIELD OFFICE PROPERTIES**

Rudin made headlines when he joined Brookfield in 2011 from the brokerage CBRE, where he'd been president of U.S. Transaction Services. At Brookfield, Rudin oversaw the firm's $250 million renovation of the World Financial Center, since renamed Brookfield Place, and the construction of Manhattan West, a 5.4 million-square-foot office, residential and hotel developmen near Hudson Yards on the far West Side. (Rudin left Brookfield in mid-201₄ after this interview, but hadn't announced his new plans as of the time c the book's publication.) *Interview by Katherine Clarke*

"I view art as a passion, not as an investment."

What's your full name?
Mitchell Eliot Rudin.

Any relation to Bill Rudin, CEO of Rudin Management?
No, but I get that almost daily. They're a wonderful family.

What's your date of birth?
April 25, 1953.

Where did you grow up?
I was born in New York City, but grew up in Atlantic Beach, on the south shore of Long Island.

What were you like as a kid?
I was probably fairly serious. I was committed to school, sports and the friendships that came with them.

What did your parents do?
My father owned and ran a hosiery company — stockings and men's socks. My brother and I worked with him on weekends when we were young. I learned the importance of hard work and ethical behavior from him.

You now live in Scarsdale?
Yes, I commute every day by car. It takes about 45 minutes.

Do you have any other homes?
We just completed construction on a house in Amagansett. We converted an old beach house into a modern beach house. We'll be out there probably 12 to 15 weekends a year.

How long have you been married?
Thirty-three years. We met in Amagansett. Bonnie was coming off the tennis court, I was coming off the basketball court, and we met at the water fountain. We ended up going to the same singles party, followed by a club, and we've been together since that night.

How many kids do you have?
We have two children, Scott and Ben. Scott is 28. He's a senior fashion designer at Ralph Lauren. Our younger son Ben is 26. He's living in Israel.

Does a passion for fashion run in the family?
Scott has a wonderful sense of design and style. I think it skipped a generation. My father was always considered a very dapper dresser; I just try to keep up.

You were previously an attorney. How did you get into real estate?
I was practicing law at [Manhattan firm] David & Gilbert. I'd been doing a deal with Saatchi and Saatchi at 375 Hudson Street. After the deal, the people at Tishman Speyer [the owner of 375 Hudson] asked me if I'd ever thought of making the switch to real estate. We had a series of discussions, and I ended up going over to the business side with them.

You left CBRE for Brookfield after being there for 21 years. Was it a tough decision?
It was an opportunity to be part of two projects that would be redefining New York City: the renovation of Brookfield Place and the West Side project. It was only an opportunity of that nature — which I was not looking for — which would have led me to make the change. CBRE could not have been more gracious when I left.

What is the status of Manhattan West?
We've been in construction since October. We're currently talking to a couple of major tenants.

You used to host an annual basketball tournament at your house for CBRE people. Do you still do that?
Yes, a number of CBRE and Brookfield people come to the house. The moment I stop playing is the moment I'll stop hosting.

Are you competitive?
Quite.

"Occupy Wall Street" protesters spent months camped out in Brookfield's Zuccotti Park last year. What did you make of the movement?
We were concerned about crime, and harm coming to individuals. There were some really bad elements mixed in among that group. ... Regardless of your view of the politics, it was a terrible missed opportunity. Their message was entirely unclear and their decision-making was dysfunctional. They could have converted their efforts into political influence, but they didn't. If you look back now, what was really accomplished?

How do you size people up when you first meet them?
I listen very carefully. Start with the fundamental decision: Is the person a good or a bad person? If the person is good, have tolerance for some of the things they do that might not be so perfect. If the person is a bad person, have no tolerance. ... When I've been involved in recruiting people, I often want to know about their significant other. I want to meet that person.

What other hobbies do you have?
I stand-up paddle board in the Hamptons and play tennis. We also collect Modern American art. At the moment, our favorites are Reginald Marsh, Charles Burchfield and other artists of that generation.

Do you view art as an investment?
I view it as a passion, not as an investment. Still, the passion won't lead me to buy something that isn't a prudent investment. **TRD**

August 2013

Photo by Hugh Hartshorne

DAUN PARIS

PRESIDENT | **EASTERN CONSOLIDATED**

Paris co-founded Eastern Consolidated in 1981 with partner Peter Hauspurg, whom she married in 1983. Since then, the company has grown into the largest single-office commercial real estate investment services firm in the United States, with over $4 billion in annual sales. Paris directs day-to-day operations and handles the firm's strategic direction. In 2013 the firm, for the first time in its history, expanded into retail leasing, a little more than a year after it launched a retail investment sales group. *Interview by Candace Taylor*

"I think he wanted to ask me to marry him when we didn't have a big commission on the horizon."

What's your date of birth?
June 4, 1955.

Where were you born?
Denver, Colorado, but I grew up in Ridgewood, N.J. My father was in the Air Force, stationed in Germany. He had family in New Jersey and that's why we ended up there. He was a builder. He built luxury homes.

Where do you live now?
We live in Bedford, N.Y., in Northern Westchester. Rockledge Farm [our 26-acre estate] keeps us very busy. We have llamas, and up until last December, we had Royal Dexter cows.

How do you have time for the animals?
We have some help, but the llamas sort of take care of themselves. The cows required more care. They were constantly breaking loose. It just became ridiculous, so we gave them as Christmas presents. They were grass-fed and they ended up being delicious.

Do you ever think about moving back to the city?
We put Rockledge Farm on the market in 2007 and then promptly took it off. We have four houses on the property, and with the kids gone there is no good reason to occupy such a large carbon footprint. But Peter refuses to give up his horses and golf around the corner, and we have wonderful friends there.

How many children do you have?
Two. A son [Philip], who's 23 and is an actor, and a daughter [Alexandra], who is 21. She's in her senior year at Duke.

What challenges did you face as a woman when you started in this business?
In commercial real estate, being a woman, I think, was an advantage. I think it was a way that we stood out from the crowd.

How did you and Peter start working together?
We were at the same firm — Whitbread Nolan — and we started teaming up on deals. I was really good at finding deals and he was really good at closing. We had been working with a group from the Arab Emirates. They had a large war chest and they were very committed to working with us, and we decided to start our own firm.

How did you start dating?
We were very slow and careful because we knew our professional life was working really well. I had tremendous regard for him and we complemented each other.

Do you put your personal relationship aside when you're at work?
We can go through the day without even seeing each other. We handle different ends of the business. I do the day-to-day operations, recruiting, and Peter does the deal-making. Sometimes we ride in together, but often we have our own schedules.

How did you learn the business?
When I started there was no training. I truly believed that if someone would give me a shot, I would be able to sell that property. I called up Sol Goldman. I ended up getting a meeting with him. I had been in the business like three months and convinced him that he should give me a building [1040 Madison Avenue], because I was going to sell it.

What are some of the deals that you're most proud of?
The deals we've done on behalf of the Durst family. Americas Tower on Sixth Avenue.

What deal has affected you personally the most?
The Lowell Hotel [in 1982]. Peter and I thought we lost that deal, and I had used all of my savings. We were walking to my apartment, and Peter proposed to me. I went from thinking, 'What am I going to do?' to being ecstatic. So I have a very special feeling about that deal. It ended up going through the next day.

Why did he choose that moment?
He was in debt at the time, and I think he wanted to ask me to marry him when we didn't have a big commission on the horizon.

So you wouldn't be marrying him for his money?
Or he wouldn't be marrying me for my money.

Tell me about the photographs above your desk.
This is a Bert Stern of Marilyn Monroe. We have a number of his works. At home we collect a lot of nudes.

Would you advise someone to go into real estate now, given the state of the economy? What was your experience in past downturns?
Absolutely, for the right kind of person. In 1989, we decided we had to get bigger, smaller or close our doors. We tripled our size at 30 Rock and went about recruiting some senior brokers. It proved to be successful and that was a turning point for us.

Do you have any family trips planned?
At Christmastime we go on a yoga retreat at Parrot Cay in Turks and Caicos. We're all very into yoga, all four of us. Peter and I have a yoga instructor who comes to the office. For a while the brokers were taking part in yoga, too.

How come you stopped?
Given the economy, the assets could be deployed more effectively elsewhere. But we're going to do it again. **TRD**

November 2009

THE CLOSING

| 119

SANDY LINDENBAUM

COUNSEL | **KRAMER LEVIN NAFTALIS & FRANKEL**

Lindenbaum, who at the time of this interview served as counsel at Kramer Levin Naftalis & Frankel, was one of the city's most high-profile land-use attorneys. Over the years his clients included some of the city's pre-eminent developers and non-profit organizations, ranging from Carnegie Hall to Weill Cornell Medical College to the Macklowe, Silverstein and Solow organizations. When he spoke to *The Real Deal* he was working on the expansion of the Museum of Modern Art and the development of the new Manhattanville campus of Columbia University. (Lindenbaum died in August 2012 of esophageal cancer.
Interview by Candace Taylor

"To some extent, that skyline is there because of what I did."

What's your full name?
Samuel Harvey Lindenbaum.

Why do people call you Sandy?
I had blond hair as a child.

What's your date of birth?
March 29, 1935.

Where did you grow up?
I grew up in Brooklyn, in the Crown Heights section.

Where do you live now?
In a co-op at 998 Fifth Avenue at 81st Street, across from the Metropolitan Museum of Art. It's very convenient.

Are you a big art lover?
Yes. My wife Linda and I do collect.

What's your favorite piece?
I have two. One is an artistic favorite — "Femme Nue Sur Un Lit," a 1907 Picasso, which is a study for "Nude with Drapery." My sentimental favorite is a 1962 crayon on paper from a sketchbook by Picasso. It's dedicated to my wife. It says "Pour Linda," but it was "poor" Sandy, because it cost me all of my bar mitzvah savings to buy it.

How did you become interested in art?
They didn't teach art in my high school in Brooklyn. After [Harvard] law school, a classmate said, 'Let's go to an art gallery.' His mother was looking at a painting. It was a Picasso. I said, 'This is the craziest thing in the world.'

How often do you go to the Met?
At least once a week, and sometimes more. We go to a lot of the openings. We have a house in East Hampton, but on Saturday and Sunday mornings when we're in town, my wife is always slower than me getting dressed, so I'll run over to the Met for an hour. Or if for some reason I get finished with a meeting early, I run over because it's right across the street.

How did you meet your wife?
My wife and I met at Camp With-A-Wind [in Pennsylvania] when she was 14 and I was 16. I was a counselor-in-training. I lived in the head counselor's office. One day a girl counselor comes and says, 'Call the doctor, one of our girls got hit in the head with a baseball.' The infirmary was locked so they put her in the office. I went and there was a beautiful blond chick in my bed. So I literally met my wife in my bed.

How many children and grandchildren do you have?
We have two married daughters and six grandchildren, ranging in age from 8 to 22. The oldest grandchild just graduated from Princeton.

What made you want to become a lawyer?
My father [Abraham "Bunny" Lindenbaum] was a lawyer, so I didn't know any better.

How did you become a land-use attorney?
The Tisch brothers, Larry and Bob, they were building six Loews Hotels in the early '60s. They had a zoning problem. They came to see us and my father said, 'We'll take care of it.' When they left, he turned to me and said, 'Go take care of it.' I said, 'What do you mean, I have no idea what you guys were talking about!' He said, 'You're not going to make a liar out of your father, go take care of it.' So I took out the zoning resolutions and believe it or not, I figured it out.

Did you know then that that's what you wanted to do?
I loved it from day one. It was exciting, it was creative. I can get in the car with you and on almost every block I can tell you what building we're looking at and how it got there. To some extent, that skyline is there because of what I did.

What projects are you proudest to be associated with?
Trump Tower. Park Avenue Plaza. The Museum of Modern Art. I did a lot of work on Rockefeller Center — that's fun work.

Why?
Because you're taking an asset that was to some extent faded and rejuvenating it. That may be getting the big NBC store approved or reopening the [Top of the Rock Observation Deck], which had been closed since World War II, in a way that makes sense in the 21st century, with more than a few deck chairs and a few guys in sailor suits.

You've worked with some of the biggest names in real estate. Who was the most colorful character?
I've had fun with them all in different ways. I guess my favorite to work with was Harry Helmsley. He had eyes like a slot machine. I could see the wheels turning in his head, and every time they stopped, the two eyes would say jackpot. Donald Trump was always very creative in his thinking. Harry Macklowe has great foresight. I would work with Steve Roth of Vornado for nothing just to be in the same room with him. He's absolutely brilliant.

Your father worked for Donald Trump's father. What's your relationship with The Donald like?
His father's legal fees to my father paid my way through college. People ask when I first started representing Donald Trump, and I say when he was in short pants. **TRD**

July 2009

THE CLOSING

| 121

Photo by Hugh Hartshorne

NORMAN STURNER

CEO | **MURRAY HILL PROPERTIES**

Sturner co-founded Murray Hill Properties in 1971 along with former partner Neil Siderow. Since then, the company has bought and sold $11 billion worth of commercial real estate — including such properties as the Brill Building at 1619 Broadway, One Park Avenue, 450 Lexington Avenue, 530 Fifth Avenue and 1180 Avenue of the Americas. The company, now known as MHP Real Estate Services, owns, leases and manages over 6 million square feet of office space. *Interview by Candace Taylor*

"Until somebody says the dog is dead, we keep walking it."

What's your full name?
Norman Sturner.

What's your date of birth?
September 6, 1940.

Where do you live?
In Short Hills, N.J.

Why no middle name?
We were poor. None of my brothers have a middle name.

Do you have a lot of siblings?
Two older brothers. We're each four years apart, with me being the youngest.

Where did you grow up?
I was born in the Bronx, then moved to Brooklyn and spent my teenage years in Bayside, Queens. That's where I met my wife, [Harriet].

How did you meet her?
Bayside High School. She was 14, I was 15. She was in a sorority, I was in a fraternity. One of her sorority sisters, who has since become my sister-in-law, set us up on a blind date.

There were fraternities and sororities in high school?
In the 1950s, everybody had a sorority or fraternity.

How many kids do you have?
We have two men. They're 42 and 45, so we can't call them boys anymore. Four grandchildren.

How do you get to work?
I'm driven in a car by a driver. Even sitting in the back of a car, I'm the type of personality that doesn't sit well in traffic. I'm not one for sitting about without doing something.

Do you think that's one of the qualities that has made you successful?
More than half of it is luck and the rest is perseverance. We never give up on a property or situation, which is not to say we win every one. But until somebody says the dog is dead, we keep walking it.

What's an example of that?
It was 135 West 50th Street, it was 225 Fifth Avenue, buildings where the broker brought it to us and said, you have 48 hours, there are bidders against you, great competition, bigger guys, better guys, smarter guys, richer guys, and we wound up with the building. Every investment sales broker in the city knows that if we say we'll do it, we'll be at the closing day. We're not tire-kickers. If we don't want it, we tell them right out that that's not for us. If we do want it, we will tell them we will do everything legal and imaginable to get it done. In 40 years of doing business, we have not been a defendant, have not had a federal audit and we've not lost money for a client.

Even now, in the current economic downturn?
That future is yet to be seen. But having lived through 1971 when the city was on its back, and owning the New York Stock Exchange building on 9/11 [Murray Hill Properties has since sold it], we've seen a great deal of what the world has thrown at New York City.

How is the current downturn different than the other downturns you've lived through?
It's different in that it's quicker. It fell off the table quicker than anything I have seen before.

What is your strategy going forward?
To acquire properties at 50 percent of their replacement value, that don't need financing. We don't believe there is any new financing at $250 million-plus.

What do you like to do for fun?
Harriet comes into Manhattan maybe once or twice a week after work. We go to the theater, restaurants.

What shows have you seen recently?
"God of Carnage," "Exit the King." Harriet brought the grandkids to "Mermaid."

Where do you like to eat in the city?
We frequent San Pietro [on East 54th Street] — a lot. It's become a real estate hangout for the pooh-bahs. I'm there certainly once a week, every 10 days, during the day with some real estate person that I need to speak with. It's not so much see-and-be-seen — Gerardo [Bruno, the president of San Pietro] has a terrific restaurant.

Do you have homes anywhere else?
We did, but we got rid of them all. We had a home in Palm Beach, we had a home in Hollywood, Florida. Harriet and I, we would rather travel. Now that the kids are old enough, we take them with us. The grandkids and the kids.

Where have you gone recently?
Portugal, Spain, Aspen, Egypt, Israel, China.

What trips do you have planned?
We're going to Alaska in two weeks. We're flying into Vancouver with all the kids and the grandkids and taking the Inland Waterway. It's a cruise, but you have to fly to Vancouver to start it. And in December, we're all going to Costa Rica.

What was your first job?
I was a short-order cook in a luncheonette while I went to school. I was 13. I went to school very young and I skipped two of the years in high school to get into college at 16.

Why?
I was one of the smart kids. I've since gone downhill. **TRD**

September 2009

THE CLOSING

MIKI NAFTALI

CHAIRMAN & CEO | **NAFTALI GROUP**

Naftali is perhaps best known for the restoration and redevelopment of the Plaza Hotel during his tenure at Elad Group. The company purchased the iconic building in 2004 for $675 million and spent $500 million to renovate. As CEO of Elad, Naftali oversaw a portfolio of 12,000 multi-family units in the U.S. and another 12,000 units in Canada. After this interview, Naftali went on to found and lead the Naftali Group, which as of early 2015 was involved in developing more than 1,000 residential units in New York City. *Interview by Candace Taylor*

"Some people might say that I'm, maybe, too aggressive. I hope that people see me as fair."

What's your full name?
Michael Naftali.

What's your date of birth?
June 7, 1962.

Where did you grow up?
Tel Aviv.

So why do people call you Miki?
I insisted from a really early age to be called Miki. I didn't like Michael. In my middle school graduation, my teacher called me to the stage and she called Michael Naftali and I refused to go up. After two, three times; she said Miki.

Where do you live now?
In Demarest, N.J.

How do you get to work?
I drive. I don't need a driver.

What kind of car do you drive?
The BMW 750 Li.

What about traffic?
I really don't care, because I leave early in the morning and the minute I'm in the car, I'm working. We work all over the world, so early in the morning, I'm speaking with Asia or Israel, and when I'm coming home late at night I'm speaking with the West Coast or, again, with Asia.

What time do you leave in the morning?
Around 6:30 a.m. I'm home as early as 8 p.m. or as late as 9:30 p.m.

How long have you been married?
17 years [to Frieda Naftali].

Do you have kids?
Two girls, Danielle, 16, and Loren, 13.

When did you first move to the United States?
I graduated in 1989 from U.S.C. My sister at the time lived in California, so it was quite convenient for me.

How did you get into real estate?
I needed to fund some of my tuition and my living expenses, so I started to work as a property manager. Then, I established my own company. I managed three buildings in rough areas in Downtown L.A. That's how I started.

When did you first set foot in the Plaza Hotel?
When I traveled in '84, like any other tourist in New York. I saw the Plaza and obviously I was very impressed. But I first looked at it seriously when Elad was bidding on what is now 15 Central Park West. The day that I found out that I lost the bid, I was walking around the park and I was looking at what is the next opportunity for us. I entered into the Plaza and said, 'Okay, let's try to buy the Plaza.'

What aspects of the project are you most proud of, and what do you wish you'd done differently?
I'm most proud of the extensive restoration work that we did. We had many challenges along the way, but I'm very proud that we put it back for New Yorkers to enjoy for the next 100 years.

What do you say to criticism about the quality of construction at the Plaza?
I encourage everyone to come and see the hotel, walk the public spaces, to see the amazing restoration of the Palm Court, to book a room, to see the amazing rooms that we have, and then to make a decision.

Switching gears, what are your hobbies?
I like boating, sailing.

Do you have a boat?
I don't, at this moment.

So do you have to rely on friends to take you sailing?
Either friends, or whenever I have time, I rent boats in different parts of the world. For example, in the Caribbean, in the British Virgin Islands. I like that part of the world because it's very natural, not too many tourists.

What are your best and worst qualities?
I think my best quality is that I'm very determined. I make things happen, I get the job done. Some people might say that I'm, maybe, too aggressive. I hope that people see me as fair.

In your family, are you the bad cop or the good cop?
I'm actually the nice cop with the girls, but I would say at work I'm probably the bad cop.

What are your daughters doing for the summer?
Loren is at sleepaway camp. Danielle is in Hawaii on a Teen Tour. It's funny how they communicate these days. She contacts me on BBM [BlackBerry Messenger].

Is that the easiest way to get in touch with you, on the BlackBerry?
If she calls, I answer. **TRD**

MICHELE KLEIER

PRESIDENT | **KLEIER RESIDENTIAL**

Since founding her eponymous boutique real estate brokerage in 1993, Kleier has worked with many a celebrity client, including Diane Keaton, Dustin Hoffman and Al Pacino. She has also become something of a celebrity in her own right; Kleier stars alongside husband, Ian, and daughters, Sabrina Kleier-Morgenstern and Samantha Kleier-Forbes, on the HGTV real estate reality television show "Selling New York." She bills herself as a "broker specialist" for some of the New York's most exclusive cooperatives along Park and Fifth avenues. Kleier and her daughters are also the authors of the 2011 novel "Hot Property" about the high-stakes world of Manhattan real estate. *Interview by Katherine Clarke*

"I heard Warren Beatty was looking for an apartment and I sent handwritten notes to every hotel he might stay at."

What's your date of birth?
My mother always said that after you're 21 you never discuss the date of your birth. My in-laws, for instance, never knew how old I was.

Where do you live?
1125 Park Avenue. I walked into it and I loved it. I've lived there since 1980. When we first moved in, Samantha ran into one of the bedrooms and announced, 'I want this to be my room because it faces Park Avenue.' I knew from then on she was going to be in real estate.

Do you own other homes?
We have an apartment overlooking the Boca Beach Club in Florida and a house in Atlantic Beach [on Long Island]. We used to have a house in the Hamptons but I never used it. I used to pray for rain on a Sunday afternoon so we could go home early.

You were born in Pittsburgh. What was it like to grow up there?
It was a wonderful place to grow up, but a wonderful place to move on from. It was very neighborhood-y, everybody knew everybody else, big trees and beautiful houses. I outgrew it when I was about 6. I broke my mother's heart, because the day I graduated college I moved to New York.

Do you have siblings?
I have a brother and a sister. They're much older. I was actually a mistake. A very happy mistake, but a mistake nevertheless.

What did your parents do?
My parents owned a gift and jewelry store. I spent summers and holiday seasons working there. I learned to sell at a very young age.

What were you like as a kid?
I had lots of friends. I moved to New York initially with the best friend I had growing up. I still speak to her all the time. We planned our pregnancies together.

How did you do that?
Well, not like, 'tonight's the night.' Not to that degree. But we said, 'Let's plan to get pregnant.' Our oldest two are almost the same age.

You worked for a few years in social work. Why didn't you stick with it?
One of the people I worked with was a 19-year-old guy — he was my favorite client. I found him a great job and helped him get housing. Then one day he came to me with a gun and robbed me. That was the end of my social work career.

How did you get into real estate?
When we were looking to buy an apartment, I met with about 25 brokers, 24 of whom were horrible. But I met one good broker — [the late] Phyllis Koch of Phyllis Koch Real Estate — and I kept sending people to her. She said to me, 'You keep sending me people, and I keep sending you gifts. I don't know what to send you anymore. Why don't you just get your license?'

What were your early days as a broker like?
I used to take Samantha along to showings in a stroller. When Sabrina was born, I would take her in a Snugli and Samantha in the stroller. They learned 'co-op' and 'condo' with the ABCs.

What was your first deal?
The first transaction that I did was a board turndown. I sold to a trumpet player in a co-op. Of course, the board thought he was going to practice at home. Phyllis Koch was so lovely, she sent me a check anyway, even though I never made one penny.

Warren Beatty was your first celebrity client. How did you connect with him?
I heard he was looking for an apartment and I sent handwritten notes to every hotel he might stay at. He was at the Carlyle, and he actually answered. I sold him and Diane Keaton an apartment and then they broke up. I worked with him for two years.

In 2009, your 25-year-old son Jonathan died suddenly as a result of a heart problem. How do you cope?
He's the first thing I think of in the morning and the last thing I think of at night. ... Honestly, ["Selling New York"] saved our lives. They're doing your hair and your make-up and they're calling you "the talent." It takes you out of your normal life. If ever you need to be taken out of your life, it's when something like that happens.

Do you ever argue with Sabrina and Samantha?
They're my clones. What would I argue with them about?

You do dress alike.
Oh my God, it's embarrassing. Even if we speak in the morning, we sometimes don't mention what we're wearing and we'll all end up with the same purple sweater on. We shop together and we like a lot of the same clothes. We have all the same bags.

What do you do in your downtime?
I play with my grandchildren. My dogs are also extremely important to me. I have three.

What are the dogs' names?
Mine are Roxy, Dolly and Lola. Sabrina has Dixie. They have diva names and show girl names. They all have their own songs. There's "Hello Dolly," "Whatever Lola Wants," "Roxie Hart" and "Deep in the Heart of Dixie." **TRD**

January 2013

DAN TISHMAN

CHAIRMAN & CEO | **TISHMAN CONSTRUCTION**

In addition to his leadership role at AECOM, Tishman serves as chairman and CEO of Tishman Construction Corporation, one of the country's largest construction companies. Founded as Tishman Realty & Construction in 1898 by Julius Tishman, the company has overseen the building of mega-projects like the original World Trade Center, Madison Square Garden and Disney World's Epcot Center. In 2010,

Tishman Construction was sold to AECOM, a global engineering firm, for $245 million. Currently the company is construction manager for the new One World Trade Center, and Tishman is on the board of the National September 11 Memorial & Museum. A leading environmentalist, he also chairs the board of the Natural Resources Defense Council. *Interview by Candace Taylor*

"The greatest thing I've done is to be involved with the rebuilding of the World Trade Center."

What's your date of birth?
I was born in July of 1955, July 3 — ruined my parents' Fourth of July holiday.

Where did you grow up?
Upper East Side. I grew up in an apartment building that the Tishman family built in the late '40s.

Which building?
It's called 885 Park Avenue. Tishman was the largest builder of residential real estate in Manhattan around World War II, and at that time, Park Avenue north of 57th Street was considered a wasteland. If you look at old newspaper articles, they predicted the demise of Tishman for making such a foolhardy decision as to build in an area where nobody would want to buy an apartment.

As a kid, you wanted to be a scientist. Did you know you would end up joining the family business instead?
I absolutely did not know. I grew up as a product of the construction industry. Some of my fondest memories were of walking the World Trade Center site when that was being originally developed. But I was also very interested in the out-of-doors. So I went off to college and took a lot of science courses.

Where did you go to college?
Evergreen State College in Washington State. I ended up being offered a job by the National Audubon Society to help them develop educational programs.

So what changed?
I had a bit of an epiphany. I just decided that if I didn't, at that point in my life, take a stab at coming into the family business, then I probably wouldn't, and I might regret that.

Did your family pressure you to join them?
My dad, who was running the business at the time, his philosophy was to go out, do your own thing, and the family business will always be there. He had been a math schoolteacher after he came out of the Navy.

I see a Red Sox hat in one of your family photos.
Well, my wife, Sheryl, is from Maine.

How long have you been married?
This will be 27 years. We met at a ski lodge in Killington, Vermont, during Christmas break. We knew each other eight years before we got married.

But you're still a New York fan?
I am, and we're a split family. Both of my sons [ages 14 and 19], unfortunately for me, related to the Red Sox and not the New York teams.

Where do you live?
In Westchester County, in Bedford. And we have a farm in Maine that was for a long time the largest commercial llama farm in New England.

That is quite a claim to fame. Why is it no longer the largest?
We don't have a breeding program anymore. They're just pets. We also grow our own organic vegetables, most of our food, and we raise chickens and pigs and sheep and have about 400 acres of managed forests.

You are distantly related to the founders of Tishman Speyer, which spun off from Tishman Realty & Construction in the 1970s. Does it bother you when people mix the two companies up?
No, I think we're used to it — they've confused us for so long.

Since selling the business to AECOM, has it been hard to give up control?
I've quite enjoyed getting to know the public company life.

What is your greatest career accomplishment so far?
I would say in my career, the greatest thing I've done is be involved for the last 10 years with the rebuilding of the World Trade Center site. You know, when the World Trade Center came down, Larry Silverstein called my father literally the next day and said, 'John, we're going to rebuild.'

What has that experience been like?
Oh, it's been very emotional. I sat here in my office and watched the towers come down on the TV with my father sitting at my side.

Could you see it from here?
You could see the dust cloud.

Your father, John, is now 85. Is he fully retired?
We don't use the R-word around my father. He likes to do special projects; there are usually two or three that he's involved with.

How did your dad react to the attacks?
The World Trade Center was one of three or four projects that in a 50-year career he always went back to as one of the centerpieces of what he had done. So to see them disappear for him was very emotional. But then from that came a real dedication to want to have as much a hand in the putting back of what was destroyed as we could, because we felt that was the most important thing we could do to say to the world: 'Listen, you might be able to knock us down, but you can't knock us out.'

Do you have any regrets about the way your career has gone?
There are moments when I think maybe a life as a scientist would have been a little less stressful, less responsibility. But I like running things. I probably regret not being able to say no — I tend to get myself a little overly involved in things. But I don't really have many regrets. **TRD**

May 2011

BARRY GOSIN

CEO | **NEWMARK GRUBB KNIGHT FRANK**

In 1978, Gosin teamed up with partner Jeffrey Gural to purchase Newmark & Company. After years of growth and several mergers, the present-day Newmark has 12,000 real estate professionals in more than 320 offices worldwide. Gosin and his partners also control a portfolio of over 40 properties totaling in excess of 10 million square feet, including New York City landmarks such as the Flatiron Building (the Italian real estate giant Sorgente Group has since bought a majority stake in the building), the former Ford Building and 55 Wall Street. *Interview by Candace Taylor*

"Don't sign personally, don't cross collateralize, and if you live long enough, your real estate will be worth a lot."

What's your date of birth?
October 2, 1950.

Where did you grow up?
Brooklyn. East Flatbush.

Where do you live now?
I have a home in Upper Westchester, in Chappaqua. And an apartment in Manhattan on Central Park South.

Where do you stay most of the time?
I kind of mix it up. I like having both.

When you stay in Chappaqua, how do you get to work?
I drive in.

What car do you drive?
I drive a GMC Yukon Hybrid. I drive a truck, so I'm doing my part for America.

Do you have kids?
Two girls. One lives in Boston and is married to a doctor at Brigham and Women's Hospital. And another in Hoboken. She's a social worker and she's about to get married in September.

That's soon. Are you going through a "Father of the Bride" thing?
No, since it's my second.

What do you like to do on the weekends?
I love to play tennis. I enjoy singing. I like to listen to music and I read.

Do you sing in a choir?
No, it's more or less in the shower or karaoke or at the piano. Actually, in one of my greatest piano bar experiences, I sang with Yo Yo Ma in Davos [Switzerland]. He was with a group of people singing songs.

Have you ever sung with [NGKF President] Jimmy Kuhn's band, "Square Feeet"?
I have sung with his band, just a couple of times.

What did you sing?
"Sweet Caroline," The Eagles, Neil Diamond, Willie Nelson — that's my genre. But I do like rhythm and blues, and I actually like hip hop. I like guys like Kanye West and Eminem. I like the beat.

What was your first job in real estate?
I worked for a small company, Feder and Company. I was a broker, so I was knocking on doors. We were working on a building owned by Lew Rudin, an office building on 26th and Madison. After three years, I rented all the space in the building.

What was your favorite job ever?
I love what I do now. It's constantly changing. It's always challenging, and I get to meet incredibly interesting and smart people. I have the opportunity to hire young people and see their careers flourish. I've watched them grow up. That gives me great satisfaction.

Do you have a personal mantra that you try to pass on to young brokers at your company?
The most important thing is the client comes first. If your objective is to do the right thing by the people you represent, regardless of what it means for you, then you will have a sustainable career. For those who are focused on the quick deal, their careers will be marginalized.

Do you have a role model or mentor in the real estate business?
Aaron Gural, who recently passed away. He sold me the business. He taught us how to buy real estate. As I said in his eulogy, he taught me three different things: Don't sign personally, don't cross collateralize, and if you live long enough, your real estate will be worth a lot of money.

When you play tennis, do you have a favorite partner or someone that you're really competitive with?
One of them is Steven Simkin, head of the real estate department at [law firm] Paul Weiss, and Bobby Bull. He was the number one player in the East in the '50s. I play almost every weekend, pretty much, with him.

So you're pretty competitive in your personal life as well as at work?
That's what gets your juices going: winning.

Have you ever played tennis on Donald Trump's tennis courts above Grand Central, which are set to close?
I've played there.

How does it measure up?
Not well. The courts are hard and short.

You're an owner of the Flatiron Building. Do you go to Shake Shack a lot?
At this age, it's hard for me to eat burgers.

Any other hobbies?
My family is the most important thing. I've been married 34 years to Jackie. We went to the same high school. We got together when I came back to New York from college [at Indiana University]. We've been together 36 years, 34 of them married. **TRD**

April 2009

THE CLOSING

| 131

SHARON BAUM

SENIOR VICE PRESIDENT | **THE CORCORAN GROUP**

A specialist in high-end properties, Baum has sold more than $2 billion of real estate in some of New York's most exclusive co-ops since she joined the Corcoran Group in 1991. A graduate of Randolph-Macon Woman's College, Baum was one of seven women in the first co-ed graduating class of Harvard Business School. Before entering the real estate field, Baum worked at Chemic Bank for 17 years, where she was Chemical's first female vice president. In 20 she received the Henry Forster Award from the Real Estate Board of New Yor for her professional achievements. *Interview by Candace Taylor*

"[What do I make of all the fuss over me having dated Mayor Bloomberg?] Not much."

What's your date of birth?
January 3, 1940.

Where did you grow up?
In Jefferson City, Missouri.

Where do you live?
On the Upper East Side, Park Avenue. We also have a home in Greenwich, Conecticut. My husband is a fourth-generation Manhattanite. I didn't even know those people existed when I was growing up in a small town in the Midwest. I have a seven-month-old baby granddaughter so I try to get to Minnesota once a month [to see baby Hannah, son Ben and daughter-in-law, Heather]. They live in a place called the Calhoun Beach Club on a big lake in Minnesota. They have two guest apartments. We can be right in the same building but not tripping over each other.

Do you still have a "Sold 1" license plate on your Rolls-Royce?
I do.

Do you really have a yellow Vespa?
It is a yellow Vespa. It has a leopard-print seat. We have it up in Connecticut. I've always been fascinated with motorcycles and motor scooters. A few years ago we did get a custom Harley Davidson. When we told our sons they said, 'We're disowning you. It's not safe.' So we owned it for like one day. We never even got one ride on it. But we do have fun with the Vespa in Connecticut.

Do you have any pets?
No pets. [But] I love pets. I especially love cats. Part of my youth was on a farm. We had every kind of pet known to man ... baby foxes whose mothers had been killed, flying squirrels, you name it, we had it. I always loved animals. When I was young I was a member of 4-H. I raised registered Black Angus cattle. I had my favorite heifer whose name was Roxanne. She was my prized show heifer. I joke that I really learned my skills as a broker by taking care of Roxanne, because she needed a lot of care and attention.

What was the first job you ever had?
I almost don't remember a time I didn't work. In fifth grade, I was maybe 11, I wanted to buy these charms out of a gum machine but my mother said it was ridiculous. I was thinking, 'How could I make money?' As I walked home from school, I noticed a men's barbershop with hair on the floor. I went in and asked if I could sweep the floor on my way home from school for 25 cents. They said that sounded like a good idea. But after about five days somebody told my mother, and that was the end of that.

What did you think you'd be when you grew up?
I really wanted to be a doctor. I had quite a few doctors in my family. But I found out that I was not cut out for physics and science. How can you be a doctor if you don't excel in science?

How did you get into real estate?
When it became clear I was not going to become the chairman of Chemical Bank, I was looking for something else to do. I had met Barbara Corcoran years before that. She said, 'You should go into real estate.' I thought, why not? That's what I did, and the rest was history. It was really a total fluke because I never would have thought about it. But I love what I do. I don't have any plans ever of retiring. I just want to keep doing it.

What do you make of all the fuss over you having dated Mayor Bloomberg?
Not much. He's a terrific person. Such a strong work ethic. He was one year behind me at Harvard, but we really met here in New York. On the day I got married in March 1969 he sent a dozen red roses with a card that said 'I wish you a lot of happiness.' That's the kind of stand-up guy he is. I can't imagine that our city could have anyone better to run it than Michael Bloomberg. **TRD**

Photo by Hugh Hartshorne

ROBERT LEVINE

PRESIDENT & CEO | **RAL COMPANIES & AFFILIATES**

Founded in 1982, RAL is a developer of luxury apartment and resort communities in New York, Colorado, Florida, Texas and elsewhere. The firm also offers architecture, construction planning and real estate management services. RAL's projects have included One Brooklyn Bridge Park, Tower 270, Loft 25, 15 Union Square West and the New Yorker Condominium. Levine's older son Ian is the COO and CFO of the company, and younger son Spencer is director of landscape architecture and site development. *Interview by Lauren Elkies*

"My biggest mistake is trusting and believing that people are going to treat me the same way that I treat them."

What's your date of birth?
February 15, 1951.

Where did you grow up?
In Flatbush — Kings Highway and 29th Street.

Where do you live now?
In Tribeca, in a building we converted at 270 Broadway.

Do all of your children live in buildings you own?
Yes. Just like anyone else. They were purchased, and we all paid the offering plan price.

Do you have any other homes?
In Madison, Connecticut, in a waterfront community up in New Haven County.

Anywhere else?
Telluride, Colorado. That's the reason I ended up developing projects there.

How long have you been married?
36 years.

On a personal level, in what ways is each kid like you?
My older son, Ian, is family-minded and I think he has an intuitive sense to deal with issues and management. Spencer, on the other hand, is a landscape architect. He's part of the design group of our business. He is very much like me. People have said he's the other side of my brain. Amanda [an in-house events coordinator at the Metropolitan Pavilion] is probably the most gregarious of the three. The commonality between us is independence, her ability to be self-motivated and her sense of humor. She's very clever, very sharp.

So you think you're very sharp?
Well, I don't know, but I've been told I'm very sharp.

What do you and your wife do on the weekends?
Ronny and I tend to spend our weekends up in Connecticut. In the winters, we go out to Telluride, but in the past year or so, we've taken advantage of being in Manhattan. We're big museum people. I collect photography. I'm an avid photographer as well.

What kind of photography do you like?
Old. Berenice Abbott, she photographed during the Depression period a lot of Lower Manhattan. There's another photographer Hiroshi Sugimoto. He did very interesting things.

Who in the real estate industry do you most respect?
I would say Larry Silverstein — just because of his tenacity and his ability to stay focused and pursue things. I've always respected him and his general demeanor and knowledge of what's going on.

When you started your firm, what were your aspirations?
My education was architecture design and planning, and I was into large-scale architecture. Strangely enough, I didn't want to do homes.

So why did you go into residential development?
The real thing that became enticing was the conversions — taking buildings and finding the highest and best use for them. That became our niche.

What's the biggest mistake you've made in the course of your career?
My biggest mistake is trusting and believing that people are going to treat me the same way that I treat them.

Do you think you'll retire soon?
No. I thought about it years ago, after the last downturn, in the early 1990s, and I thought about doing some other things, but it was pretty apparent that my sons wanted to be involved in this business going forward.

Is that why you didn't retire?
Yeah, and also my interest. I'm really driven by this. I really have a passion for it.

Do you have any vices? Gambling? Drinking?
Not gambling. I don't drink. It goes back to college.

Drinking didn't work out for you?
It didn't. Is it a vice to have interesting cars, clothing, things of that nature?

How many cars do you have?
I have five or six. **TRD**

February 2009

Photo by Hugh Hartshorne

WILLIAM THOMPSON

COMPTROLLER | **THE CITY OF NEW YORK**

From 2002 to 2009, Thompson served as New York City comptroller, essentially the city's chief financial officer. Thompson has spent most of his life in public service, working as an aide to a Brooklyn congressman, and later as the youngest Brooklyn deputy borough president. Thompson was the Democratic candidate for mayor in 2009, narrowly losing to Mayor Michael Bloomberg. (In 2013, he again sought, but lost, the Democratic nomination for the city's highest office. He is now senior managing director at investment banking firm Siebert Brandford Shank & Co.) *Interview by Lauren Elkies*

"We've been here before. After 9/11, we lost 235,000 jobs. We bounced back stronger than ever."

What's your date of birth?
July 10, 1953.

Where do you live?
In West Harlem, for the last three and a half months.

Where did you live before that?
In the four-story house in Bed-Stuy where I grew up. My daughter lives in it now. It's been in the family since 1939.

Why did you move?
I got married in the middle of September.

Is this your first marriage?
Third.

How did you meet?
[Elsie McCabe and I] knew each other over the years. She worked in government years ago. Now, she's building a project. She's the president of the Museum for African Art, which is building a new home at 110th and Fifth Avenue.

Do you have any other homes?
We have my mom's home in Cape Cod. We built it when I was 15. My sister and I are keeping the place. She is three years younger and lives in Jersey.

What do you do on weekends?
I work [laughs].

How old is your daughter?
She is 29. Her name is Jennifer, and she's a public school teacher. My wife has two 11-year-olds, a girl and a boy — Erin and Eugene.

With kids around the house again, how is life different?
The sound of screams in the morning — little things like that. There are different kinds of movies that you select to see.

What was the last movie you saw?
They were out of town, and my daughter and I just went to see "Quantum of Solace." However, I have seen "Wall-E." I haven't seen "High School Musical 3," thank God.

What time do you get up in the morning?
Somewhere around 6, and if I have any energy, I'll try to go to the gym — New York Sports Club — two or three times a week.

You're pretty trim.
Just bigger suits [laughs].

What time do you get home at the end of the day?
Normally somewhere around 10.

How do you decompress at the end of the day?
Getting home at 10 gives you a little time to maybe watch an hour and a half of something on TV.

What do you watch?
I'll TiVo "24." There are a couple of sporting events — a basketball game or football game. What else? "Fringe."

What's the greatest challenge in your life you've had to overcome?
I don't know that there is one. Maybe Mayor Bloomberg's money [when I run for his office].

What keeps you up at night?
If the market keeps tanking, that's going to keep me up at night. What concerns me is: How difficult will it get in the city?

When do you think things will look up?
The truth is, we've been here before. If you look at the recession the city was in after Sept. 11, we lost 235,000 jobs. We bounced back stronger than ever. I think we will bounce back — probably the latter part of this year or the beginning of 2010.

Do you invest money personally?
When I became comptroller, any individual stocks that I had, I got rid of.

What's the best place to put your money now?
Under your mattress [laughs]. We just went through a cycle where people were buying short-term government debt and willing to lose 2 basis points because at least they knew how much they would lose. Right now, you want to be as liquid as you can, so put money in a short-term money market account.

What is the safest real estate investment right now?
I still think some of the smaller mortgages that we've done on the affordable housing side with various organizations are safe. The default rate there is almost zero.

If a developer asked for advice about what to do in this economy, what would you tell them?
I would still say to identify projects and start to develop them in phases. The credit market will start to loosen.

How is the current economy affecting your personal life?
I will be cutting my spending in general. I just leased a Nissan Maxima. My lease was up on the Lexus GS. Cost was a factor. **TRD**

January 2009

Photo by Hugh Hartshorne

JOSEPH CAYRE

CEO | **MIDTOWN EQUITIES**

Cayre was part of a group of investors that bought the World Trade Center in 2001, and he also invested in the purchase of the Sears Tower in 2004. His New York-based real estate investment firm's portfolio includes more than 100 properties, comprising some 14 million square feet of space in the residential, office, retail, industrial and hospitality sectors. Cayre is also the co-founder of residential marketing and sales brokerage firm, CORE Group Marketing. *Interview by Lauren Elkies*

"Don't do it the fastest way. Try to do it the slow and steady way."

What's your date of birth?
August 1, 1941.

Where did you grow up?
I was born in Brooklyn on 20th Avenue and 65th Street [on the border of Bensonhurst and Borough Park]. When I was 1, we moved to Kansas City, Missouri. I was there from 1 to 8 years old. From 8 to 20 years old, I was in Miami Beach, Florida.

When you think of your childhood, what memory stands out the most?
Moving from Kansas City to Miami. It was a traumatic experience. I left all my friends in Missouri.

What was your first job ever?
Working in my father's retail store in Miami Beach. I was 13. I got out of school at 3 p.m.. I got to the store at 4. It was open until 10. We sold Miami Beach souvenirs.

Did you have to work or was it something you wanted to do?
We had to work to eat — me, my brother and my dad — and we barely made a living. Things were so tough in the store that I worked as a bellhop at the National Hotel in South Beach.

To what do you attribute your success?
Learning in a retail store. You would sell a lot of stuff, but you were really selling yourself.

Did you graduate from college?
I enrolled in the University of Miami but I never went there because I was a playboy. I went out with girls all day long.

When and why did you get into real estate?
Eleven years ago. When I grew up in Miami Beach, the nicest home sold when I was a senior in high school for $100,000. I saw that house sell for $38 million about 11 years ago.

Where do you live?
Central Park South.

Do you have any other homes?
In Brooklyn, the Jersey Shore and Aventura, Florida. We spend half the week here, half the week in Brooklyn. We spend the summertime on the Jersey Shore and the wintertime in Aventura.

Why do you have a home in Brooklyn when you have an apartment in Manhattan?
My kids live there.

How long have you been married?
Thirty-seven years. She's the love of my life. I love her more every day.

What's the trick to staying married that long?
Resolve everything before you go to sleep and don't be afraid to say you're sorry.

How many kids do you have?
Four sons and one daughter.

Do they work for you?
My sons are all equal partners with me. I gave them all an equal share of every company. My daughter just graduated Barnard College and is taking her masters at Columbia University.

What are the challenges of working with your family?
In the beginning it was to keep all of them happy, to keep all of them from fighting with each other. It took a couple of years, but we got it down. We have five different skill sets.

What is yours?
Experience. I've been there before.

What do you think is the fastest way to make it rich?
Don't do it the fastest way. Try to do it the slow and steady way.

Do you cook?
I do cook.

What did you make this week?
Vegetarian curry noodle soup [minus the noodles]. I copied [restaurant] Zen Palate's recipe.

Are you and your wife vegetarians?
No. I'm seeing a nutritionist to lose weight.

How many pounds do you want to lose?
Twelve.

You were a bidder for the General Motors Building at 767 Fifth Avenue. Are you happy that you didn't win it?
[Mort Zuckerman's Boston Properties acquired the building for a record $2.8 billion in June.] I'm delighted. I was as high as the selling price and then I backed out. I just didn't like the returns. I like to make money on all my deals. I think that in the General Motors deal initially you'd lose your arm. **TRD**

PAUL J. MASSEY JR.

CEO | **MASSEY KNAKAL REALTY SERVICES**

Massey and partner Robert Knakal founded their commercial real estate firm in 1988. The brokerage has created a niche for itself, focusing on mid-size building sales and operating on a territory system. With more than $2 billion in sales annually, Massey Knakal ranks among the nation's largest privately-owned real estate brokerage firms. Its 150 employees serve New York City's five boroughs, nearby suburbs and New Jersey. In December 2014, Cushman & Wakefield acquired Massey Knakal in a $100 million deal. *Interview by Lauren Elkies*

"I'm a bit of a conflict avoider."

What's your date of birth?
February 19, 1960.

Where do you live?
Larchmont, N.Y.

Do you have any other homes?
No.

Where did you grow up?
Dedham, Mass.

What was your first job?
Washing dishes at a Woolworth's luncheonette counter. I was 15 years old, and it was the summer. I wanted money, and my parents weren't giving me any.

How long have you been married?
20 years this past May.

What do you do in your free time?
Coach soccer for all three children [Paul III, 18, Sarah, 16, and Greta, 12]. I have a racing sailboat, a Shields, which is a 1962 one-design boat. I am part of the Long Island racing circuit. I box for exercise, three days a week, with some of the young kids from the office [at Mendez Boxing at 25 West 26th Street].

Do they hold their punches?
They might say they do [laughs], but I don't think so.

How'd you get into boxing?
When we first started this company, I worked out at a taekwondo gym [Henry Cho's Karate Institute at 46 West 56 Street]. I did that for 15 years. I always wanted to do karate and box, and when Henry Cho retired and closed the gym in 2001, I needed to do something. I still work out one day a week with some of the old black belts [Massey has a black belt].

Do you have a mentor?
My stepfather Jack Holler [who started the John H. Holler Co. in New Jersey], who's technically my wife's stepfather. He was a very successful mortgage broker both in New York City and New Jersey. In the early '90s, Bob [Knakal] and I were broke, and he lent us $75,000 to keep Massey Knakal going. We offered him a piece of the company, but he wouldn't take it. He just said, 'Repay me whenever you can,' which we did earlier than we had promised. He's retired, but he and I always talk about business, and it's always very helpful.

What quality could you improve in yourself?
I'm a bit of a conflict avoider.

If you weren't in the real estate industry, what would you be doing?
Coaching wrestling.

Did you wrestle?
In high school and college.

What worries keep you up at night?
Keeping my schedule straight.

You don't have an assistant?
Yes I do. The Crackberry helps a lot, too.

What do you generally eat for lunch?
Usually I go a year straight eating the same thing.

What is it this year?
Chicken salad in a wrap with bacon, lettuce and tomato.

Are you obsessive compulsive?
I don't know. Growing up, my mom would make the same thing every day — bologna and mayonnaise on white bread. I hated it. I'd trade it for anything I could.

How often are you at home for meals?
I have this thing where I'm home for dinner one night a week and home for breakfast one day a week. I started this when my children were really young. I usually make my mom's buttermilk pancake recipe from scratch for breakfast, take them to school and say hi to their teachers. In the summer, we go up to the Cape and spend time up there. Every kid in the neighborhood comes by for pancakes, which I love.

Do you miss being a broker?
I still work with select clients, but I don't have a territory.

How many times has your firm sued or been sued?
We're probably in 15 or 16 litigations either as collection actions or some nominal nonsense at any given time, but never anything substantive.

How'd you get to be the first name in the company name? Was it alphabetical?
No, we agreed to flip a coin. We bought a silver dollar at the bank, went to the clock tower in the Waldorf lobby, and we flipped a coin — the best out of seven. I told Bob that was divine intervention, because who can spell 'Knakal'? And the trade-off was he got to be chairman. **TRD**

November 2008

YOUNG S. WOO

FOUNDER | **YOUNGWOO & ASSOCIATES**

Woo made headlines in August 2009 when his firm bought embattled AIG's two office towers, 70 Pine Street and 72 Wall Street, for $150 million, with South Korea's Kumho Investment Bank. The company built the Sky Garage condominium at 200 Eleventh Avenue, which has an elevator that takes cars to their owners' units. Woo's firm has also been chosen to develop Pier 57 along the Hudson River, where a massive retail complex, or "SuperPier," is planned. He started his real estate development company in 1979 after earning a degree in architecture from the Pratt Institute. *Interview by Candace Taylor*

"The only thing I had at the time was confidence. I thought I could create something very different."

What's your full name?
Young Woo. Middle initial is S for Sik — it means green and growing.

What's your date of birth?
April 23, 1953.

Where do you live?
In Chelsea. I can walk to work, less than 15 minutes. It's a townhouse — I've been there since '81.

Sounds like you made a smart real estate decision.
Yes, but without knowing it [laughs].

Where were you born?
Seoul. My family came from North Korea in the war. And my father had a very good impression about America. He thought it was a dream country to go to, but it was so difficult. So he said, 'Let's go to South America, and someday we're going to reach to the U.S.' So that's what happened; we went to South America [first to Paraguay and then to Argentina].

You came to New York when you were very young?
I came here when I was 19. The intention was to go to school. Eventually, I went to Pratt.

What did you do before Pratt?
I was driving taxis. I did a lot of things: I was working in a kosher butcher shop, I was driving trucks. But most of the time I was driving taxis, while I was going to NYU Language School to learn English.

Were you scared when you first arrived here?
Nothing scared me. Even now, nothing scares me. The funny story is this: I decided to come to the U.S. to follow my father's dream. So I went to the U.S. Consulate and they interviewed me and they said, 'You're not going to come back.' So I failed the interview and I could not get a visa. So I decided to cross the Mexican border ... but my brother-in-law's friend said, 'Don't do that. Come to my office tomorrow.' And he actually took me the very next day to the American Consulate. And I got a visa.

Sounds like you owe him one.
I owe him a lot — too bad I forgot his name! As he was driving me back, he said, 'I know a person named John Boggart who owns a supermarket in Boca Raton. Why don't you go to see him, and maybe he can help you.' When I arrived in Miami, all the taxi drivers were speaking Spanish. So, proudly I got into the taxi and I spoke in Spanish and I said, 'I want to go to Boca Raton. I don't have the address but I know the name of the person; he owns a supermarket.' The driver said, 'Come on!' [laughs]

Did you find him?
I kept going to different gas stations and asking. The driver was translating for me. When we found the place, [Boggart] said, 'Don't stay here, you've got to go to New York, because you'd be the only illegal alien Asian immigrant in Boca Raton.'

You went to architecture school, but became a developer instead. How did that happen?
When I applied to school, I thought it was more engineering, because Asian families usually say you have to become a doctor or engineer or scientist. So I was disappointed when I saw so much art going on. But I became more interested, because they make you think differently; they make you create something.

How did you get your start in real estate?
The first building I bought was at 45 West 33rd Street, in 1979. I went to two friends and I convinced them to invest money. I paid $800,000. Apparently, two months before, the previous owner only paid $400,000. So I overpaid. [laughs] The only thing I had at the time was confidence. I thought I could create something very different, which I did. In less than eight months, we sold for $1.8 million. So that was how we began the journey, from there.

What do you think is your greatest achievement?
Actually, how to write e-mail was a great thing. I have this very creative side, but I'm so bad on the tech side.

How did you meet your wife?
I was a delivery boy. [laughs] I was working for a Korean grocery in New York. I had to deliver rice — rice is heavy to carry. That's how I met her. That was in 1972. We have two children — one is 27, and the other one is 23.

How did you come up with the car elevator idea at Sky Garage?
[Architect] Annabelle Selldorf came up with this unbelievable design. Even so, we said, it's not enough — we've got to do something so different. That idea was Sky Garage. The concept is nothing new. A lot of parking lots in New York City, they actually have car elevators going up and down. Everybody said, 'Don't do it, it's impossible to do it.' But we believed in our procedures.

What is your next big project?
We're opening DeKalb Market in a few months, at DeKalb and Flatbush in Brooklyn. We're going to build this open market with food, creative merchandise, and farming. Retailers will make their own jewelry so people can see. We're going to have hydroponic vertical farms in containers.

What's that bracelet?
It's honoring my mother; she's Buddhist. She wears one, and so do my two kids. She lives with me, but this way I have my mother with me all day.

Does she have her own apartment in your house?
My wife and I live on one floor, my mother has one floor, and my brother lives on another floor.

How is that — do you guys ever have fights?
Fighting is good. Otherwise it's boring. **TRD**

February 2011

FREDERICK PETERS

PRESIDENT | **WARBURG REALTY PARTNERSHIP**

After starting in the business as a residential agent in 1980, Peters worked his way up to manager at the real estate firm Albert B. Ashforth. In 1991, he bought a majority stake in the firm's New York residential arm and renamed it Ashforth Warburg Associates. Twelve years later, he renamed the firm again, this time to Warburg Realty Partnership; today Warburg is home to some 150 brokers. Peters has been a cast member of the hit HGTV series "Selling New York."
Interview by Lauren Elkies

"I feel like in my middle years, which hopefully these are, I am trying to cultivate a more Zen attitude."

What's your full name?
Frederick Warburg Peters.

What's your family history?
I decided to name the firm after my middle name because the Warburgs have a lot of resonance in New York. My great-great-grandfather, Jacob Schiff, was the head of an investment banking firm, Kuhn, Loeb & Co. (It merged with Lehman Brothers in 1977.) He was probably the most significant Jewish investment banker in the city at the turn of the last century. My great-grandparents, Frieda and Felix Warburg, were also big philanthropists in New York, and their house is now the Jewish Museum. My father [C. Brooks Peters] was a New York Times reporter (who was credited with contributing to the Times' foreign reporting Pulitzer Prize in 1941).

What's your date of birth?
February 9, 1952.

Where did you grow up?
Manhattan.

Where do you live?
86th Street and Central Park West. We've been in the apartment for 31 years. We bought it two weeks after we got married.

Are you going to stay there forever?
Yes. Feet first, that's how I'm leaving. People say to me, 'Isn't it hard for you not to move when you see so many apartments?' But the truth is, I look at them and think, 'Hmm, can we sell this?'

Do you have any other homes?
We own a house in Sharon, Connecticut [in Litchfield County].

What's a weekend like in the country?
Weekends tend to include a lot of reading, at least one trip to the nursery, hours of planting and weeding, and garden tours and house tours. There's a fair amount of meal preparation, and we'll often go to the nearby town on a Saturday or Sunday night for dinner and a movie.

How do you get to work?
I walk through the park every day [to Warburg's office at 969 Madison Avenue at 76th Street]. It's like the best commute you could ask for. I'm a big user of public transportation. Diane [Ramirez, president of Halstead Property] and I leave REBNY's board of directors meetings, and the cars are lined up outside with all the drivers, and we cross the street and get on the subway.

What restaurants do you frequent?
We go to neighborhood places. [My wife] Alexandra and I have a place we go to all the time on the East Side — E.A.T. [at 1064 Madison Avenue, between 80th and 81st streets]. Not with each other necessarily, but I often run into her there. Another place in the neighborhood of my office I like is Serafina [at 1022 Madison Avenue at 79th Street]. I have a standing date, even though we haven't done it much lately, with Barbara Fox [president of real estate firm Fox Residential Group] once a month there.

Is your wife OK with that friendship?
As my wife likes to say, 'I have a career in which I take women alone into apartments.' She had to make her peace with that long ago.

Do you consider yourself a cynic?
No, actually the opposite. I think often, people's best quality and their worst quality is the same. And for me, in business, I'd say it is that I give everyone a million chances.

Are you tough during a job interview?
As an organization, we aren't great at weeding people out once they're here, which means that it's better to not make too many mistakes up front.

What's the craziest thing one of your brokers has done?
I had a broker who had a kind of breakdown in 2003 [reportedly getting naked, screaming and relieving herself on furniture and in a closet] in the apartment of a client. That's all I'm going to say because there's ongoing litigation.

How do you express anger?
I'm embarrassed to admit there's probably an annual moment in the office when I scream.

Would you rather be right or happy?
Happy. I feel like in my middle years, which hopefully these are, I am trying to cultivate a more Zen attitude.

How are you doing to do that?
I have done yoga for 15 or 16 years.

Are you a big clothes shopper?
I was an incredible shoe groupie for many years. A year ago, I had this catastrophic break with my ankle, so that's broken me of my shoe habit. I haven't been able to wear anything except Merrell's or sneakers.

Are you a metrosexual?
I suppose. I don't quite know what that means.

If you weren't in real estate, what would you do?
Run an orchestra. Run an opera company. In addition to being a shoe groupie, I'm an opera groupie. That's just another nail in my metrosexual coffin, isn't it? **TRD**

October 2008

Photo by Hugh Hartshorn

JULIEN STUDLEY

FOUNDER | **STUDLEY NEW VISTA ASSOCIATES**

Studley founded the eponymous commercial real estate firm Julien J. Studley in 1954. In 2002, he sold his shares to younger associates and then founded Studley New Vista Associates, which manages properties he and his Studley associates own. He is a member and former chair of the board of trustees at the New School; the school's graduate program in international affairs is named for Studley. *Interview by Lauren Elkies*

"I was never a great broker because you have to be able to tell people, 'this is what's good for you.'"

What's your date of birth?
May 14, 1927.

Where do you live?
East 60th Street between Park and Lexington avenues. I'm the president of the co-op.

Do you have any other homes?
I have a house outside of New Paltz. And we have a barn on 50 acres six miles from the house in the town of New Paltz.

When did you come to the U.S.?
When I was 16.

Where did you grow up?
I was born in Brussels, Belgium. On the 10th of May [1940], the Germans attacked Belgium. We went to the Belgium coast near the French border. We decided the Germans were moving quickly and crossed the French border with a Boy Scout patch I had posted on the car. They thought it was a pass. We stayed in a little town that night. There was a lot of machine gunning and we went farther south. Eventually we ended up in Nice [France]. We left there because we knew things were dangerous. Finally we came to Cuba with $50 rolled up in a pen. My mother's brother lived in New York at the time, and he was able to get us Cuban visas. You would have been cooked by the time you got an American visa.

What was your first job?
I started working in diamonds right away when I came to the U.S.

When did you learn the trade?
I went to high school [which is the equivalent of up to eighth grade in the United States] in Cuba and the students went on strike in 1943, saying, 'we will not continue going to a school for a corrupt government.' I was 15. That's when I learned to cut diamonds because there was nothing to do.

What was the first place you lived in the United States?
On the floor in my uncle's third bedroom, on 101st Street and West End Avenue, where my cousin still lives.

Were you in the army?
I was drafted in 1950 when I was 23. My assignment was to be in the 278th Regimental Combat Team [of the Tennessee National Guard]. They filled this southern reserve unit with people from the Northeast. I was hardly from the Northeast. I wasn't a citizen. My English was abominable. I had never gone to school. I was supposed to go to the front of the line and zero in on enemy short-term artillery. You had to climb up a tree, put up speakers, and if they shot, you could triangulate where they were located. It's a long story, but I went to the Pentagon and got transferred into psychological warfare.

What was the first real estate firm you worked at?
Brett, Wyckoff, Potter & Hamilton. I stayed there for two years. I averaged $2 a month. But I also cut and polished diamonds at night.

Were you ever a successful broker?
I was never a great broker because you have to be able to tell people, 'this is what's good for you.' My job, I think, is to make you understand each of the alternatives, both the good and bad parts.

Where was the first Studley office?
In my fourth-floor walk-up apartment at 400 East 53rd Street.

Do you have any siblings?
I have a brother, George, who is three years younger than me. He worked at Studley for 15 years [until 1972]. He's totally lost the use of both of his legs. I see him at least three times a week.

Do you play poker?
I'm a third-class poker player. I'm exactly what the poker professionals like — someone who plays it as a hobby. I've been playing for probably 40 years.

What's the most you put up for a game?
$10,000 for the World Series of Poker. I used to play poker for as long as 20 hours a day. It was like going to a sauna or something. I felt completely relaxed even though I had stupidly lost my money.

When did you get married?
I was 49 years old. It was like a revolution — Julien's getting married. What's going to happen to the company? I never thought I would be married. I got married to the most junior person who worked for the company. She was 19 years old. It was the most stupid thing I've ever done and it didn't last very long. We had a son [Joseph, 31].

Did you remarry?
After we got divorced, I decided, I'm not going to look for a wife; I'm going to look for someone to take care of me. Ultimately I married Jane, and we have been married almost 20 years now. She is 20 years younger than I am. I have two grandchildren with her — I mean not real grandchildren — who are 3 and 6.

What's the deal you are proudest of?
Bringing Bob Kerrey [former governor and U.S. senator from Nebraska] to the New School [as president]. It was really a brokerage transaction. **TRD**

September 2008

Photo by Hugh Hartshorn

DIANE RAMIREZ

CEO | **HALSTEAD PROPERTY**

Together with Clark Halstead, Ramirez started the residential brokerage Halstead Property in 1984. Ramirez was a partner in the firm until 2001, when it was acquired by Terra Holdings, also a parent company of brokerage Brown Harris Stevens. Halstead has nearly 1,000 sales and rental agents in more than two-dozen offices in Manhattan, the Bronx, Brooklyn, the Hamptons, and several New York-area suburbs.

Interview by Lauren Elkies

"We eat dinner out seven days a week. I used to be embarrassed but I'm not really anymore."

What's your full name?
Diane Marie Ramirez. Say that one three times! It's a tongue twister, but I love it anyway.

What's your date of birth?
February 22, 1947.

Where did you grow up?
Jackson Heights, Queens. That's where I spent my entire life until I got married [to Samuel Ramirez, founder and CEO of the investment banking firm, Samuel A. Ramirez & Company] on May 11, 1968.

How did you and your husband meet?
In an after-work singles club, where you go after five to have a cold drink and meet guys with your best girlfriend.

Did you hit it off right away?
Actually, no. He met my girlfriend and was interested in her. He and his best friend invited us to go dancing, and he escorted me in and we spent the evening together. I must have been married 15 years when I told the story to a girlfriend. I said, 'I think he found something very charming about me and that's why he switched [dates].' He heard me and said, 'What are you talking about, charming? You were too tall to dance with Dominick.' So, thank God I'm tall.

Where do you live?
67th and Lexington in a 100-year-old co-op.

Would you ever live in 15 Central Park West or the Plaza?
The Plaza is not me. I'd rather a more private place. But 15 Central Park West, yes.

How do you get to and from work?
I'm a subway gal. I either hop on the subway one stop or I walk it. It's only 10 blocks.

What other real estate firms have you worked at?
Key Ventures in New York and Claude D. Reese Agency and Gardens Insurance in Palm Beach, Florida [where Ramirez still holds a real estate license]. And I started to open my own firm but instead very happily went with Halstead Property.

What was the last real estate deal you brokered?
It was 1987, and I sold a townhouse to Calvin Klein on East 76th Street.

What was the commission check?
Oh God, I honestly can't remember, but it was sizable. It was a multi-million dollar transaction.

How many children and grandchildren do you have?
Two children and five grandchildren, ages 9, 7, 5, 4 and 8 months.

Do you have any other homes?
We have a partnership with my son and his wife and his two children on a farm in Patterson, N.Y., in Putnam County. My son has a polo team, and the farm will be an active polo club by September. It also has a couple of fields, stables and an indoor riding rink.

What's your favorite restaurant?
We tend to go for low-key local ones like Bella Blu. We're members of the Lotos Club. We'll go for a fabulous lobster over there.

Do you cook?
We eat dinner out seven days a week. I used to be embarrassed, but I'm not really anymore.

What do you do for breakfast?
My husband makes the coffee, and I usually just have something simple like yogurt. We literally sit down for maybe only 10 minutes, and we just talk. It's a way to connect each day, and then I literally walk him to the door and say goodbye, like a little schoolboy. Maybe that's why we're married after 40 years.

What quality do you like best about your husband?
I would say it's his heart.

What annoys you the most about him?
He loves to shop and I don't. That annoys me a bit. His closet is bigger than mine.

How do you stay calm in the face of difficulty?
I think it's just my nature. My mom was a very nervous, anxious person. She reached out to me often when she was anxious, so if she saw my brother [Ramirez is one of five siblings] fall down a flight of stairs, she would run the other way and say, your brother fell down the stairs, and I would rush over to him.

If you could change one aspect of your life, what would it be?
Could I just get more time? There are a lot of little things I'd like to do — silly things like playing more golf and learning a language. My son married a Brazilian gal and the 7-year-old is fluent in Portuguese and understands Spanish really well. I sit there with her other grandmother, who speaks no English, with a 7-year-old between us who translates. I mean, it's ridiculous. But I will learn Spanish.

If you could do your life over again, would you do anything differently?
I wouldn't lose my dad so young. He died in 1967 when I was 19. He had colon cancer.

Is your mom still alive?
She just passed away in December, also of cancer. I thought she would live forever. **TRD**

Photo by Michael Toola

BRUCE EICHNER

CHAIRMAN | CONTINUUM COMPANY

Eichner's Continuum is a privately held firm that has focused on the acquisition and development of residential, office, hospitality and retail space in New York, Miami and Las Vegas. Eichner's projects have included CitySpire, which was the tallest mixed-use building when built in 1987; the Manhattan Club, which opened in 1997 as the city's first time-share resort; the Continuum, a 2 million-square-foot condo community in South Beach that had openings in 2002 and 2008; and the 3,000-room Cosmopolitan Resort & Casino in Las Vegas, which opened in 2010. Eichner started his career as a lawyer and assistant district attorney in Brooklyn. *Interview by Lauren Elkies*

"I'm not a genius when I make $50 million. I'm not a failure if I lose it."

What's your full name?
Ian Bruce Eichner.

Why don't people call you Ian?
Because when I was a kid, you don't like being called "Peein' Ian."
Also, my mother — and she pronounces it "I-on" — she'd say:
'Ian Bruce Eichner, get up here now!'

What's your date of birth?
June 25, 1945. Are you aware that that year is the single greatest
vintage of the 20th century in Bordeaux?

Where did you grow up?
Sunnyside, Queens.

Where do you live now?
I've been living at 52 Park Avenue. I'm about to move into a new
apartment at One Morton Square.

Do you have other homes?
In East Hampton, Las Vegas and South Beach.

How long have you been married to Linda, who is in charge of marketing and interior design for your projects, and how did you meet?
Twenty-five years. We met at a pool party in East Hampton.
I was dating someone else. I talked to her for three hours
and then didn't see her again for two years.

Have you been married before?
For an hour, when I was in college.

Do you have any children?
We have a 25-year-old, Lindsay, and we have Alexandra, the
magnificent, who's 23. Alexandra just came back from China. After
graduating from the University of Pennsylvania, she decided to go to
Shanghai and seek her fortune.

Did she find it?
[Laughs] I don't think so. She's back — she's "beeacck." She and Arnold Schwarzenegger are "beeeacck." And Lindsay works for the new
start-up Town Residential by Andrew Heiberger. Lindsay has a better
Rolodex than I do.

How'd you get into real estate?
I liked working for the nonprofit world ... but they pay you $1.95 and
all the Hi-C orange drink you can drink. So, I started ferreting around,
and I had shared an office, when I was working for the DA, with a guy
who lived in Park Slope. [I'd] never heard of it. ... I went into the Slope
in 1969 and '70 and I said, "This thing looks to me like Greenwich
Village." I realized there was an opportunity. Only problem was — no
money, no family in the business. And so I started, in 1973, with a borrowed $10,000 and I bought a rooming house at number 40 Montgomery Place from Mrs. Fitzpatrick. And then I went to a Shylock and
borrowed 40,000 bucks to renovate it and I turned it into a rental.

Do you have a trademark?
Maybe my ties ... the designer is Leonard. I have about 100
or 150 of them.

How would you describe your personality?
I'm reasonably chatty, as you've ascertained. I have a semblance
of a sense of humor. I have a real bevy of interests. I travel to
rather esoteric places. I'm a collector. I play a lot of tennis;
I still play tournaments sometimes — doubles.

You're going on vacation tomorrow. Where are you headed?
I'm going to Rwanda to see silverback mountain gorillas and
to northwest Kenya to go leopard trekking. This will be my 11th
safari. I've been all over — Botswana, Kenya, Tanzania,
Zimbabwe, South Africa, Uganda.

**You are not a New York City household name like Trump and
Durst and Tishman. Why do you think that is?**
Number one is that a bunch of the people you just mentioned
are families — family businesses. Number two, I have spent the
preponderance of the last eight-plus years doing developments
elsewhere. There were a zillion articles in the Vegas papers
about the Cosmopolitan, and same thing in South Beach
with the Continuum.

**What's going on at One Madison Park, a condo project you've
expressed interest in getting involved with?**
One of the creditors put it into bankruptcy in Delaware in June
of last year. And I came along and proposed to inject new money
[$40 million] into the building to recapitalize it and offered
to finish it.

**Late last month, developer Ira Shapiro and investor Cevdet
Caner tentatively agreed to sell the property to HFZ Capital
Group. Where does that leave you?**
It is highly likely we will actively pursue a competing plan for
the benefit of the creditors.

**What's the deal with the condo you bought there for $5
million, a big discount from the asking price?**
I bought an apartment at One Madison Park to live in. It's part of
the bankruptcy. It's a claim that I have along with everybody else.

**You defaulted on CitySpire on 56th Street and the Bertelsmann
Building at 1540 Broadway, both in the early 1990s,
and at the Cosmopolitan in Vegas in 2007. Are you feeling
discouraged today?**
No. Like I try to explain to my kids, there's only one thing you're
in control of — your level of effort. I'm not a genius when I make
$50 million. I'm not a failure if I lose it. **TRD**

March 2011

ELIZABETH STRIBLING

CHAIRMAN | **STRIBLING & ASSOCIATES**

Stribling founded the high-end residential firm in 1980 with partner Connie Tysen. She served as the company's president until 2013, when she announced that her daughter, Elizabeth Ann Stribling-Kivlan, would take on that role. Currently, she is the company's chairman. Long focused on Manhattan, the company opened its first Brooklyn office in 2013. In total, Stribling has some 250 agents. *Interview by Lauren Elkies*

"People think I look a certain way, but I've got a real sense of adventure. I don't consider myself stuffy."

What's your full name?
Elizabeth French Stribling. French was my grandmother's maiden name.

Is your family French?
No, but I'm a great, great Francophile. I have a home in the South of France, an apartment in Paris, and I'm involved in many, many Franco-American cultural and charitable societies.

What's your date of birth?
August 7, 1944.

Where did you grow up?
I was born in Atlanta, Ga. I have lived in New York City since I was 7 years old. I first lived in the Sutton Place area, and then we moved to East 79th Street. I would go down to Georgia every summer to visit my grandmother and my great aunt. I would curtsy. I would pass hors d'oeuvres. I would get all starched up and be on call when all the callers and friends came.

Where do you live?
I live in a townhouse on East 84th Street. I rent it. But I'm moving to [a $6.6 million condo at] One Brooklyn Bridge Park in Brooklyn Heights.

Why are you moving to Brooklyn?
I thought it would be nice to move to a condominium, high in the sky, with a fabulous view. People think I look a certain way, but I've got a real sense of adventure. I don't consider myself a stuffy person at all. I've been going to Brooklyn for 20 years, going out to all of the productions at the Brooklyn Academy of Music and to all sorts of ethnic neighborhoods. Brooklyn's a pretty swell place.

Why didn't you buy in the Plaza?
Coming from a house, I wanted more space than I myself could have afforded at the Plaza. I'm a real estate broker. I'm not the mogul type that is buying into the Plaza.

Do you have any pets?
I used to have a Jack Russell terrier. He went to dog heaven about five years ago. His name was Franklin, and I was crazy about him. He would go to the South of France with me all the time. Franklin liked France, he loved French food and he understood French.

What was the first job you ever had?
During a summer vacation from Vassar I worked at Revlon as a receptionist, then in accounts payable, then for the chairman of the board and later the president. I got, that summer, the equivalent of a Harvard Business School education.

When you founded your firm, did you have a mentor?
No. Connie and I met our accountant at Schrafft's [restaurant and ice cream shop]. We said we wanted to form a real estate firm, and I mean, he looked at these two dizzy dames like we were absolutely crazy and it wouldn't last long. I still use the same accountant, and he laughs every time he looks at the annual statements.

Are you a socialite?
I go to a lot of parties and I participate in a lot of charitable events in New York, so I'm a gal about town, but I think the word has a pejorative connotation.

If you weren't in real estate, what would you be doing?
I'd be an actress.

What kind of actress?
I'm hoping a fabulous actress.

Did you ever pursue acting?
Yes, I did summer stock at the Gateway Playhouse in Bellport, Long Island, when I was 18 years old. I acted in all the things at Hewitt.

What did you think you'd be when you grew up?
I thought I would get married, live on Park Avenue, have two kids and a dog. That's what everyone else did when I was 14.

Do you ever throw on jeans and a T-shirt, wear no makeup and not style your hair?
Probably not, but I can tell you this: Practically all my Saturdays, I'm in my dressing gown all day long surrounded by piles of the New York Times, piles of books, just having the most marvelous lazy, lazy day. So I don't get dressed on Saturdays or go out.

What is your husband up to then?
He is in his study on the computer, and he really leaves me alone. We meet for lunch in the kitchen and have a fabulous kind of catch-up and go over all sorts of things.

Do you cook at all?
I love to cook.

Do you have a specialty dish?
I'll tell you what I made for dinner this week. I started off with a butternut squash soup garnished with Stilton cheese, toasted nuts and sage. I made that myself from scratch. Then I made medallions of saddle of lamb with a sweet roasted garlic cream sauce. I made gaufrette potatoes, which you make on a mandoline. They're like crispy homemade potato chips. For dessert, I made my signature dessert dish, which is a hazelnut cheesecake. You roast the hazelnuts, you grind them all up and put them in the cake. My guests seemed to enjoy it a lot.

Who is the boss at home — you or your husband?
I plan the schedule.

What does he do?
He cheerfully puts on his dinner jacket and dancing shoes practically every night and accompanies me around New York. **TRD**

June 2008

JEFFREY LEVINE

CHAIRMAN | **DOUGLASTON DEVELOPMENT**

Chairman and principal of three affiliated companies: Douglaston Development, Levine Builders, and Clinton Management, Levine has overseen the new construction and rehabilitation of thousands of rental and condo apartments, including many affordable housing units. His companies have also built or renovated millions of square feet of commercial space. Notably, Levine developed the Edge condominiums in the rezoned 175-block area along the Williamsburg/Greenpoint waterfront. Back in 2010, the 565-unit building sold more units than any other residential building in New York City that year. *Interview by Lauren Elkies*

"The key to being successful is having a high threshold for aggravation."

What's your date of birth?
May 15, 1953.

Where did you grow up?
In Brooklyn, initially East Flatbush/Brownsville, and then East New York. And then we moved out to Queens, to the Bayside area. I actually started my office in the two-bedroom apartment I shared with my younger brother in Queens, and the phone number, which is still the Levine Builders phone number, was the phone number that rang in our apartment. I refuse to change it.

Where do you live now?
I have a home in Old Westbury, and I have an apartment in a project that I built at 555 West 23rd Street.

Which one is your primary residence?
I've just become, in theory, an empty-nester. The last of our children is off at college at the University of Arizona, and it's only occurred in the last five months, so we're working to figure out what our primary residence is.

Do you have any other homes?
We have a house in Westhampton.

Where did you go to college?
The City College of New York School of Architecture. That's a four year degree, but I went at night, so it probably took me closer to five or six years. I was working for a contractor during the day.

What did your father do for a living?
He drove a cab and later had an auto repair shop.

Did your mother work?
No. She raised four children.

Did your siblings go to college?
No.

What are they doing today?
My sisters work for me part time, and my brother is in a successful air-conditioning service business.

What was the first job you ever had?
I delivered kosher meat in Brooklyn by bicycle. I guess I was about 11 years old.

How long have you been married?
Twenty-five years this past December.

So you're not on your second marriage to a woman half your age.
If you want to really do me a great big favor, you can say that I married the love of my life and a trophy bride in one fell swoop. I would really get a lot of points for that.

How have you stayed married all these years?
Well, we were first too poor to divorce. Now we're too opulent to divorce [laughs]. We love each other and have a respect for our respective qualities.

How do you handle anxiety?
Obviously, you can worry about everything, or you can worry about nothing. I choose to worry about things that I can alter.

Are you religious?
I am very observant. I belong to a Conservative temple. I'm probably one of the only Jewish boys to receive the National Museum of Catholic Art and History recognition.

Why'd you receive that?
I was very active working in the East Harlem community years ago, where they were based.

What is your definition of courage?
Courage, I guess, would be the ability to say and do what you believe is right at any time.

Do you think you have courage?
I like to believe I have it. Maybe other people should make that judgment.

What qualities do you look for in an employee?
You've got to be honest, hard-working and capable. There are times when obviously people make mistakes. I have no problem with that as long as their intentions were good. But I have no tolerance whatsoever for a lack of integrity.

Do you think your kids will come into the business?
It's very apparent that my son loves this business much the way I do. I hope one day that he makes a decision to come work with me. My daughters are somewhat younger, and I would love for them to come to work with me.

What makes you angry?
The key to being successful is having a high threshold for aggravation. What upsets me is when people don't do what they say they are going to do — when people are not honest.

What one word would people use to describe you?
I would like to think that I'm a mensch [Yiddish for a decent person] and a hamish person [Yiddish for easy to be with]. **TRD**

HOWARD MICHAELS

CHAIRMAN & CEO | **CARLTON GROUP**

Founded in 1991, the company started by Michaels specializes in equity and debt placement, investment sales and commercial and residential loan sales. The firm has closed some $100 billion in transactions, and has offices in the U.S., Europe and Israel. Some of its more notable deals include the financing of the $350 million Trump Soho in 2007; the $825 million equity and condo conversion financing of Manhattan House in 2005; and the $1.7 billion recapitalization of the GM Building in 2004. In 2014, Carlton launched a crowdfunding site for accredited investors. Carlton has crowdfunded several big transactions, including $240 million in equity and debt for developer Michael Shvo's 125 Greenwich Street. *Interview by Lauren Elkies*

"When you own your own company it's not like work. It's a way of life."

What's your date of birth?
November 3, 1955.

Where do you live?
I split my residence between Manhattan and Old Westbury. I have my new wife [Jennifer Bayer Michaels] and kids in the city. And my old kids in Old Westbury. We live at 79th and Park, in a rental building. But we just bought at the Stanhope and the Lucida. We needed something for our growing family so we're moving into the Stanhope [in early March], but it really isn't big enough, so when the Lucida's ready in a year and a half, we're going to move into that.

How old are your kids?
From 2-and-a-half to 19. There are three boys and one girl, and there is a fifth coming. It's another girl. We like to be very productive at Carlton.

Do you have a weekend home?
I have a house in Bridgehampton.

Where did you grow up?
I grew up in Deer Park, which is in Suffolk County, Long Island, but I was born in Flatbush, Brooklyn.

What was your first job?
Sweeping the floor at a place called Holzman Carpet [in Flushing, Queens, before it closed]. I was 9. My dad worked for the guy that owned it. I grew up a fat Jewish kid in an all-Italian neighborhood. I wasn't that athletic, although I loved sports. What I liked about work was that I was good at it. Then [my father and I] worked for this other place Raphan Carpet, all over Queens and Long Island. I was 11 or 12 and worked there for 10 years. I started as a stock boy working my way up to sales. I liked making the sale and convincing people to buy the carpets.

Did you always like money?
Yeah, I did. My family was more blue-collar. When I worked at Raphan Carpet, it was a family business, and they did very well and had nice cars. I felt like this was for me.

How do you think you compare to your father?
My father's a nice guy. He never reached his potential, and I think he was always frustrated by that. I think that's one of the things that keeps driving me to try and reach my full potential.

Do you like to watch sports on TV?
I love to play sports. I don't like to watch them. I realized a long time ago that it was great to watch them, but my life was never going to change — this may be a cynical thing to say — watching them.

Does your wife work?
For eight years, she was [Sen.] Chuck Schumer's chief fundraiser and then a senior fundraiser/advisor for two years at the DSCC — the Democratic Senatorial Campaign Committee. Now she has her own company operating on a consulting basis. She's hosted a bunch of different fundraisers for Hillary Clinton and some of the other candidates. But I'm a Republican.

How does that work out?
[Laughs] I'm like a quasi-Republican. Not always great.

Walk me through your day.
A typical day is getting up at 6:30 a.m., reading publications, organizing voicemails and emails from 7 to 9. From 9 to 10, I'm on the bike in my apartment and on the phone having conference calls with my office and clients. People who know me also know I'm breathing heavy because I'm working out. I'm usually in the office by 11. Then I'm home every night. I'd be the easiest guy to assassinate because I'm very routine-oriented. Other than when I travel, I have the same day every day.

How do you relax?
I get massages. I work out. I travel a lot. I just came back from Israel with my three boys [David, 19; Josh, 17; and Sam, 12]. We had a great time. I'm going to take a Jacuzzi right now with them. They just came home from tennis.

What do you typically do on the weekends?
Nothing too exciting. I get up early, and my wife tends to sleep late. I make the kids breakfast and take them to whatever activities they have. My wife and I typically go to the [David Barton] gym together on 85th and Madison. Then we usually do an afternoon activity and come back and take a nap. And then we typically go out with friends Saturday night. I watch "Meet the Press" Sunday morning with my wife, and then I have an 11 o'clock conference call. After that, I am kind of on the BlackBerry, and we do family stuff for the rest of the day.

Is it hard for you to put work aside?
Why should I put it aside? When you own your own company it's not like work. It's a way of life.

Does your wife view it as work?
Sometimes. Sometimes it's too much and she'll tell me to chill out, and I do. **TRD**

April 2008

JEFF BLAU

CEO | **THE RELATED COMPANIES**

Blau leads one of the largest private real estate development firms in the country, with a portfolio valued at over $15 billion. The company, which was behind the creation of the Time Warner Center at Columbus Circle, is also developing the 26-acre Hudson Yards, the largest development site remaining in Manhattan. It is also the biggest private development in United States history. Plans for the site include five office towers, 5,000 residences, 100 stores, and 14 acres of public space. *Interview by Candace Taylor*

"There are times when the best thing to do is not do anything, when the market gets overheated."

What's your date of birth?
April 11, 1968.

Where were you born and where did you grow up?
Born in New York City, lived in Bayside [in Queens] until I was 9, and then moved to Woodbury on Long Island.

What did your parents do?
My dad was a contractor, a builder, in New York, and probably got me started liking real estate. I used to work on construction sites over the summer. You know, if you're in real estate you have to love the physical building side of it. It's more than just finance and dollars.

What kind of kid were you?
I wasn't the best student. I didn't particularly love school — I liked doing things on my own outside of school.

What did you do outside of school?
I had a whole bunch of businesses growing up, from flea markets to paper routes to lemonade stands. [In college at the University of Michigan], I bought some houses and converted them into student apartments with some local guys there.

How did you meet Related Chairman Stephen Ross?
He's a Michigan grad. He was up for a conference, and the head of the real estate department introduced me. We wound up sitting together in the back row at the conference, talking, and he offered me a summer job.

What did you say to him that made him want to spend so much time talking to you?
I think we were probably talking more about Michigan football than anything else. We just hit it off. I actually give his secretary more credit because he was difficult to get in touch with afterwards, and I kept hounding her. It's always good to know the secretaries.

You and your wife, Lisa, just moved into a $21.5 million penthouse at 1040 Fifth Avenue, a co-op built in 1930. Why not live in a Related building, like Superior Ink?
I actually just moved to 1040 from a building Related did build on 65th and Third Avenue, the Chatham. I loved living in that building — the apartment was great. It's sad to move out, but as two kids come along and you need more space, we opted to make the move.

How old are your kids?
The young one's 9 months and the other one's 3. The 3-year-old is really into cars and all sorts of boy things.

How do you balance work and young kids?
I see the kids in the morning. I usually don't see them during the week at night, and then on the weekends, it's all about the kids, 100 percent. It's a trade-off.

Before you bought at 1040, you had a board turndown at the exclusive co-op 820 Fifth Avenue. Why do you think you got turned down?
Technically it never went to the board, so it's unclear.

Why even bother with a fancy co-op — why not live in a new condo, especially since you build them for a living?
I agree with you — I think that goes in the "lessons learned" category.

Is there any one development that you are particularly proud of?
Of course, the Time Warner Center was really a game-changer for us. Also, I think the first real development that I did was a very small building on the north end of Union Square, the Barnes & Noble building on 17th Street. I remember when we went in and it was an abandoned shell of a building, and there were pigeons flying through it.

What kind of rents are you getting at your project MiMA in Midtown?
We're averaging about $75 a foot.

That building has a "pet spa" — didn't pet spas go the way of the real estate boom?
It's not just a pet spa; they do dog-walking, so they'll come up to your apartment during the day and get your pets, and feed them, and let them play outside. It's been a tremendous leasing tool. People really love it.

What is a mistake you've made in your career that you've learned from?
There are times when the best thing to do is not do anything, when the market gets overheated. In the '06-'07 timeframe, there were plenty of deals that, had you gone on vacation, that would have been the best outcome.

Related agreed in 2008 to a $1 billion long-term lease with the MTA to become the developer of Hudson Yards. How did you decide to take that gamble?
Well, Hudson Yards could be our greatest accomplishment yet. It's the future growth corridor of the city. It's where companies are going to go. Our office building stock is old here. We're falling behind as a city. ... Obviously the project didn't start as quickly as we'd like, but in the last 12 months or so, I'd say the mindset of the large companies has changed dramatically. And what you're seeing now is that people have the confidence once again to make that type of leasing commitment.

Related has said it needs a large tenant to begin construction. What's the latest leasing update?
I believe we'll start with two 2 million-square-foot office towers and 1 million square feet of retail, and we'll announce those commitments within the next 12 months. **TRD**

Photo by Hugh Hartshorn

K. THOMAS ELGHANAYAN

CHAIRMAN & CO-FOUNDER | **TF CORNERSTONE**

At the time of the interview, Elghanyan was President of Rockrose Development Corp., which he co-founded in 1970. The family business, in which his brothers Henry and Frederick Elghanyan were also partners, built up a portfolio of more than 30 residential and commercial buildings in New York City and Washington, D.C., including more than 5,500 apartments. In 2009, Thomas and Frederick split from Rockrose to found TF Cornerstone. The new company owns and manages an 8 million square-foot portfolio of luxury residential properties, as well as office and retail spaces. *Interview by Lauren Elkies*

"We have a rule here, me and my brothers: Everyone pays market rate, no matter what."

What's your full name?
Kamran (pronounced Kum-run) Elghanayan. Kamran is Iranian. I was born in Iran, and so was Henry. Henry's name is actually Houchang (pronounced Who-shang).

Why don't you go by your first name?
It's just too big a handful — Kamran Elghanayan — you know, spelling it 30 times a day. Actually, I really got the name Tommy in grade school. My name was Kamran, and the short name for Kamran was Kammy (pronounced Commee) in Persian. And so there I was, I was going to school in Forest Hills in the early '50s with the name Kammy, and all the kids used to make fun of me. That was when the whole Red Scare, Communist thing was going on. So my teacher said, 'We're not going to call you Kammy anymore, we're going to call you Tommy,' because it sounded like Kammy, and her husband's name was Tommy.

What's your date of birth?
August 5, 1945.

How old are your siblings?
Fred is 58. Henry is like 66. Jeffrey is — I always think of him as being a baby — he's like 52. I have a sister, Lili, who is — she wouldn't want me to say this — one year older than me.

How old do you feel?
I feel like I'm 30. I work out a lot. I go at things with a lot of gusto. I work very hard. I play very hard. I just got divorced a couple of years ago, finalized in August of 2006.

That must have really changed your life.
It was a jarring experience. I was married for 29 years.

Do you have kids?
A daughter, who is 30, married, has a child, so I'm a grandfather. And I have a son who's 24.

How old were you when you came to this country?
I was 4 years old. I have no memories of Iran at all.

Where did you grow up?
I'd have to say I grew up in Forest Hills, though I never felt part of Forest Hills. I went to grade school there at P.S. 101 until fifth or sixth grade. By the way, we lived on Rockrose Place in Forest Hills, Queens. That's where the name Rockrose came from. Then I went to [the now-shuttered] Nyack Boys School, a boarding school; and then to Blair Academy, a boarding school in Blairstown, New Jersey. So I was always sort of a transient.

Where do you live now?
I live on 72nd and Madison in a co-op.

Do you have any other homes?
A house out in Southampton. I bought all these things since I got divorced. When I was married, I lived at Fifth Avenue in the 70s, and I had a house in East Hampton.

Do you feel like you're American?
I'm American — 100 percent. Look, I relate to my father some, but he's very Persian and has strong emotional ties to the place. But I think even that has weakened because when they had the revolution, they executed my uncle [Habib Elghanayan] when the ayatollah came to Iran. My uncle was the leader of the Jewish community in Iran.

What's the best advice you received from your parents?
When I got married, my father took me for a walk around the block, and he said, 'Kammy, I want to tell you three things that you should do when you're married. First, you should always wear pajamas at night; second, always have a separate bathroom; third, never tell your wife anything about your business.' Now, the last two things I can understand, and they turned out to be good advice. The first thing about the pajamas — I'm still a little puzzled about [laughs]. I think what he may have meant — I should ask him before he dies — is that we have a lot of body hair, me and my brothers, and maybe he felt that that would frighten women.

How many times have you been married?
Once. I'm now engaged to a girl [Madeline Hult, 37, a sales director at Corcoran Sunshine Marketing Group] I met subsequent to the divorce.

Have you ever lived in a Rockrose building?
Actually, I've had two stints at the Fairfax [at 201 East 69th Street and Third Avenue], first when I got divorced — when I was leaving the house — and then afterwards, after I bought the apartment that I'm living in now, when I was renovating it, for three or four months.

What was your rent?
I was paying, I think, $8,700.

Why wouldn't you live there rent-free?
We have a rule here, me and my brothers, because we have lots of relatives, lots of friends, lots of kids: Everyone pays market rate, no matter what.

How do you measure success?
Whether you've lived according to your own ethical standard you've set yourself and also according to the absolute standard of the whole community.

Are you successful?
By that standard, yes. Just on a financial basis, I'd say I'm pretty successful, too. Have I been successful as a father and a husband and those other things? I think I've been successful as a father. I don't think I was that great a husband. **TRD**

EDWARD MINSKOFF
PRESIDENT | **EDWARD J. MINSKOFF EQUITIES**

Minskoff founded the real estate acquisition and development company in 1987. The firm oversees all aspects of its properties, including design and development, management, leasing and financing. Among its projects are the residential condominium development at 101 Warren Street, and the office buildings at 1325 Avenue of the Americas, 590 Madison Avenue and 5 Astor Place. Before founding his company, Minskoff was at Olympia & York, whose development projects included the 7.5 million-square-foot Worl Financial Center, now known as Brookfield Place. *Interview by Lauren Elkie*

"I got nothing from my family. I got incentives to do better than all of them."

What's your date of birth?
I don't discuss my birth date.

Why?
I don't know. I just don't. My mother never did. My mother was 39 her whole entire life until she died at 93. She never looked her age, so no one ever knew.

When's your birthday then?
Dec. 31 — New Year's Eve.

What was it like having both on the same day?
It was shitty. I got screwed every year as a kid because they used to give me my birthday and Christmas present as one.

Was your family affluent, middle-class or lower-class?
They were pretty well off.

How do you compare to them financially?
I don't like to talk about wealth, but when I got out of business school my father had nothing. He lost all his money gambling. I came to New York with a two-year-old Chevy and two grand in the bank, and that's all I ever got from my family.

Did your father have a job?
He was a developer. My mother and father were divorced when I was 12.

That's unusual, no?
Back then it was. So I lived out of a suitcase until I got out of business school. I was going to prep school near Princeton. My mother was living in Detroit. My father was living in Southern California.

What did you want to be when you grew up?
A developer. When I was a little kid in Washington I was curious, and I used to ask people about their jobs. I went to some job sites with my father when he was building in Washington and I said, 'This is kind of cool to build buildings. It seems like a cool business to be in.'

Are you a gambler?
I was never inclined. I gamble for fun with my friends on the golf course. That's the extent of my gambling, and I gamble big in business.

Are you a good golfer?
A seven handicap. The two sports I am active in today are squash and golf. I retired from skiing.

What are your hobbies?
Collecting art. Art's a passion really for both of us [him and his wife of 14 years, Julie (Chai) Minskoff]. She oversees the entire collection.

How many pieces of art do you have?
Oh, I don't know—somewhere between 450 and 500.

What does your collection consist of?
It's 100 percent 20th-century Contemporary. It ranges from the old guard, which is Picasso — we have huge numbers of his works in our collection — paintings, drawings, sculpture. Jackson Pollock, Roy Lichtenstein, Willem de Kooning ... right up to the new guard, which we have quite a few of including Richard Prince, Damien Hirst, Jean-Michel Basquiat and Jeff Koons.

Where do you keep the collection?
Home in the city, home in Southampton, my office ... and every single building that I own has my art in it.

Do you have children?
I have three — 13, 21, 30.

Where do you live in the city?
71st Street and Park Avenue.

Did you build your house in Southampton?
Yes.

What kind of home is it?
It's a beautiful Robert A.M. Stern-designed house.

Do you have any other homes?
We have a place — not a home — in Palm Beach, but we never use it.

Did you think your company would be a success?
It wasn't even a question in my mind.

Where did you get your confidence from — your family?
I got nothing from my family — zero. I got incentives from my family — incentives to do better than all of them.

What's your favorite movie?
I don't like depressing movies. If I go to a movie, I want to be totally entertained.

If you don't like depressing movies, how do you feel about things like the crime coverage in the city papers?
I was saying to my driver, why is it so important for them to tell me about some guy in Massapequa that got shot? Who cares about somebody that got murdered in Newark? If it, God forbid, is some important politician or world leader or something, that's news. That, they should report. There are so many important things in the world today ... why is it necessary, day in and day out, every friggin' day of the week, to tell me about somebody else that got murdered? **TRD**

February 2008

BOB TOLL

EXECUTIVE CHAIRMAN | **TOLL BROTHERS**

Toll founded Toll Brothers with his brother Bruce in 1967, and today it is a massive, publicly traded Fortune 500 home-building company. The firm entered the New York City market in 2004, and in the decade since has been behind such residential condo developments as Northside Piers in Williamsburg, Pierhouse at Brooklyn Bridge Park (which has set condominium price records in the borough) and the Touraine and 400 Park Avenue South in Manhattan.

Interview by Lauren Elkies

"It's a wise man who knows what he doesn't know."

What's your date of birth?
December 30, 1940.

Where did you grow up?
Elkins Park, Pennsylvania., a suburb of Philadelphia.

Where do you live?
I live in Bucks County, Pennsylvania.

Do you have any other homes?
Yes. In Telluride [Colorado]; Casco, Maine; and New York City.

Where in New York City?
On 85th and Madison.

What's your favorite thing to do in New York City?
Go to the opera.

What's your favorite New York City restaurant?
Babbo [at 110 Waverly Place].

What is your favorite borough and why?
Manhattan, because it's got more action, more food, more shows, more opera, more music than the others.

Toll Brothers is known for building McMansions. Are your homes all McMansions?
No, not at all. The home in Bucks County has an 8-foot ceiling on the first floor. There's no vaulted ceiling. It's not a big home compared to many of the homes that we have built. I would guess that it's under 5,000 square feet. It's an old Pennsylvania farmhouse, the first part of which was built in the early 1700s.

What is the first job you ever had?
I was a counselor at Camp Powhatan in Otisfield, Maine, at about age 18, and then I came back and ran the boating department at the waterfront at that camp for a couple of years. It no longer exists. It's now known as Seeds of Peace, which my wife and I are very much involved in. The camp brings teenage Arabs and Israelis together for summer sessions.

What is the best piece of advice you have received?
In Plato's "Apology of Socrates," he said, and I'm paraphrasing, 'It's a wise man who knows what he doesn't know.'

So what don't you know?
Almost everything.

What's the last book you read?
I just completed the biography of Andrew Jackson ["Andrew Jackson: His Life and Times," by H. W. Brands].

What was the biggest obstacle to your success?
It was in 1974, when the country was running out of money. You couldn't get a mortgage — not to be confused with these times. You can still get a mortgage today. There were literally no mortgages in '74.

What has been your toughest time on a personal level?
Probably a divorce about 30-some-odd years ago. I'm now married 30-some-odd years to my second wife. I met my honey [Jane] at the end of '74. A friend hooked us up.

How do you deal with antagonists?
Some I ignore. Some I try to reduce the level of antagonism. Some I guess we go to battle. But I don't have personal antagonists I battle with.

Do you have any remorse about any of your projects?
Sure.

Which one?
I don't care to say. There was one out of 1,000 communities we've had that I wasn't proud of. I felt bad that I didn't leave the quality and the value behind that we should have. Then there are more than several communities that have been a financial failure, and I wish I hadn't done those.

How do you blow off steam?
I play a lot of tennis, I play a lot of golf, I ski a lot, I sail a lot, I swim, I fish, I read, I go to a lot of opera, I see a couple of shows, I love to go out to eat.

Do you cook at all?
I don't cook. My honey cooks quite a bit.

What do you read every day?
I try to read the New York Times and the Wall Street Journal.

What's your worst vice?
I don't know. I smoke cigars once in a while, but I don't think that's bad. Maybe I play too much golf, but I only play once a week. In the past, it was leaving my family too much to sail competitively. That was a mistake.

What's your most prized possession?
I like my dogs. I've got a Goldendoodle, a cross between a Poodle and a Golden Retriever. I've got two Labradors. My most prized possession? I guess my artwork.

What's the most money you've spent on a piece of art?
Not for publication.

What kind of art collection do you have?
Extensive and eclectic. **TRD**

September 2007

Photo by Hugh Hartshor

HALL WILLKIE

PRESIDENT | **BROWN HARRIS STEVENS**

Willkie oversees the residential sales company, managing over 350 agents with sales totaling in excess of $4.2 billion at Manhattan's most white-shoe residential brokerage. The firm has offices in Manhattan, Brooklyn, Long Island and Palm Beach.

The brokerage's parent company is Terra Holdings, which also owns Halstead Property. Willkie has been a recipient of REBNY's prestigious Henry Forster Award for professional achievement. *Interview by Lauren Elkies*

"My mother always told me my father was an honorable man, and I think I am too."

What's your full name?
Hall Francis Willkie.

What's the origin of your first name?
My mother gave me her maiden name as my first name.

Do people tell you that it's an unusual name?
Usually when people hear it, they call me Paul, and if they read it, they call me Hal. But once they get it, they tend to remember it.

Have you ever met anyone with the same name?
I'm very proud to say I have a goddaughter whose first name is Hall. Other than that, I haven't met anybody.

What's your date of birth?
April 7, 1949.

Where did you grow up?
I was born in Kentucky. Then, between the ages of 11 and 17, I lived in Madrid. I went to a boarding school for one year in Scotland and graduated from high school in Bermuda.

What was family life like for you?
I'm one of four children, and my mother moved to Madrid when I was 10 or 11. My father passed away when I was 10. He died of heart trouble, but he had been hospitalized for eight and a half years before he died, so I never really knew him. I'm the last child of the last wife.

How many wives were there?
Three.

How has the absence of your father affected you?
I think it's more of a challenge. Certainly I wish I had known him.

Where do you live?
On East 72nd Street in a four-unit co-op. I also have a farm in upstate New York in Delaware County, in Bovina. I love it up there.

How do you get to work?
I walk. It's about 17 or 18 blocks.

How many miles is your country house from the city?
About 160.

How do you get up there?
I drive.

What kind car do you own?
I have an Infinity M35, which is an all-wheel drive car. The farm is up in the mountains, and we get a lot of snow. My other car is a pickup truck, which is also all-wheel drive.

Do you have a life partner?
Yes. He is an architect and works for himself.

Do you have any children?
No.

What was the first job you ever had?
On a thoroughbred horse-breeding and training farm. I did whatever job there was. I actually delayed going to college for two years in order to continue to work there. I've always been a horse person. I've always been a rider. I have four horses, and I'm a chicken farmer.

Are people stunned that you're a farmer?
I don't know. I think they see the hayseed in me [chuckles].

How does someone get into your inner circle?
I'm very much a people person. I work with a lot of people. I'm involved in our local community in the country. I'm involved in our little co-op. I have a few very close friends. I'd be happy to have that group be larger, but there's not enough time in my life.

What one word would people use to describe you?
I'm a problem solver. That's not one word, I know.

What kind of character do you have?
Honor's an important thing to me — to be truthful, to be honest. My mother always told me my father was an honorable man, and I think I am that too.

Do you cook?
On the weekends in the country.

What's your specialty dish?
A few things. I make a mean paella, and I am famous for my short ribs of beef amongst my friends.

What publications do you read regularly?
My favorite magazine is The Week. I read that without fail. It is so smart, especially for busy people that don't have a lot of time to read. I also read Time magazine. I look at Architectural Digest, and I read Vanity Fair.

If you could do it again, what would you do differently?
I would buy a co-op sooner. For many years in New York, I lived in a rent-stabilized apartment at 85th Street and West End Avenue. It seemed like I had this great apartment for very little money, and to buy something would have been half as nice and cost me four times as much.

How many brokers have your cell phone number?
All of the brokers that work with me, but I don't have voicemail on my cell. I won't have it. If you call me on my cell and I can answer it, great. **TRD**

January 2008

Photo by Hugh Hartshorne

MITCHELL STEIR

CHAIRMAN & CEO | **SAVILLS STUDLEY**

Steir heads an international commercial real estate services firm specializing in tenant representation that has more than two dozen offices in major cities throughout the U.S., as well as two in China. He has helped secure major leases for companies such as Tiffany & Co., Ralph Lauren and Accenture. Steir started at the firm in 1988 and, along with a group of partners, bought the company from founder Julien Studley in 2002. In 2014, after this interview, the London-based Savills acquired Studley for $260 million, with Steir retaining his chairman and CEO position. *Interview by Lauren Elkies*

"Please tell my competitors that I'm mellowing a little."

What's your full name?
Mitchell Shubow Steir.

What is the origin of Shubow?
It was my grandfather's name, who was a rabbinical scholar in Boston. My mother changed my middle name to Shubow after he passed away in the late '60s.

What was your original middle name?
I don't even know.

What's your date of birth?
August 3, 1955.

Where did you grow up?
Brookline, Massachusetts.

Where do you live now?
On East End Avenue.

Do you have any other homes?
In Sagaponack [in the Hamptons].

How old are your kids?
My son is 16, and my daughter is 11.

What's your favorite restaurant?
My favorite restaurant du jour is chez Steir – my kitchen. I got so tired of eating out and ordering in, so I said to my wife, 'Let's hire a chef.' As for actual restaurants, it's Nicola's, on East 84th Street, and the Four Seasons.

What's your favorite sports team?
The Red Sox. Red Sox is a religion when one grows up in Boston, so having to carry the flag in New York only increases the passion. It's finally paid dividends.

What outside interests do you have?
I love to ski. It's a passion of mine. And I love swimming in the ocean, film and collecting photography.

What was the first job you ever had?
I had two jobs: a garbage man in South Boston at 13 or 14, and on the floor of the Boston Stock Exchange. That was the same summer.

What did you want to be when you grew up?
I think a comedian. I never had the nerve to pursue it.

Are you funny?
You probably wouldn't think so. My close friends think I am. I'm reasonably entertaining in an intimate setting.

How many deals have you personally done this year?
I couldn't tell you for certain, but approximately 20.

How much revenue do you expect your company to bring in this year?
Studley will do north of $250 million.

How'd the company do last year?
2006 was a record year; 2007 should be 20 percent better.

What is the best piece of advice you have received?
Treat people the way you would like to be treated. It was preached to me by my father.

Are you a micromanager?
Absolutely not. From a transactional standpoint, one might say I'm a stickler for quality control, not a micromanager.

What one word would you use to describe yourself?
Competitive.

What one word would people use to describe you?
Tenacious. Please tell my competitors that I'm mellowing a little.

How do you deal with antagonists?
Well, if they're rational, I would look to reason with them because I believe I'm a pretty good communicator. If they're not, then I would try to figure out how to outsmart them and accomplish what I need while having as little interaction with them as possible.

How do you size up people when you first meet them?
Fairly easily. It happens to be a strength of mine. I'm pretty good at reading a person as sincere or not. And I'm pretty good at sensing what kind of character they have.

What publications do you read every day?
Typically in order, the Journal, the Sun and the New York Times. And when the Yankees are losing, I love to read the back page of the Daily News or the Post.

What's the last book you read?
I usually read two books at a time. I love sports, and I love history. The last two were "The Blind Side [Evolution of a Game]" by Michael Lewis, and "Presidential Courage [Brave Leaders and How They Changed America, 1789-1989]" by Michael Beschloss.

If you could do it all over again, what would you do differently?
Be more attentive in high school and in college.

What was on your mind?
Enjoying myself. I was majoring in having fun and chasing girls. **TRD**

December 2007

Photo by Hugh Hartshorne

ARA HOVNANIAN

PRESIDENT | **HOVNANIAN ENTERPRISES**

As one of the largest homebuilders in the United States, Hovnanian Enterprises has delivered hundreds of thousands of homes under the leadership of Hovnanian, who became president of the company in 1988. Hovnanian's father, Kevork, founded the Red Bank, N.J.-based company in 1959. Over the years, it has expanded its reach into well over a dozen residential markets throughout the U.S. *Interview by Lauren Elkies*

"Losing my 15-year-old son in a boating accident ... made me a more sensitive and caring person."

What's your date of birth?
July 4, 1957.

Where do you live?
I live on the Upper East Side, and I have a home in Rumson, N.J.

What was the first job you ever had?
My whole career has been spent at Hovnanian Enterprises. In the summers, before I graduated high school, I started on the construction sites, cleaning houses and carrying kitchen cabinets and appliances from the trucks into the homes.

What is your total compensation?
The salary is fixed at about $1 million. In 2006 other compensation went down dramatically [from 2005]. The bonus went from about $15 million to $5.8 million. The value of the stock options went down to $7 million from $19 million. In 2007 the bonus will likely be close to zero, and the value of the stock options will be considerably less than in 2006. [Hovnanian's stock, in the middle of 2007, had lost 49 percent of its value.]

Still, you are wealthy. How does it feel?
My father [Kevork] is 84. He still works every day. He lives in the same house he lived in 35 years ago. He could have retired many years ago or sold out. He's not driven by the financial rewards, but the dream to build a world-class homebuilding company. I don't quite have his stock ownership [Ara owns less than 10 percent, and his father owns around 30 percent] and therefore don't have his wealth, but I could have retired, sold stock and lived very comfortably for some time, but that's not what drives me either. I love the business. I eat, sleep and breathe it. Obviously we are in America and the financial rewards are wonderful, and I believe in capitalism, but it's far more than the compensation which is driving me.

When it comes to homebuilding, is bigger better?
I think better is better. It's more important to be a really good homebuilder than a really big homebuilder. But if you do things well and you reinvest in the company, bigness does come as a natural outgrowth, and has for us.

What is a personal example of a time when you turned calamity into success?
I suppose the biggest personal calamity I had was losing my 15-year-old son in a boating accident five years ago. I wouldn't be able to say I turned that into a success, but I think it made me a more sensitive and caring person.

How do you unwind?
I like good food, so my wife and I love to go to different restaurants. I'm very active in sports and like to work out regularly, either on a bike in Central Park or in the gym in my building. I developed a bad knee, so biking has become better because it's a little more kind on the knee. I'm a squash player as well. I play at the Racquet and Tennis Club on Park Avenue. And I like to travel. I'm just giving you the tip of the iceberg.

What's your favorite restaurant?
We are regulars at three different places. Number one is Harry Cipriani, number two is Nello, and number three is Le Bilboquet. They're all within a few blocks of our home.

Do you and your wife cook?
My wife loves to cook. Her mother ran a gourmet cooking school for a number of years in Texas, where my wife is from. Interestingly, I went to Le Cordon Bleu one summer, a cooking school in Paris, when I was in college, but I think it was more to impress the girls than serious long-term interest. I gave that up after college. My son, incidentally, went to Cordon Bleu this past summer. He's 17, and he has a passion for cooking.

Does your wife work?
She is an artist. She's at her studio painting every day. She drops off the children at school in the morning and goes straight to the studio, and comes home at the end of the day when they're coming home from school. She has a big show coming up in November at a gallery, Jason McCoy, on 57th Street.

What was the last book you read?
One of the last I read was "Everyman," by Philip Roth. I went to school at the University of Pennsylvania, and Philip Roth was a professor when I was there, although I didn't take any of his courses.

What is your apartment like?
I have a traditional apartment in its bones and moldings, but my wife and I designed it with a Dutch designer, Piet Boon, and it's quite contemporary inside.

What's one thing that people don't know about you?
They probably don't know that I am a big sports nut. I don't like to watch any sports, but I like to participate in sports. And they probably don't realize what a fabulous dancer I am. I attend a lot of philanthropic events, and if there's a good band you'll always find me on the dance floor with my wife, whether it's swing dancing or hip-hop.

Are your kids like — "Oh my God!"?
No, they're used to it. They only say that when I sing, because I'm so bad. **TRD**

August 2007

Photo by Hugh Hartshorne

JONATHAN MECHANIC

CHAIRMAN | **FRIED, FRANK, HARRIS, SHRIVER & JACOBSON**

As partner and chairman of the real estate department at the law firm Fried, Frank, Harris, Shriver & Jacobson, Mechanic negotiated the record $5.4 billion purchase of Peter Cooper Village and Stuyvesant Town in 2006, setting a record for the largest single asset sale in the U.S., and many other high-profile deals. In addition to his work counseling developers, property owners, real estate investment trusts and lenders, he teaches a real estate transactions course at Harvard Law School. *Interview by Lauren Elkies*

"The key to negotiation is to care, but not too much. You need to negotiate hard, but be able to walk away."

What's your date of birth?
October 1, 1952.

Where did you grow up?
In Paterson, N.J.

Where do you live?
In the East Village.

Do you have any other homes?
In East Hampton.

When did you realize you wanted to be an attorney?
Early on. My household was a very outspoken one. Everyone had an opinion, and everyone loved sharing them. You needed to be on top of your game to be sitting at the dining room table. I thought I'd use those advocacy skills to make a living. I think when I was in college, I thought that law school offered a lot of career opportunities.

Why did you want to be in real estate?
My father, in addition to being a dentist, was a real estate developer in New Jersey on a small scale. He used to buy and renovate buildings in the area where we lived. I have a clear recollection of when I was 12 or 13; he had bought a ShopRite, which had gone out of business, and he decided to turn it into an office building, which he leased to IBM. I remember walking to the site with him as they were tearing out the guts of the building and reconfiguring it as a swanky new building. I liked that.

What's your best childhood memory?
Probably playing tennis with my father as a kid — when he set aside time for us to do things together.

How many deals do you work on in a given year?
About 100.

What's it like to be behind the scenes rather than in the limelight?
Well, I guess I don't see myself as being behind the scenes. The press has always been kind to me. I think my clients believe I contribute a lot to the transactions that close. I don't think I'm in the foreground or in the background. I'm just part of the team that gets it done.

What word would you use to describe yourself?
Optimistic.

What word would others use to describe you?
I think some would say charismatic.

How do you deal with high-pressure situations?
Humor is always a big help.

What's the best piece of advice you've ever received?
Someone taught me about the art of negotiation: They said the key to negotiation is to care, but not too much. You need to negotiate hard, but you need to always be able to walk away.

What's the greatest mistake you have ever made?
Maybe not getting a business degree at the same time I got my law degree.

What activity do you do most regularly in your free time?
I play tennis a couple of times a week at Tennisport in Long Island City.

Do you work out too?
Three times a week at Harry Hanson [Fitness One-on-One] on Lower Broadway.

What's the last book you read?
To connect with my kids [two boys, ages 12 and 17], I read the final version of "Harry Potter" a couple of weeks ago. It was a way to see what they were talking about.

What is your greatest professional achievement?
The building of the real estate department at Fried Frank.

What was the biggest obstacle on your path to success?
I'm never satisfied that things are as good as they can be. There are some people that can sit back and rest on their accomplishments. I am always looking for ways to expand and grow the practice. It is a good thing in terms of being ambitious, but it is always like trying to hit a moving target — that every time you approach it, it moves a little farther away. I imagine there are people in the world that say, 'I met my goal, I am done.' Not me.

How do you deal with confrontation in your personal life?
Head-on.

What quality do you think you could improve in yourself?
Patience.

How many days do you eat dinner with your family?
Not as often as I'd like — maybe once or twice a week at best.

What if you lost it all tomorrow? How would you start over again?
The good news is I have a pretty significant skill set and relationships, so it's not like I can't transport that or do that all over again.

Have you ever had to hire a lawyer for yourself?
Yes.

Do you care to share the circumstances?
No. **TRD**

October 2007

SAM CHANG

CEO | **MCSAM HOTEL GROUP**

One of the most prolific hotel developers during the aughts, Chang leads a Great Neck-based development, construction, management and investment company, which has built countless numbers of moderately priced hotels in New York City and has more in the pipeline. Despite Chang's claims that he would retire by age 50, among his current planned projects are a 594-room hotel on West 40th Street, and an 80-room hotel on West 36th Street. *Interview by Lauren Elkies*

"I don't think I am successful yet. My dream is to be a billionaire."

What's your full name?
Sam Chang. When I became a U.S. citizen, that's the name I got. My Chinese name is Shen Leong Chang.

What's your date of birth?
July 29, 1960.

Where did you grow up?
Taiwan. I was born in Taipei.

Where do you live now?
Long Island, on Centre Island.

How many bedrooms are there in your house?
Seven.

Do you need all those bedrooms?
I don't. I saw the house. It was wild. It's on 18 acres. There is a private lake on my property.

Are you married?
I'm single. How do you think I can work this hard if I have a family? My first marriage was 10 years. I got divorced in 1993. My second wife was for two years. I got divorced in 2001.

Do you have children?
I have four. They're 15 (Danny), 18 (Kevin), 23 (Jeffrey) and 24 (Jennifer).

Are you dating?
No. I'm too busy to date. I just want to finish all my work and then retire, and then I will have a relationship.

When are you going to retire?
50.

What are you going to do upon retirement?
Just relax. I'm going to build one hotel at a time after I retire. Right now I'm building 30 hotels at a time.

What was the first job you ever had?
I delivered newspapers in Tokyo, Japan when I was 14 years old. I had a fight with my mom, and I ran away from home and I moved into the dormitory for the newspaper company and delivered newspapers

What was the fight about?
I was crazy about martial arts. I came home one day and asked my mom for money to pay for my tuition for martial arts school, and my mom told me I should concentrate on studying and she wasn't going to give me any more money to pay for it. I packed up and left.

What did you do after you were in the newspaper business?
When I was working at the newspaper company, a carrier of mine knew a chef in a Chinese restaurant. I got a job in the restaurant as a dishwasher. Three months later, the chef took me in as his student. I started to learn how to cook. At that time I thought I would grow up, save enough money and open a small restaurant, and that would be it for my life. That was my dream.

Did you fulfill it?
When I turned 18, I saved a little money and I went out and I bought my first restaurant. Between 18 and 23, I probably opened about 15 Chinese and Japanese restaurants.

Do you consider yourself successful?
I don't think I am successful yet. My dream is to be a billionaire.

Do you like to drink?
Yes. I'm a good drinker. I'm well-known on the street — Sam Chang is a good drinker. Last night there was a cocktail party in the Four Seasons restaurant on 52nd Street, a cocktail party by Cushman & Wakefield's capital markets group, from 6 to 9. After I finished work, I walked in at 6:30. All the brokers, when they saw me, they went right to the bar and they said, 'Sam, are you ready?' I said, 'I'm ready.' We drank five shots of tequila.

Where do you vacation?
I go back to my country once a month. Not many people know me in my country, so I can go out with a lot of freedom.

Do you have a driver?
Yes. And I have a bodyguard.

Why?
Before we had some problems with the construction union, remember? [Chang had labor battles at his sites in 2006 because of his use of non-union general contractors.] We already made up, but at that time I had a lot of people threatening me.

What's the deal with the large diamond ring you're wearing?
This one is a ring for Hersha Hospitality Management, my partner company. All the Hersha partners have this ring [with a diamond, number of carats determined by number of years of service] and this Rolex watch [with diamonds].

What's one thing people don't know about you?
People who don't know me think that I'm a real tough guy. But I'm a very easy person to get along with. I have all different kinds of friends. If you're a janitor, you can be my friend, all the way up to Donald Trump, who's my friend. **TRD**

LOUISE SUNSHINE

FORMER CEO | **SUNSHINE GROUP**

Sunshine is a real estate marketing legend, who has played a hand in such developments as the Time Warner Center, One Beacon Court and 165 Charles Street. She is the founder and former CEO of the Sunshine Group, the real estate marketing and sales company that was bought by NRT in 2002 and merged with the Corcoran Group. Currently a real estate consultant, Sunshine was at the time of the interview development director of Alexico Group, the development firm formed by Izak Senbaha and Simon Elias. She started her career at the Trump Organization *Interview by Lauren Elkies*

"Trump turned out to be the greatest teacher I ever had, and I probably was one of his greatest students."

What's your date of birth?
December 2, 1940.

Where do you live?
Palm Beach, Florida; Roxbury, Connecticut; and I maintain a pied-à-terre at One Beacon Court [at 151 East 58th Street, at the top of the Bloomberg Tower].

Where is your office?
I have an office at Alexico. But my real love is my kitchen. Right now I am actually working from my kitchen. I call it "my kitchen cabinet."

What was the first job you ever had?
The first job I ever had was with Donald Trump. [Sunshine was executive vice president of the Trump Organization between 1975 and 1985.] He turned out to be the greatest teacher I ever had, and I probably turned out to be one of his greatest students.

Did you have any jobs earlier in your life?
I never worked a day in my life before that.

What did you want to be when you grew up?
A wife and a mother.

What's something people don't know about you?
I guess they don't know that I'm shy and insecure.

How do you cover it up?
By being bold and outspoken.

What is the best piece of advice you have received?
To always be honest with myself and everybody else around me.

Who's the boss at home?
Do you think somebody has to be the boss? I think second marriages are collaborative relationships. [Sunshine is on her second marriage; her husband, Martin Begun, is on his first.] Nobody has the upper hand.

How do you deal with antagonists?
Ignore them.

What's the last book you read?
"Brandscapes: Architecture in the Experience Economy," by Anna Klingmann. I'm just finishing it now. I find it extremely interesting. Anna Klingmann wrote a beautiful inscription to me. It says: 'To Louise: I am dedicating my first copy of this book to Louise Sunshine, the founder of brandism in architecture. Best wishes, Anna.'

What do you have on your night table?
I have baby orchids in a beautiful Daum vase. I have photographs of my children, my grandchildren, my husband and my dogs.

How did you start your day today?
I awoke at 5:30 a.m., and I went down to the fitness center at One Beacon Court where I worked out for one hour with my trainer and physical therapist. She has also given me therapy for my frozen shoulder, which is a real pain in many different ways. I took my two loving dogs, Sundance and Domino, for a one-hour walk. They are twin Lowchens and will be four on my birthday. They're adorable and love unconditionally. Even picking up their poop is just a pleasure for me because they're just fantastic. I mean, the process of picking up their poop and giving them a treat is fun.

Do you cook?
I don't eat at home. Do you know that I got a notice from Con Edison that said they're going to turn off the gas because I've never turned on my stove? I must say, however, that I am hiring a chef who cooks organic foods in the hopes that I will eat at home once in a while.

Where do you eat?
I'm taking this diet pill called Acomplia. It completely makes you lose your appetite. I've lost 30 pounds in the past two months. It's not approved here by the FDA, but my doctor greatly recommends it. But I will have a delicious dinner tonight at Le Cirque with my husband.

Do you have anything in your refrigerator?
Some coffee, yogurt, Diet Coke, bottled water, apricots, carrots and dog food — oh, and cottage cheese. Know what I do have a lot of in my house, though? Webkinz [a stuffed animal with a virtual life on the Web]. I have the two most luscious grandchildren, and they are members of the Webkinz club. Wherever I go, I collect Webkinz for them, and I have one whole closet in my house full of them.

Do you watch television?
Not much. I watch anything that helps keep me apprised of global issues. I watch a lot on the History Channel, and I watch the news.

How about any shows for entertainment?
"Desperate Housewives."

What do you like about the show?
I was once one of them ... Been there, done that. **TRD**

Photo by Hugh Hartshorn

FRANCIS GREENBURGER

CHAIRMAN | **TIME EQUITIES**

Greenberger founded the full-service New York real estate development and investment company, which has some 20 million square feet of property, including nearly 3,000 residential units. Its holdings are spread throughout the United States, Germany and Canada. Among its properties is 50 West Street, where sales launched in 2014 on a 64-story luxury condo tower. *Interview by Lauren Elkies*

"One area I always feel I could improve on is being less preoccupied, giving people more feedback."

What's your date of birth?
February 13, 1949.

Where did you grow up?
Forest Hills, Queens, although I moved into Manhattan when I was 15 and lived with my girlfriend who was 18.

What were the first jobs you ever had?
Delivering newspapers when I was around 11, and then when I was 12 I worked for my father after school. He was a literary agent. By the time I was 15, I had a couple of mail order book companies. And I was also a buyer for a German book club, Bertelsmann, which is now world-famous, but at the time was less known. I also had a start in the real estate business at that point. I rented an office that was too big for me, sublet half of it and figured out that that was an easier way to make money than selling books.

Did you finish high school?
I dropped out of Stuyvesant High School, went to Washington Irving High School in the evening and then I went to Baruch College and got my degree in public administration.

Did you dislike high school?
I was interested in business. I was interested in my girlfriend. I was interested in life. School wasn't my main priority.

Where do you live?
I live in the Village near Washington Square Park.

Are you involved in any other business ventures?
I own a literary agency called Sanford J. Greenburger Associates. I'm chairman and CEO.

Have you personally worked with any authors?
I did that for the first 10 years, so that would have been in the 1970s. One of the authors that I helped get started is James Patterson. It was very difficult to sell his first book, "The Thomas Berryman Number" [Little, Brown and Company, 1976]. I think 35 publishers rejected it, but I persevered and sold it and in the end it won an Edgar [The Edgar Allan Poe Awards for mystery and crime writing]. We no longer represent him.

How do you deal with antagonists?
It depends on what kind of antagonists they are. If they're bullies, I'm extremely stubborn and I'll fight them tooth and nail. If they're crazy people, then I try to figure out how to work around them and not waste my time with them. If they are people who have a reasonable point of view that's different than mine, I try to understand it and work with it.

What do you think you could improve in yourself?
One area I always feel I could improve on is being less preoccupied, giving people more feedback and complimenting them more overtly on their successes, and just being more interactive with people than sometimes I am. I don't do it, not because I don't feel that way, just because I'm distracted by millions of things that are on my mind.

How do you unwind?
Right now, for instance, I'm in Anguilla, in the Caribbean. I'm here with 10 friends playing in a kind of informal tennis tournament. We started coming here last year and discovered that it was a nice getaway.

Do you have a hero?
Hillary Clinton is one. I've supported both of Hillary's senatorial campaigns and I'm certainly supporting her presidential campaign.

Do you have a mentor?
Charlie Benenson [of Benenson Capital Partners]. Charlie is someone I respected for a lot of reasons, not only his real estate acumen, but his whole approach to life. [Benenson died in 2004.] He and I shared an interest in philanthropic causes, art, and in ethical business dealings, just very much a kindred spirit.

What do you read every day?
I start the day with the New York Times. It depends on how much time I have that morning. At worst, I'll read the front page of the first section, the front page of the metro section, the front page of the business section. I usually try to skim the editorials and check the obituaries. I'll read the Wall Street Journal if I have a little extra time.

Have you ever come across someone you know in the obits?
Maybe 10 years ago, there was an obituary in the paper for Charlie Benenson. I was shocked because I would've thought that if something had happened his office would have called. And of course I was very sad. I didn't quite know what to do but I decided to call his office and just ask for him and see what people said. When I called up they said, 'We'll connect you.' Charlie answered the phone. I said, 'Charlie, it's good to talk to you.' He said, 'What do you mean?' I said, 'There is something strange in the newspaper about you.' He said, 'Oh, you mean that obituary? That's a cousin of mine. He's got the same name and he's in the real estate business.'

What's one thing that people don't know about you?
Even though I like to run my life as an open book, I do have areas that I keep private.

Will you tell us which ones?
No. **TRD**

June 2007

CHARLES KUSHNER

FOUNDER | **KUSHNER COMPANIES**

Started by Kushner in 1985, the real estate company's portfolio now includes upwards of 20,000 multifamily apartments and 10 million square feet of industrial, office and retail spaces in six states. In 2013 alone, the company acquired more than 2 million square feet of commercial properties in Manhattan and Brooklyn. Earlier, in 2005, Kushner was sentenced to two years in prison, after pleading guilty to 18 felony counts of filing false tax returns, making illegal campaign donations and one count of retaliating against a witness. Kushner was angry with his sister's husband for cooperating with the government in its investigation of him, so he hired a prostitute to seduce his brother-in-law, videotaped the liaison and sent the tape to his sister. Kushner was released within a year, in 2006 (Kushner's son Jared Kushner now serves as the company's president.)

Interview by Lauren Elkies

"One liberty I had in prison is that those walls kept me in but also kept out people."

What's your full name?
Charles Kushner.

You don't have a middle name?
My parents were poor immigrants when they came to this country. My mom didn't really speak English, so when the nurse, who happened to be African-American, asked what my name was going to be, my mother answered with a Yiddish name, Chanan. I was named after her brother, who was killed in the Holocaust. The nurse said they don't name children like that in America. The nurse named me Charles. Chanan is the Hebrew name I kept.

What's your date of birth?
May 16, 1954.

Where did you grow up?
Elizabeth, N.J.

Where do you live?
We have four residences. My wife [Seryl] and I spend a couple of nights a week at our apartment on Fifth Avenue at 67th Street and two nights a week in Livingston, N.J., where we have lived for 26 years. We spend summers on the beach in the Jersey Shore in Elberon, N.J., and we have a place in Bal Harbor, Florida., where we go occasionally in the winter.

Which home do you like best?
I love the Jersey Shore. It's the only place I can really go that I feel I have peace and serenity.

Did you start your company with the chairman title?
In '85 I was the chairman, I was the manager, I was the dishwasher. I started the business with one secretary.

Then you had to step down.
Yes, when I went to jail I stepped down, until August '06.

What is your greatest professional achievement?
Building the Joseph Kushner Hebrew Academy in Livingston [a Modern Orthodox yeshiva day school].

What was the biggest obstacle on your path to success?
In the late 80s and early 90s, people called our industry in a recession, but in truth, it was a depression. It was a great obstacle trying to get debt or refinance debt.

What did being in jail do to you?
It gave me an opportunity to learn a lot about myself. I learned a lot about other people. I learned a lot about different areas I've always had an interest to learn about, whether it be Jewish history or derivative financing. I didn't waste my time in jail. I was able to read the Wall Street Journal cover to cover every day.

What did you learn about other people?
That there are just so many people that are stripped of their means, that don't have families, that don't have ways to make a living. When they go to prison, they lose their hope of having a life. I tried to help the young kids write their resumes. I used to give mock interviews and try to give them some direction.

It sounds like prison wasn't so bad.
I'm an adaptable person, so living in a bunk bed was not a great sacrifice; living out of a locker was not a great sacrifice; having one pair of pants was not a sacrifice. The biggest hardship that I experienced was being separated from my wife and children and my grandchildren. They'd visit me once a week.

Did you find yourself abandoned by people you didn't expect to do so, or find people who were able to show up for you whom you didn't think would?
When the guards delivered mail, they made fun of me that I should have gotten my own P.O. box number because I used to get [two-thirds of the mail coming into the barracks]. I got letters from people all over, wishing me well, giving support. One liberty I had in prison is that those walls kept me in but also kept out people. I only wanted to see my family and three, four, five of my closest friends. It's almost a liberty I don't have now.

Are you in contact with any of the inmates?
I'm not allowed to because I'm on probation until August '08. [At that time,] I know I will be.

Have you had any resolution with your sister and her husband?
I believe that God and my parents in heaven forgive me for what I did, which was wrong. I don't believe God and my parents will ever forgive my brother and sister for instigating a criminal investigation and being cheerleaders for the government and putting their brother in jail because of jealousy, hatred and spite.

What quality do you think you could improve in yourself?
I think I could be more patient with people who can't accomplish goals I think they can or within the time frame I think that they can.

Do you read the New York Observer [the publication his son, Jared, owns] every week?
I read it from back to front. I don't spend too much time on the culture. I like the politics, and I love the real estate.

Has your son ever given you bad press?
No. Not bad nor positive.

What do you think of your record deal last year?
We still hold the record for the most money paid for a single asset [666 Fifth Avenue]. Every day I want to see somebody break that record. I'd rather be the guy that loses that contest, not who wins it. **TRD**

November 2007

EDWARD LEE CAVE

FOUNDER | EDWARD LEE CAVE INC.

Cave was for decades a top sales broker in some of New York's most prestigious residential buildings, particularly along Central Park West, Park Avenue and Fifth Avenue. In 1976, he co-founded Sotheby's International Realty; six years later he struck out on his own with an eponymous firm, Edward Lee Cave Inc., that was later acquired by Brown Harris Stevens in 2002. Cave's notable clients have included Sting, Edgar Bronfman Jr., Steve Schwarzman, Billy Joel and Richard Nixon, who he once advised against buying a Manhattan co-op in favor of purchasing a private home. Cave found him a townhouse that had once been owned by the great progressive federal judge Learned Hand, a rather interesting twist of fate.

Interview by Lauren Elkies

"That's why I sell in prewar buildings, each of which is a private club."

What's your date of birth?
August 5, 1939. I'm a Leo.

Where do you live?
I live at 70th and Park, and I have a country house in Union, Connecticut.

Do you spend more time in New York or Connecticut?
I can't wait to get to Connecticut, and then by Sunday night I can't wait to get back to New York.

Are you married?
I'm a widower.

Do you date?
Not at my age. There are people I see and enjoy being with. There's no nefarious intent.

Where did you grow up?
I grew up in Northern Virginia.

What was your first job?
My first job was a perfect way to begin. I was hired right after I got out of school by Parish-Hadley, the decorating firm, because they were just starting to do the White House with Mrs. Kennedy and they needed someone who knew about art.

How did you get started in real estate?
I really started in '68 because my father helped me buy a small apartment building in New York. It was a very, very prudent real estate lesson, because I bought it in '68 for $110,000. I sold it in '77 — when the city was going bust — for $115,000.

What advice would you offer a younger version of yourself?
You've got to learn your product. You see, I'd been in and out of these buildings for 20 years by the time I started. When they wanted something, they'd call me because they knew I knew all about their Picassos — which was a Blue Period, which was Cubist. So they knew I knew how to live. That's why I sell in prewar buildings, each of which is a private club that represents a way of life — because I've lived in those buildings, I understand the way of life, the nuances.

Is it true that that Richard Nixon turned to you for help with an apartment, and you advised him to give up trying to find a co-op and instead purchase a private home, as it says in the book "The Sky's the Limit" [by Steven Gaines]?
That's what it was, but it was his attorney, not Nixon himself.

Though you travel in very refined circles, have you ever made what you'd consider a major social gaffe?
Oh, wonderful, [chuckles]. I went to a really grand dinner party in a Fifth Avenue building, and we're having cocktails in the library, then we walked into the dining room. It was, you know, ladies first and all that, I was the last one out. You know what I did? I flipped the switch to turn the lights out because I often do that when I leave an apartment. That was a real occupational hazard. Nobody noticed at all, but I did and I just thought it was so funny. There I am in a dinner jacket turning the lights off.

What do you do in your free time?
I read voraciously. I don't watch television because in my boarding school we didn't have television. I never got hooked on it. I'm a great gardener. Maybe my plants don't agree. I started gardening when I was in sixth grade. I would train myself to get up when the sun came out because I had to go to school at 8:30, and run out and work in the garden.

How much money do you have in your wallet right now?
Two $100 bills, which I always carry, two blank checks — because all of a sudden I see something, maybe in an antique store, and they don't take a credit card so I write them a check — and three credit cards, I don't know how many $20 bills, and I always have six or eight $1 bills.

How often do you read?
I read every night and I usually wake up in the middle of the night and read for 10 minutes.

What do you have on your night table?
A new biography, "Andrew Carnegie" [by David Nasaw] is underneath "The Green Hat" [by Michael Arlen]. I have a letter opener because I sit in bed and open my mail when I get home at night. I usually have a pot of flowers.

What keeps you up at night?
I've had somebody's apartment to sell for a long time — about nine months — and I haven't sold it yet, and it really makes me mad.

What did you eat for dinner last night?
I had Christmas dinner with a friend. We always have Christmas dinner together at the Carlyle. We always have grilled sole, because she's always worried about her figure. And we each have a martini; I have mine on the rocks, she has hers straight up. We never have dessert. And we've probably been doing that for 20 years.

What should someone give you for Christmas?
A book that I haven't read. And I dare them to do that. **TRD**

January 2007

Photo by Rick Kopstein

STEVE WITKOFF

FOUNDER & CEO | **WITKOFF GROUP**

A real estate attorney by training, Witkoff founded and leads the Witkoff Group, a real estate investment and development firm known for its embrace of strategic partnerships. Its portfolio comprises residential, industrial, office and hospitality properties. Projects include a hotel building at 701 Seventh Avenue in Times Square and the conversion of the International Toy Center to the 10 Madson Square West condos in the Flatiron District. In 2013, a partnership led by the Witkoff Group purchased the Park Lane Hotel for $660 million from the estate of Leona Helmsley. *Interview by Lauren Elkies*

"Success belongs to those who believe in it the most."

What's your date of birth?
March 15, 1957.

Where do you live?
On the Upper East Side.

Do you have a second home?
Yes, in Southampton.

Where did you grow up?
I was born in the Bronx and grew up on Long Island.

What was the first job you ever had?
When I was 17, I was an ice cream salesman. I had a truck and a route.

What is the best piece of advice you have ever received?
Success belongs to those who believe in it the most. I don't remember who told me that. It might have been my father.

Who do you look up to?
I would say my father was my No. 1 mentor. He was a manufacturer of ladies' coats in the city. He instilled in me a desire to be in business. From an industry perspective, the person that I always sort of looked up to is Lenny Litwin [owner of Glenwood Management, one of the biggest owner-developers of rental buildings in the city]. I did legal work for them when I was a lawyer at Dreyer and Traub. I'm certainly not comparing myself to him. He is one of the largest and one of the most admirable real estate people out there. He wasn't a mentor to me, but he's certainly somebody who built a business on his own terms in an honest and highly ethical way.

What would you do if you weren't in real estate?
You know what, it scares me to think. I hope I wouldn't be a [practicing] lawyer. Personally I didn't find it redeeming.

What was your greatest professional gaffe?
I began buying office buildings in the mid-1990s because New York City was at its low, and we were buying very, very cheap. I sold a big chunk of office properties from 1999 to 2000. That was probably my greatest mistake, because they've soared in value.

How much money do you have in your wallet right now?
I'm not going to talk about my net worth here.

What kind of philanthropic work do you do?
I'm very active in a lot of different things, including any police-related cause. I try to be heavily involved because I'm a big believer in the police department in New York City.

What was your greatest professional achievement?
I tell you honestly, I think it's buying my first building, 164 Sherman Avenue in Washington Heights. This is 21 years ago, and there seemed to be such large obstacles to getting into the business, so after buying and closing on my first building, I was able to say, 'I did it.'

What was the biggest obstacle on your path to success?
When they changed the tax laws in 1989, and real estate was really a dirty word out there, we managed to maintain our portfolio and not lose any buildings, and then we continued to buy as well. Those were very difficult times for many people that I know — friends of mine, smart people with great portfolios — lost their properties in the early 1990s. We were able to sort of skate through, and, as I look back, it was much about luck. Also, I think I worked hard. I'm not sure I took a vacation in the first five years I was in the business.

What do you read every day?
I read a lot. I read the Post, the Daily News, the Wall Street Journal, the Financial Times, New York Times, Barron's, every business magazine, and then, on top of that, I read books. I just finished Robert Rubin's book ["In an Uncertain World: Tough Choices from Wall Street to Washington"], which is fascinating. And I finished "Charlie Wilson's War: [The Extraordinary Story of the Largest Covert Operation in History," by George Crile], which is another fantastic book.

What kind of car do you drive?
I don't drive a lot. I really walk everywhere in the city. I do not have a driver, but when I drive, I drive a Mercedes.

Do you think your children will follow in your footsteps?
Maybe, but I certainly don't push them. My mantra for raising my kids is just to give them self-esteem. To me that's the most important thing I can give them. Then they can choose wherever they want to go.

What do you think you could do better?
Maybe I could improve on how I was as a father. Maybe I could've spent more time with them, which is actually what I am starting to do now. All my kids play sports. I don't miss a game now.

What would you want people to say about you after you die?
I was a good guy. **TRD**

April 2007

COSTAS KONDYLIS

PRINCIPAL & CEO | KONDYLIS ARCHITECTURE

Kondylis, known as the "developer's architect," is one of city's most prolific (and controversial) architects. He has designed more than 86 high-rise towers throughout New York City, including the Trump World Tower at United Nations Plaza, the massive Riverside South residential complex on the West Side, and the Trump International Hotel and Tower at Columbus Circle. Kondylis was the subject of a PBS documentary produced by *The Real Deal* in 2012. *Interview by Lauren Elkies*

"I wanted to prove you could marry commerce and art."

What's your date of birth?
April 17, 1940. I'm an Aries.

Where do you live?
I live on 81st Street and Lexington Avenue. My apartment is my sanctuary, my shelter. I don't use my house as a place to impress people with my architectural skills.

Do you have a country house?
I bought a potato barn in Southampton. It's like a loft — a huge Soho loft inside a barn. I exhibit my sports cars in my living room.

Is that home more about showing off your architectural skills?
Yes.

How often do you go out there?
I try to go out most weekends.

What are your passions?
I'm passionate about architecture and another passion of mine is automotive design. When I was small, I thought I would become an automotive designer.

Why didn't you go in that direction with your career?
Back then there were no schools for the study of automotive design.

Where are you from?
I tell people I'm an island boy — Manhattan, Long Island and Samos [a Greek island] — the three islands.

Do you have family in Greece?
I have family in Greece, friends in Paris, and very good friends in Geneva. One of my hobbies is sports cars — racing cars — so I keep a Ferrari at a dealer in Geneva. When I fly to Europe for vacation, I pick up my car and go to Southern France or to Italy, Tuscany or Venice. I love traveling by car in Europe.

Do you have a girlfriend?
Yes.

How long have you and your girlfriend been together?
Six months.

How old is she?
37.

Were you ever married?
My wife died of breast cancer about 11 years ago. We lived together for 17 years. I sit on the board of directors of a cancer research organization called the Samuel Waxman Cancer Research Foundation. I do that in memory of my late wife.

You design a lot of buildings for Donald Trump. Some critics have said your work is formulaic. Do you agree?
I think every project is designed to stand on its own merits in its own context. There's never been a formula to apply in development. People buy real estate with the idea of an investment. I wanted to prove you could marry commerce and art.

What advice would you give someone starting out as an architect?
Persevere and go into the business if you are passionate about the business. If your purpose is to make a lot of money, don't become an architect.

How much money do you have on you?
$100. I typically have $200 to $300 in petty cash.

What was your first job?
My first job was when I was at the University of Geneva School of Architecture. I got a summer job as an architectural draftsman at a Swiss firm.

What do you read every day?
I read the New York Times, automotive magazines and the International Herald Tribune, because it has more news on what's happening in Europe. It's the paper I read when I'm on vacation in Europe. When I read it, I feel like I'm in Europe.

What's your greatest vice?
Staying up late at night. I feel like I'm wasting time going to bed.

What is the last movie you saw?
I saw the new James Bond movie ["Casino Royale"].

What would you want people to say about you after you die?
He was a great pragmatic architect. **TRD**

March 2007

Photo by Michael Spears

DOUGLAS DURST

CHAIRMAN | **DURST ORGANIZATION**

Durst is the third generation in his family to lead the Durst Organization, which has been a building owner and real estate developer since 1915. Notably, the company is overseeing development, management and leasing at One World Trade Center. Other high-profile Durst projects have included 4 Times Square, the Bank of America Tower at One Bryant Park and the glass pyramid-like tower at 625 West 57th Street, designed by Bjarke Ingels. The company owns or manages some 13 million square feet of office space and 1,800 residential units. *Interview by Lauren Elkies*

"You have to know what tenants want. You have to know how buildings operate."

What's your date of birth?
December 19, 1944.

Where did you grow up?
Scarsdale.

Where do you live?
Katonah, New York.

What was the first job you ever had?
The very first job I ever had was working in a dry cleaning shop. I think I was 14 or 15.

What's the upside of working in a family business?
That you're working with people that have the same or similar thought processes and that you can rely on.

What's the downside of working in a family business?
There's emotional and other relationship baggage that comes with working in a family business.

Which members of your family work at the Durst Organization?
My cousin, Jody; his brother and my cousin, Kristoffer; my son, Alexander; and daughter, Helena.

What about your other children?
My daughter Anita is artistic director of a not-for-profit, which she founded, called Chashama, which provides space for artists.

You are known for developing environmentally friendly "green" buildings — most notably the Condé Nast office tower at 4 Times Square. How are you personally environmentally responsible?
My wife and I own one of the largest organic farms in New York — McEnroe Organic Farm in Millerton. Our partner is the actual farmer, Ray McEnroe. We're very careful in what we buy. Our kids were brought up as vegetarian. I used to be a vegetarian, but not anymore. We eat as healthy as possible. We drive hybrid cars. We recycle, and I always wear green socks.

How big is the farm?
It's about 600 acres.

How often do you go up there?
In the summer, just about every week we're up there; less frequently in the wintertime.

What's your favorite thing to do on West 42nd Street?
I go to the movies there on 42nd Street. My favorite thing is to walk on 42nd Street and see all the changes that have taken place in the last 30 years.

What was the last movie you saw there?
The last movie I saw was "Monster-in-Law." My wife thought she would like it. We did not like it.

How much money do you have in your wallet right now?
Probably about $400.

What's your biggest professional gaffe?
When I came back to New York in the late '60s, I was looking at making an investment and I looked at property in Soho and decided that nobody would ever want to live in Soho. So I invested with [Manhattan grocer] Eli Zabar in a project on Columbus Avenue and 78th Street. That was five years too soon. Five years after I finished selling the units, one unit sold for the same amount that I sold all of them for.

Give advice to someone younger and in the same field.
When people ask me how to get started I always advise them to start as a broker or in operations, that you can't just suddenly become a developer. You have to know what tenants want. You have to know how buildings operate.

What's one thing people don't know about you?
That I'm a grandfather.

Who's your hero?
My father [Seymour Durst, who died in 1995] because he was always trying to do what was best even if it was not very popular.

What do you miss most about him?
His advice. I often think that 'I've got to ask Dad about that.' Of course I can't.

What's your greatest vice?
Bridge.

Are you a good player?
Not as good as I would like to be.

What was the last book you read?
Right now I'm reading the new biography of Andrew Carnegie ["Andrew Carnegie" by David Nasaw].

What do you have on your night table?
The book I'm reading. I also have the report of the Iraq study group my daughter wants me to read, alarm clock, my reading glasses.

Who is the boss at home, you or your wife?
I make the big decisions — world peace [chuckles], things like that. She makes the other decisions. She's the boss.

What would you want said about you after you die?
He sure knew how to party [laughs]. No, no, I'd like them to say, "He was a good father." **TRD**

THE CLOSING

| 189

PAMELA LIEBMAN

PRESIDENT | **THE CORCORAN GROUP**

Since 2000, Liebman has led the Corcoran Group, one of Manhattan's largest residential real estate brokerages. Notably, she was responsible for the negotiations that led to Corcoran's acquisition of the brokerage Citi Habitats and the merger of the Sunshine Group and Corcoran Group Marketing, thus creating the new development marketing brand Corcoran Sunshine. She has also expanded Corcoran's reach into other markets including the Hamptons and South Florida. The firm has more than 2,000 agents and some two-dozen offices. *Interview by Lauren Elkies*

"I liked the idea that you could create your own destiny in real estate."

What's your date of birth?
July 4, 1962.

Where did you grow up?
Staten Island.

Were you a good student?
Yes. Still, I was one of those students that they said, 'Imagine if she applied herself, she'd be a great student.'

Where do you live?
I live in New Jersey, and I have a second home. I'm waiting for it to be done. It's at Canyon Ranch in Miami, and I plan to spend a lot of time there. I also just bought at the new Element [Condominiums at 555 West 59th Street]. Right now I'm thinking about keeping it as a pied-à-terre.

What was the first job you ever had?
Babysitter, when I was 13. Then I was a lifeguard, and that was pretty much my job through high school. Then in college one summer I was a camp counselor, which I hated. That was the only job I really hated.

Why did you hate it?
The kids [laughs]. The kids didn't listen as well as I would have expected, and they tried my patience, which back then was very little to begin with.

When did you join Corcoran?
In 1984, pretty much right after I graduated from college [at the University of Massachusetts, Amherst].

Why did you decide to go into real estate?
I just always had a thing for real estate. When I was a little kid my aunt lived in California, and she was a real estate broker. I wanted to go to work with her, so she took me to see some houses, and I thought it was fun. I liked the idea that you could create your own destiny in real estate.

Do you earn as much money as you'd like?
Does anybody? [laughs] I do OK.

What is the biggest professional gaffe you ever made?
One time early on when I was still doing deals, I had this client I really didn't like, and I had to send him a fax. I wrote a really not nice, but sort of funny, fax and accidentally sent it. And then I had my assistant call and beg his secretary to rip it up and throw it away, which she did. It said how much I couldn't stand dealing with him and what I thought of him as a client — everything I really would like to say, but would never say.

What was the biggest obstacle on your path to success?
If I had any one personal obstacle, it's probably my impatience and my desire to get something done right away. And as time has gone on, I've tempered that.

Barbara Corcoran, the founder of Corcoran and your predecessor as CEO, was referred to as the Queen of New York City Real Estate. Are you a queen, too?
My friends and kids will sometimes refer to me as, 'Oh, the queen wants her — whatever.' I like to be catered to in a queen-like way.

If someone wrote a book about you, what would the title be?
"The Pocket Rocket." Twice when I played golf, people called me that because I'm like 5'1". So, the pocket rocket, you know — small but with a lot of power.

What's something people don't know about you?
I like rap music. My iPod is full of rap music with everyone from Ludacris to Jay-Z to the Game. When people borrow my iPod, they're like, 'What is this?'

What do you read every day?
I read the New York Post with my coffee and the Wall Street Journal in the car.

Cover to cover or headlines only?
In the Post I read everything through Page Six, and then the business section. In the Journal, I read whatever stories interest me. And I know I probably should say I read the New York Times, but I do only on Sunday.

What's the last book you read?
I just finished one on vacation by Michael Palmer called "The Fifth Vial."

Where did you go on vacation?
I was at Casa de Campo [resort in the Dominican Republic].

What did you eat for dinner last night?
A bowl of cereal. I had just come back from vacation and ate probably more than I wanted to for the week. I'm not a big dinner person anyway. I eat a big breakfast, and I'll have lunch, but dinner is very light unless I am out.

Who cooks at home?
My housekeeper.

What do you eat for a snack?
I'm a rice cake kind of person.

Who is the boss at home, you or your husband?
As my husband says, "You're the boss until I want to be the boss" [laughs]. Although, sometimes I think my eight-year-old is the boss. She's got a lot to say. **TRD**

May 2007

A B Y   R O S E N

CO-FOUNDER & PRINCIPAL | **RFR HOLDING**

Rosen is one of the most prominent developers and landlords in New York City, noted for boutique office buildings and luxury condos controlled by the RFR Holding firm he co-founded in 1991. RFR's Manhattan properties include the Lever House and the Seagram Building as well as luxury condominium projects such as 530 Park Avenue and One Jackson Square.

The firm also owns the Paramount Hotel and the Gramercy Park Hotel. The Casa Lever Restaurant in the Lever House is festooned with Warhols, among other artists' work, from Rosen's own collection. RFR also has extensive holdings in Stamford, Connecticut; Tel Aviv; Las Vegas; and South Florida. *Interview by Lauren Elkies*

"Most of the stuff I ever did, I did it right on the spot."

What's your date of birth?
May 16, 1960.

Where did you grow up?
Frankfurt, Germany.

What was your childhood like?
I had a great childhood growing up in Frankfurt, born to nice parents, lots of friends. Growing up as a Jewish child in Germany, I was a little bit of an outsider. It was rough at some points of my life.

Where do you live?
I live in the East 80s in a townhouse.

What was the first job you ever had?
My first job I ever had in New York, I was an investment associate, selling real estate to German institutions and private investors.

Do you have a mentor?
Not really. Is that bad?

How much money do you have in your wallet right now?
Probably a couple thousand bucks. This is not a cash society anymore, but I always have a couple of thousand bucks in my pocket.

Aren't you afraid of getting mugged?
No. Nobody mugs anybody in New York City anymore. This is the safest city, I swear to God.

Do you earn as much money as you'd like to?
Yeah. I always spent more than I earned. Finally a couple of years ago, I caught up with all that stuff and I make more than I can spend.

Where do you invest your money?
Eighty percent of my money is in my own business, 10 percent is in art, another 10 percent is with various types of very conservative money managers. I buy very low-yielding paper, stuff that you sleep well at night with.

What is your greatest professional achievement?
Probably to own the Seagram and the Lever House [located at 375 and 390 Park Avenue, respectively]. Those are two of the greatest office buildings in America I think. They are basically pieces of art. It fits exactly what I want to do — meld the art and the architecture together.

What's your greatest social gaffe?
I walk around with a T-shirt and some jeans while other people get dressed up. If they call that a social screw-up, that's OK with me.

What's your biggest professional gaffe?
I wish I would have been less conforming earlier on, break the mold earlier on. Today, when you're established, it's easier to break the mold and do things that are more challenging and more out of the box.

Given your success, are you arrogant?
No, but I'm very cautious. I'm very selective when it comes to people. But, I do make instant judgments, which I think is a mistake sometimes, but I still do that.

Who is your favorite celebrity and why?
I love Henry Kissinger because this guy came over here almost 65 years ago and still has a strong German accent. It's a guy that doesn't want to fit in somewhere with his accent. Also, I like him as a person.

Are you impulsive?
Most of the stuff I ever did, I did it right on the spot. I bought my townhouse on the spot. I saw it at noon and by three o'clock I had a signed contract.

How do you deal with antagonists? Confront or ignore them?
I think ignore them. People don't change.

What piece of artwork would you love to own?
I would like to own a lot more work from the '60s by lots of different painters like Warhol.

What's the most expensive piece of art you own?
A Francis Bacon.

What do you have on your night table?
A photo of my kids and my wife, an alarm clock and some water, gummy bears and white chocolate. I like sweets. I eat white chocolate every day and I eat gummy bears every day.

Who is the boss at home, you or your wife?
I think we're both pretty much even.

What kind of staff do you have at home?
Lots of people helping with the house, to clean, a chef, a nanny, a laundry lady, people who serve. It's a huge house and we entertain a lot. You need people there. The worst thing is to invite people and not give them decent service.

What's your favorite music?
I love Pink Floyd. I just saw Roger Waters a couple of weeks ago and it was insane.

What do you like to read?
I read tons of magazines. It's a mirror of what's going on in this world, a very focused mirror. I have like 50, 100 magazines around me all the time.

If you could work on any real estate project, what would it be?
I would like to do something in the area of the High Line.

What would you want people to say about you after you die?
That I had a great eye and lots of fun. **TRD**

December 2006

STEPHEN SIEGEL

CHAIRMAN OF GLOBAL BROKERAGE | **CBRE GROUP**

Siegel has long been one of the most influential commercial real estate brokers in New York City and has led its two biggest commercial firms during his career. He has negotiated office leases for myriad big-name clients, including Simon & Schuster, the Trump Organization, Silverstein Properties, JPMorgan Chase, Showtime, Cerberus Capital Management and the law firm Stroock & Stroock & Lavan. A Bronx native, Siegel got his first job in real estate at age 17 at Cushman & Wakefield, which he went on to lead as CEO and chairman 20 years later. He held identical roles at Insignia/ESG, growing it into a global firm by the time it was acquired by CBRE in 2003. *Interview by Lauren Elkies*

"There's no such thing as a white lie. There's only a lie."

What's your date of birth?
September 13, 1944.

Where did you grow up?
I grew up in the Bronx.

Where do you live now?
I live in a townhouse on Park Avenue.

What was the first job you ever had?
I was delivering leaflets and groceries at age 11. Then I worked in a local candy store with a fountain after school every day and on Saturdays all day. My first job in the city, at age 15, was in the mail room of a company called Bing & Bing, a residential management company. And I was really fortunate that I got that job because I actually met somebody there who left and got a job in the accounting department of Cushman & Wakefield. He called me one day and said that there was an opening — 'you want to interview for it?' So, I joined Cushman & Wakefield at age 17, and 20 years later I was chairman and chief executive officer.

Tell one of your most significant childhood memories.
I remember going every Thursday for tests, a variety of tests, to see which allergies I had. I was allergic to so much stuff that it was unbelievable — chocolate, corn, coffee, you name it. I couldn't even eat cookies because they all had cornstarch and corn syrup. One of the reasons that prompted my wife and I to establish the Stephen B. and Wendy Siegel Fund for Pediatric Asthma and Allergy Research was because of my history with asthma.

What is the best piece of advice you have ever received?
It's to always treat people honestly. There's no such thing as a white lie. There's only a lie.

Who is your mentor?
My friend-slash-mentor was a man by the name of Earl Reiss. He was very good to me when I was a young guy breaking into the sales side of the business at Cushman & Wakefield. He was a senior broker. He would talk about deals and structures and he'd go over actual transactions that had occurred, talk about how business was developed, how business was implemented, how to create opportunity. He had no hesitancy to give me everything he had, and I was fortunate that I was able to absorb it.

Do you earn as much money as you'd like to?
Oh boy. That's a tough question. I make a very nice income and yes, you can always earn more and then I would have more to give away. I do mean that sincerely. I know that sounds like bullshit, but it's real.

What was the biggest obstacle on your path to success?
I guess time. I'd always like more time in the day, more time to get things done. And I wouldn't hesitate to be smarter than I am.

How do you invest your money?
Right now, primarily in real estate.

How do you remain humble?
You're assuming I am [laughs]. Maybe there's an aspect of me that's insecure, that'll always keep me in balance.

What do you read every day?
I read every newspaper I can get my hands on.

What's the last book you read?
I read "The Bronx is Burning" ["Ladies and Gentlemen, the Bronx is Burning: 1977, Baseball, Politics, and the Battle for the Soul of a City," by Jonathan Mahler]. Before that, I read "740 Park" ["740 Park: The Story of the World's Richest Apartment Building," by Michael Gross]. I'm also reading fiction — "Tell No One," by Harlan Coben.

What do you have on your night table?
I have an automated battery-operated Yahtzee game and a telephone. I just play Yahtzee to take my mind off of everything else, so I can relax. It's more mindless than a mindless book. It's a great tranquilizer before bed.

What did you eat for breakfast today?
I had low-fat yogurt — and some fruit. I've been actually eating very healthily the last three months because I didn't like the way I looked at the beginning of July. I decided it was time to lose some weight, and I've done that.

Who is the boss at home, you or your wife?
My wife says, 'my husband's the boss, sit up straight, honey.' That's her standard line. I think it might be a partnership, but I think the edge goes to her.

How do you deal with antagonists? Confront or ignore them?
I confront them. I believe in confronting issues and getting them resolved as much as possible.

If you were mayor of New York, what is the first thing you would change?
You know what, it would've been an easier question to answer two mayors ago, but I think they've done a lot of the right things.

What would you want people to say about you after you die?
I'd want them to say, 'I miss him.' And that would say it all, frankly. **TRD**

November 2006

DAVID WALENTAS

FOUNDER | **TWO TREES MANAGEMENT**

Walentas almost single-handedly pioneered the development of Brooklyn's Dumbo neighborhood. His firm, Two Trees, has owned, managed and developed more than $3 billion in property since Walentas started it in 1968. The Dumbo transformation began in earnest in 1978, with Walentas' purchase of the Clock Tower Building; the firm's holdings in the neighborhood now spread over more than 8 million square feet. The firm ventured into Manhattan for the first time in 2011, building Mercedes House on West 54th Street, and is undertaking the massive transformation of the former Domino Sugar Factory in Williamsburg into a mixed-use project. *Interview by Lauren Elkies*

"Dumbo has defined my life for the last 25 years, my whole adult life."

Where did you grow up?
I grew up in Rochester, N.Y.

Which college did you attend?
I went to the University of Virginia on a Navy ROTC scholarship and graduated in 19-something, in mechanical engineering. I also went to Darden business school, also at the University of Virginia, and graduated in 1964. As a poor kid from Upstate, engineering is what you did in the 50s. I would have gone to architecture school, but that was a five-year program and I only had a four-year scholarship.

What has been your biggest contribution to society?
My kid, Jed, who is terrific. But, in a larger sense, probably Dumbo. As a large urban development, it is one of the few things that will matter in 100 years.

You make it sound like you are solely responsible for Dumbo.
I am solely responsible. My wife, Jane, who has been my partner, certainly she was responsible, but we didn't get a lot of help from the government and nobody wanted to work with us for a long time. Nobody really got it. The planning people didn't get it. The community board voted against every rezoning we proposed down there. The banks all quit. My partners all quit, so we ended up with all the marbles.

So that's obviously your greatest achievement professionally.
Clearly Dumbo has defined my life for the last 25 years, my whole adult life. And it has been entirely successful on every level. When I first got there, it was vacant industrial buildings. We bought 2 million square feet from Harry Helmsley for $12 million. We are going to sell one apartment in the Clock Tower [Building] probably for twice that.

If you were mayor of New York, what is the first thing you would change about the city, and what would you fight to keep the same?
I would bring Mike Bloomberg as my first deputy mayor. He really is the best. He runs the city like a business.

What is your philosophy on love? Money?
I love them both. Money is interesting. I grew up a very poor boy. I didn't know anybody who had gone to college. I was happy when I was poor and hitchhiking, drinking beer and chasing girls. And I am happy now. Money loses its value. It's like eating. Once you are full, food doesn't seem as appealing. Right now, I am only thinking about giving money away.

Who is your mentor?
I never had a mentor. My mother was terrific. My father was paralyzed when I was 5, so my mother would have to work and take care of everything.

What's your idea of the perfect Sunday afternoon?
Sunday is just another day. But we do like to spend weekends on our farm in Southampton.

How big is your farm?
It's a 115-acre farm. It's a nice piece of land.

Do you feel the world needs more people like you?
I am an entrepreneur, and I think entrepreneurs are the people that make this country great.

Give advice to someone 20 years younger and in the same field.
I don't know. I can only say what I would do if I was young today. I would find an Asian woman, get married, and move to China or India or somewhere like that.

What do you read every day?
I read the New York Times, unfortunately. Other than that, I don't read the papers every day; maybe the New York Post for entertainment.

What's your biggest pet peeve?
Obnoxious people.

What time do you get in on Mondays and what time do you leave on Fridays?
I live across the street so the commute is short, but I am in the office everyday by 8 a.m. I like to work. I am better when I work.

Do you have a Donald Trump story?
My son, Jed, worked for Donald. When he graduated from the University of Pennsylvania, I told him that he couldn't work for me. So, Trump gave him an offer and Donald loved him. After two years with him, we converted the Clock Tower, and I called Donald and told him that I needed Jed and Donald says, 'No, you can't take him. I taught him everything he knows.' I said, 'But I am converting the Clock Tower and I need him here.' He didn't skip a beat; he said, 'OK, give me 10 percent of that project and put my name on it.' Of course, we didn't do that, because it has my son's name on it.

How much money do you have in your wallet right now?
I don't have a wallet.

Where did the name of your firm, Two Trees, come from?
I used to have a business partner, but he died 30 years ago. His grandmother had a farm in South Carolina called that, and we were two people; hence, the Two Trees.

How do you deal with antagonists? Confront or ignore them?
I definitely am confrontational, but I've mellowed.

What should be the first sentence of your eulogy, and who should give it?
I am not thinking about that. I am not there yet. TRD

October 2006

Photo by Hugh Hartshorne

HOWARD LORBER

PRESIDENT & CEO | **VECTOR GROUP**

Lorber is head of the largest residential brokerage in the New York City area. He is also president and CEO of the Vector Group, which controls Douglas Elliman. The brokerage boasts 22 offices in the five boroughs alone, as well as dozens more throughout Long Island, South Florida and California. The firm also produces some of the most oft-quoted reports on the New York City housing markets with appraisal firm Miller Samuel. Lorber is also the executive chairman of the fast-food chain Nathan's Famous and a partner in numerous high profile developments. *Interview by Amir Korangy*

"It's easy, if you work like a dog."

What's your date of birth and what's your sign?
September 8, 1948. Virgo.

Who are your parents?
Charles and Celia.

How much money do you have in your wallet now?
I don't carry my money in a wallet. I have a money clip and there is $1,640 in it right now.

Where were you born and where did you grow up?
I was born in the Bronx and grew up in Paramus, N.J., until I moved to Long Island for college.

What is your greatest achievement professionally?
The restructuring of the Western Union corporation as a board member, where the stock went from $1 to $240 a share in three years.

What is your motto?
Come to me if you want to hear the truth. Don't come to me if you want to hear what you want to hear.

What do you read every day?
The New York Post and the Wall Street Journal. Not the New York Times because it is too liberal for me.

Are there any public buildings bearing your name?
I donated the building that houses the school of professional accountancy at my alma mater, Long Island University. It's called Lorber Hall.

What is your favorite saying?
'It is better to remain quiet and be thought a fool than to open your mouth and remove all doubt.' — Abraham Lincoln

What should be the first sentence of your eulogy and who should give it?
I gave the eulogy for my father. I'd want my children to give mine. And the first sentence should say, 'He was a great guy.'

Who is your consigliere?
I have many.

Who is your mentor?
My business partner, Bennett LeBow.

Who is your hero?
Donald Trump, because of everything he's accomplished. Everything he does is first class, be it developing a building, a golf course, casinos, or producing a television show. A first-rate guy.

Do you feel the world needs more people like you?
Not necessarily just like me, but more people who are willing to help others.

Give advice to someone 20 years younger.
It's easy, if you work like a dog.

What gadget can you not live without, besides a cell phone?
My Bloomberg machine.

Do you have your own plane?
Yes, I am also a pilot of 15 years.

What's the biggest professional gaffe you've ever made?
I make mistakes every day, but I try not to make the same ones.

What do you consider to be the greatest vice?
Not being thankful for what you have.

What is your job?
My job is to help those who work for me make money.

What's the secret to a happy marriage?
A spouse who understands what you are trying to accomplish. Additionally, separate bathrooms and lots of living space helps.

What is people's biggest misperception about you?
I am a very outspoken guy, so they never have a chance to have one.

What's been your greatest disappointment?
Not winning the Westminster Dog Show with my champion English springer spaniel, Jagger, named after Mick.

You have a few Picassos and Cézannes hanging in your office. Are you a big art collector?
I am an art collector, but I must admit the ones in the office are fakes. **TRD**

July 2006

ROBERT SHILLER

CO-FOUNDER | **S&P/CASE-SHILLER HOME PRICE INDICES**

Shiller is a Nobel Prize-winning economics professor at Yale University widely known as the co-founder of the S&P/Case-Shiller Home Price Indices, composites of housing markets in several metro regions, including New York City. The indices are some of the most oft-quoted measures of U.S. real estate. Shiller is also well-known as one of the few prominent economists to warn of a housing collapse during the national real estate boom of the 2000s. The prominence that the prediction afforded him helped lead Shiller to sharing the 2013 Nobel Prize in economics. He had made a similar prediction about the bull stock market in 2000, right before it also nosedived. *Interview by Amir Korangy*

"My mission in life has been to use our wit and intellect to reduce the role of chance as much as possible."

What's your date of birth and what's your sign?
March 29, 1946. I am an Aries, not that I believe in such things.

Who are your parents?
Benjamin and Ruth.

Where did you grow up and where did you attend college?
Detroit. I went to the University of Michigan in Ann Arbor and then I got a PhD at MIT in economics.

What is your job?
Professor of Economics at Yale.

What are your greatest achievements professionally?
I wrote the first edition of "Irrational Exuberance" in 2000, about the stock market [which correctly predicted the dot-com bust]. The second edition was then released, on the real estate market as I interpreted it. I've written five books and over 100 journal articles.

What has been your biggest contribution to society?
Education. I've been teaching since 1972. I also co-developed a futures and options market on real estate [which began trading on the Chicago Mercantile Exchange].

Who is your hero? Why?
The original Adam Smith, who wrote The Wealth of Nations in 1776. He launched the field of economics, and because he was a moral philosopher, he had a sense of law and purpose in what he did.

What do you read every day?
I have an addiction to reading, and I've always been very broad. But I subscribe to the Wall Street Journal, the New York Times, Forbes, the Economist, BusinessWeek, and I particularly enjoy Science and Nature.

Do you feel rich? Successful? Happy?
Yes. I am happily married. I have two fine children. I have a wonderful job which brings me in contact with young people.

What is your philosophy on love and money?
I've been married to the same woman for 30 years, so I believe in long-term consistency, and money is just a game to me as long as you have enough. My parents would be surprised, because as a child I never showed any interest in monetary things. I wanted to be a professor. I found it amusing to make money.

What's the secret to a happy marriage?
Mutual support. I try to look at the positive things of it. I married a psychologist, so she thinks there is a science to it.

What's your idea of the perfect Sunday afternoon?
Sitting by the seashore thinking about the intricacies of economics with my wife sitting beside me.

How do you size up people when you first meet them?
I value sincerity and if they look you in the eye.

If you were mayor of New York, what is the first thing you would change about the city?
I might not rebuild the World Trade Center. It's challenging the terrorists. A little park and monument is not backing down.

And what would you fight to keep the same?
I guess it was under Mayor Giuliani that we got rid of a lot of the graffiti and trash, and it's a brighter, safer and more civilized place, and I would want to keep that.

How do you deal with antagonists?
Going back to my childhood, I would tend to not pacify people, but I would tend to stall and hope they would turn their aggression to someone else.

What's your biggest pet peeve?
Conventional thinking.

What do you consider to be your greatest vice?
I work too hard. It sometimes takes away from the finer things in life.

Give advice to someone 20 years younger.
I think young people often underestimate their own human capital. Your investment in yourself is to improve yourself with education, improve your knowledge, your skills. With every decision you have to ask yourself, 'How will I grow from this experience?'

What's the biggest professional gaffe you've ever made?
Waiting too long to take a broader view of economics. I started out in economics studying some very narrow things. As I got confidence, I became a lot more of a broad thinker.

What was the biggest obstacle on the path to succeeding?
I am always short of time. There is a famous quote from Napoleon: 'Ask anything of me but my time.'

What should be the first sentence of your eulogy?
'Time and chance happeneth to them all.' It's Ecclesiastes 9:11. I don't always quote the Bible, but I thought that was a very profound passage about the role of chance in our lives. My mission in life has been to use our wit and intellect to reduce the role of chance as much as possible. But there is an irreducible component.

What is people's biggest misperception about you?
I wish I knew the answer to that. **TRD**

August 2006

BARBARA CORCORAN

FOUNDER | **THE CORCORAN GROUP**

Corcoran is best known as the founder of the Corcoran Group, which grew from a one-person operation in 1973 into one of the largest residential brokerages in New York City, with more than 1,500 agents in the five boroughs. Corcoran famously started the firm with $1,000 borrowed from a boyfriend and sold it in 2001 to conglomerate NRT for a reported $66 million. Following the sale, Corcoran turned to television and books. She has written extensively about her life and business, and acts as a judge and investor on ABC's "Shark Tank," a reality show about business startups. Corcoran has also been a regular real estate pundit on NBC's "Today" show. *Interview by Amir Korangy*

"The only important thing is love, and money makes everything more lovable."

What's your date of birth and what's your sign?
March 10, 1949. Pisces.

Where did you grow up?
I was born in Teaneck, New Jersey, and grew up in Edgewater.

What is your greatest achievement professionally?
Building the Corcoran Group and all the people that came along for the ride.

What do you think of your old firm under the new management?
They've grown tremendously. I never saw it as anything other than a city firm. They've grown the Corcoran brand to different cities and states, and I could've never envisioned that.

Do you feel rich? Successful?
I've always felt successful. I've never felt rich and still don't. But I guess relative to a lot of people, I am. My family tells me I am rich.

But you are a legitimate millionaire?
I didn't worry about money when I didn't have any, and I don't worry about money when I lose it, because it's not so important. The only important thing is love, and money makes everything more lovable. Helps out. It takes away the edges.

What has been your biggest contribution to society?
I don't think I've made any contributions to society as a whole. I give a million little donations to a million little people but nothing that you could build a hospital with.

Are there any public buildings bearing your name?
Not a chance. Not a chance.

If you were mayor of New York, what is the first thing you would change?
I would definitely put mature trees on every block and have bike lanes on every avenue.

What's your idea of the perfect Sunday afternoon?
Sitting on the beach with my 2-month-old daughter, Kate, in her bucket.

What's been your greatest disappointment and how did you cope?
The first thing that comes to mind is not being able to have a baby. The seven years of in vitro trying to have my son was very disappointing. I coped with the help of my husband and was fueled by the determination that I wanted to have a baby.

What's your favorite street in New York?
My favorite street for me is where I am living, because I love my home. And I've moved like 20 times. But I guess Fifth Avenue along the park — but, then again, because I live around there.

Who is your consigliere?
My husband of 16 years, Bill.

Will you ever recreate the sort of success you had with the Corcoran Group?
I will because I need to. I just need to be involved in a big creative project. And I need a lot of attention. I probably need a shrink, but instead I'll build a business.

Going back to the time when you sold the Corcoran Group, would you still sell?
I would still sell it, because I had accomplished my goal to become the number one firm. After that was done, I was like, 'OK, now what do I do?' It was time for a change. I had worked that beat for 30 years, which is long enough. It was almost like raising a family where the kids were mature enough to be on their own.

What do you read every day?
The truth is, nothing. Ever. I never read the papers. I love being unplugged and always have. It makes space for creative thinking and being different from the next guy. Ignorance is bliss.

What gadget can you not live without, besides a cell phone and email?
I can definitely live without my email and cell phone. I don't even read or answer my own email. The gadget I can't live without is my DustBuster. I love to be tidy.

How do you size up people when you first meet them?
I have two categories and two sub-categories for everyone. First, if they are good or bad; then, if they are an expander or a container. Expanders want to push out and create bigger things. Containers want to control, and they are both good. One is not less important than the other.

Do you prefer to be feared or loved?
Who wants to be feared? I want to be surrounded by people who want to give me kisses.

What was your biggest obstacle on the path to succeeding?
My belief that I had the right to be there. **TRD**

September 2006

ACKNOWLEDGMENTS

•••••

Many contributors were responsible for interviewing, photographing, laying out, and editing these conversations. We wish to thank them for their efforts over the years and more recently, in producing this book.

For being unafraid to ask the tough questions of the real estate industry's elite, we wish to thank past and current reporters Lauren Elkies Schram, Candace Taylor, Leigh Kamping-Carder, Katherine Clarke, Sarabeth Sanders and E.B. Solomont.

We extend our gratitude to the photographers who have captured the essence of our subjects throughout the years: Marc Scrivo and StudioScrivo, Ben Baker, Hugh Hartshorne, Max Dworkin, Michael Toolan, Rick Kopstein, Michael Spears, Karl Rivenburgh and Chance Yeh.

We wish to acknowledge Yoav Barilan, our director of marketing operations, who has been there since the very beginning.

Art director Kéziah Makoundou and designer Juan Zielaskowski created this book with great style and laid out all the pages on top of their daily work. They regularly work on this feature in the monthly magazine, as Ron Gross and Derek Zahedi did in the past.

We thank the editors who have worked on The Closing over the past decade: Jill Noonan, Eileen AJ Connelly, Jennifer White Karp and Matthew Strozier, and the editors who worked on this book, specifically Jennifer White Karp, Gabrielle Birkner and Tom Acitelli.

This book would not have been possible without the contributions of interns Alexandra Barrett and Maya Kaufman, or production staff Linden Lim and Victoria Tuturice, who have worked on the magazine feature as well.

We also wish to acknowledge our senior advertising staff members Eran Evron and Ross Fox, in addition to administrative staff who supported the book, Virginia Durso, Junaid Zahid and Ken Cyrus. Thank you to our proofer, Stephen Vesecky, and to all our colleagues at *The Real Deal* and *Luxury Listings NYC*.

A special thank you to Julie, Sophie and Jonah, and to Ali, Jaleh, Ghazal and Ahmad.

A tip of the hat to the book, Vanity Fair's "Proust Questionnaire," which gave us the inspiration to create The Closing interview, and to Vanity Fair Editor Graydon Carter, who gave us the idea for the book.

A special note of appreciation to all of our subjects for opening up to us and to Howard Lorber, for being our first interview. Look at what you started.

•••••

INDEX

ABOUT THE REAL DEAL

•••••

About *The Real Deal*

Considered the bible of New York City real estate, *The Real Deal* has become mandatory reading for everyone in the real estate industry and beyond. Since 2003, *TRD* has provided up-to-the-minute news and in-depth reports on the big deals and major players in the most closely watched real estate market in the world. Our monthly print magazine has a circulation of more than 60,000 and TheRealDeal.com receives more than 1 million unique visitors a month. Our South Florida website, TheRealDeal.com/Miami, features the latest real estate news and trends in the Sunshine State, along with quarterly print editions and conferences. And our annual *Data Book* has become the essential almanac of statistics and facts for real estate. *The Real Deal* has been repeatedly recognized for its journalism prowess, most recently receiving the Society of American Business Editors and Writers' 2013 award for general excellence.

Luxury Listings NYC, *The Real Deal's* sister publication geared to Manhattan residents, is a tabloid-sized glossy magazine focusing on apartment and townhouse listings, plus stories on design trends and dedicated real estate news that lets readers know what's going on specifically in their neighborhood. The magazine provides a cheat sheet on the latest new buildings, store openings, and celebrity moves that keeps affluent readers up to date. *Luxury Listings* is delivered to more than 105,000 Manhattan homes, which is more than the daily distribution of the New York Times or the Wall Street Journal.

•••••